A History of Modern Trinidad 1783-1962

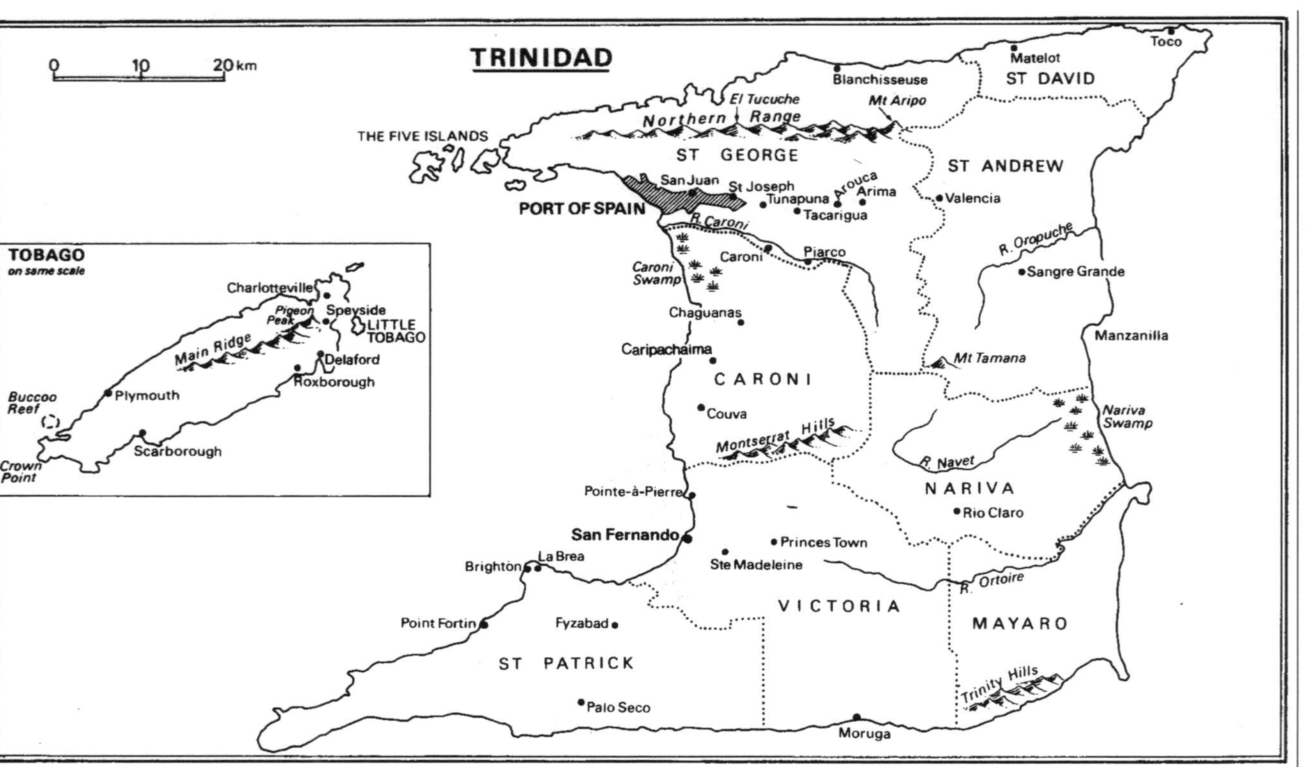

Map 1 Trinidad and Tobago

BRIDGET BRERETON
Professor of History, University of the West Indies, St Augustine, Trinidad

A History of Modern Trinidad 1783-1962

Champs Fleurs, Trinidad

Terra Verde Resource Centre

14 Hilltop Drive, Champs Fleurs, Trinidad and Tobago.

ISBN 0 435 98116 1 (paper)

First published by Heinemann Educational Books Ltd, 1981
Reprinted 1985, 1989

Republished by Terra Verde Resource Centre, 2009

For my favourite Trinidadians: Ashton, Stephen, Michael

Printed in Trinidad and Tobago by Zenith Printing Services Ltd.

Contents

List of Plates and Maps

The author and publishers thank Neal & Massy Ltd, Trinidad, Plates 1, 2, 4, 5, & 8; Oilfield Workers Trade Union, Trinidad, Plates 7 & 10; Royal Commonwealth Society, London, Plate 3; Sampson Studios, Plate 14; Texaco Trinidad Inc, Plate 9; the *Trinidad Express*, Plates 11, 12 & 13.

Map 2 The Eastern Caribbean and South America

Preface

This book attempts to provide a scholarly and interpretative account of the history of Trinidad since the 1780s, when its settlement really began. It is based primarily on the work of academics, many at the University of the West Indies, who have written books, theses and articles on the subject, particularly over the last ten years or so. Unfortunately, much of this work is still unpublished (graduate theses, conference papers, mimeographed seminar presentations); even if published, it is often to be found in journals that are inaccessible outside the university community. A major purpose of this book, therefore, is to synthesize and interpret for a wider public the recent work by researchers and academics. It is written for senior pupils in the secondary schools and their teachers, for students in universities and teacher-training colleges, and for the general public in Trinidad and Tobago, and elsewhere.

Many readers will wonder why the title of the book is not 'A History of Modern Trinidad and Tobago', and my treatment of Tobago requires a word of explanation. Up to 1889, Tobago was a completely separate entity with no administrative links to Trinidad. Its historical experience was quite different from Trinidad's, and had more in common with that of St Vincent or even Barbados. Furthermore, little academic research has been carried out on the history of Tobago between 1763, when its real development began, and 1889, when it was linked administratively to Trinidad. For these reasons, I decided not to include Tobago's history before 1889. Tobago awaits a serious and scholarly history; it is to be hoped that research being conducted now by teachers and graduate students at the St Augustine campus of the University of the West Indies will soon see the light of day.

I have tried to include material on Tobago's historical experience in the twentieth century, that is, after 1889, and especially after 1898 when Tobago became a Ward of Trinidad and Tobago. I have found it difficult, however, to locate suitable sources (although the work by C. R.Ottley was useful) and this explains why my treatment of Tobago after 1898 is so sketchy. Here again, more research will have to be carried out and published before a really comprehensive history of Trinidad and Tobago can be written.

In a book of this kind, intended as a general though scholarly history for the lay public rather than academics, it is impossible to please everyone or include everything of importance. I am very conscious of serious omissions. For instance, I say nothing about Trinidad's role in the Federation of the West Indies (1958-62) or about relations with Venezuela in the twentieth century. I have neglected the social and cultural contributions of the smaller minorities in Trinidad's population, such as the Chinese and the Syrians. I have not said enough about education and the role of the churches, and I have said absolutely nothing about cricket. My coverage of cultural, artistic and intellectual affairs is thin. In what was always envisaged as a fairly short book, I have concentrated on what seemed to be the crucial historical developments and tendencies between 1783 and 1962.

I owe a great deal to people who have contributed to the writing of this book. It is based on the work of colleagues who have written on the history of Trinidad. Most of these are at the University of the West Indies, and I have ‘borrowed’ from their writings to a degree that is probably professionally improper. In particular, the work of Sahadeo Basdeo, Carl Campbell, Howard Johnson, Keith Laurence, Kemlin Laurence, James Millette, Brinsley Samaroo, Kelvin Singh, Gerad Tikasingh and Donald Wood has been of fundamental importance. I have gained new ideas and perceptions about the history of Trinidad from post-graduate students and undergraduates in the Department of History of the St Augustine campus of the University of the West Indies since 1969. The staff of the university library at St Augustine have always been helpful and efficient.

The manuscript of the book was read wholly or in part by Edward Kamau Braithwaite, Patrick Cruttwell, Keith Hunte, Franklin Knight and Donald Wood, and I am grateful for their incisive criticisms and advice which helped me to improve it. Finally, Ian Randle and Kennetia Lam Pow of Heinemann Educational Books (Caribbean) Ltd, based respectively in Jamaica and Trinidad, have been encouraging and sympathetic beyond the call of duty.

Bridget Brereton,
St Augustine, Trinidad
August 1980

ONE

The Deserted Island, 1498-1783

The Colonization of Trinidad

Christopher Columbus did not, of course, discover Trinidad on 31 July 1498. Trinidad was 'discovered' by Amerindian peoples of the Arawakan group, who had lived there for many centuries, and by Kalinago (Caribs) who had begun to raid the island long before 1498 and had established settlements on the north coast at least by the end of the sixteenth century. What Columbus did was to establish contact between two worlds, both already very old; between the restless, expansionist, technologically advanced states of Western Europe and the Amerindian communities of Central and South America. Even the three great native American civilizations, the Maya, the Aztec and the Inca, suffered from fatal weaknesses which enabled the small Spanish forces to conquer and subjugate them with astonishing speed. In Trinidad Columbus and his successors, Spanish adventurers and seamen, found simple communities of Arawakan farmers cultivating the soil, hunting in the extensive forests, gathering shellfish. No great or sophisticated civilization had been created in the lush, wooded island that Columbus named Trinidad (after the Trinity), but the Arawaks had built up a selfsufficient economy which efficiently exploited the abundant natural resources of the land, the forests and the sea; and they had evolved a simple but effective political organization of villages and chiefs. Before they were dragged into that great historical drama, the collision of Europeans and Americans, they feared only natural disasters, and the increasingly frequent raids by their Kalinago neighbours based in the Lesser Antilles. But once the fatal contact was made, on that July morning in 1498, the Arawaks of Trinidad would suffer the tragic fate shared, in varying degrees, by all the Amerindian peoples of the Americas.

Yet the colonization of Trinidad by Spain was anything but rapid or effective. Nearly a century was to pass after Columbus's chance landing before a permanent settlement of Spaniards was established. In 1592 Domingo de Vera, acting in the name of Antonio de Berrio, Governor of Trinidad, formally founded the city of San Josef de Oruna (St Joseph). In the stately Spanish ceremony, conducted all over Central and Southern America during the early years of the empire, he marked out the sites of the Church, the Governor's residence, the cabildo or town council building and the prison. A city had been duly and properly founded, even if for decades it remained little more than a clearing in the bush; and the handful of Spaniards with de Vera elected a cabildo (town council) with two alcaldes or magistrates and six regidors or councillors. The year after, in 1593, de Berrio assumed his governorship and settled in his 'city' of San Josef, henceforward the seat of government and, until the early seventeenth century, the only European settlement.

The formal structure of a Spanish colony had been established in 1592, but for nearly two centuries Trinidad remained undeveloped and isolated. The island was an insignificant part of a vast empire, an outpost of Spanish colonialism; few people in Madrid were sure exactly where it was located; it lacked precious metals, it had no established productive peasantry to be taken over and exploited by the settlers. Spain's weakness as a colonial power in the seventeenth and eighteenth centuries meant that Trinidad would fail to develop a viable economy, at a time when the West Indian colonies of France, England and Holland were becoming major producers and exporters of tropical staples. Most of the island remained untouched by European enterprise until the last decades of the eighteenth century. There were no plantations producing tropical crops for export to Europe, worked by gangs of African slaves, creating vast wealth for a handful of planters and businessmen. Instead, a few Spaniards and mestizos (of mixed Spanish-Amerindian descent) cultivated a little tobacco, then cocoa, for export; but mostly they were preoccupied with survival and subsistence on their scattered clearings in the forest.

Tobacco production began, on a small scale, early in the seventeenth century, and it was sold to Dutch and English ships which called to trade illegally with the settlers. The tobacco industry prospered for a time; an English observer reported seeing fifteen foreign ships in the Gulf of Paria in 1611 awaiting shipments. But this modest export industry was virtually destroyed by competition from the English colonies in North America, and by the efforts of Spain to end the contraband trade with foreign ships.

In the later seventeenth century cocoa became important; in 1668 a British officer reported that the cocoa grown in Trinidad was the best in the Indies. Cocoa soon became Trinidad's major industry, cultivated by Indian labourers on Spanish-owned plantations. Production rose rapidly in the early eighteenth century, after the Spanish government allowed the settlers to employ Indians from the mission villages on their estates, and Trinidad cocoa fetched high prices because of its superior quality. By 1725 the settlers depended almost entirely on this export crop, and it supported a fairly prosperous trade: in 1719 the settlers could afford to equip a warship to protect the island's cocoa trade. Disaster struck in 1725 and the cocoa industry failed, probably as a result of a fungus disease. Trinidad's trade was crippled, and many settlers emigrated. Although cocoa was revived in 1756, when a hardier variety of tree was introduced, it never regained its pre-1725 importance as Trinidad's major staple.

Cotton, sugar and coffee were grown in very small quantities for local consumption. The Indians cultivated maize (corn) and provisions on their conucos or gardens, and around the mid-eighteenth century the Spanish settlers made some efforts to grow food crops to ensure their survival. There was no ranching, and domesticated livestock were scarce. Except for the short-lived prosperity of the tobacco and cocoa export industries, the Spanish settlers were nothing more than subsistence farmers scratching at the soil around the edge of the forest. They lacked the essentials for agricultural development. In 1662 the governor wrote home that the colonists had no knives, hatchets, cutlasses or agricultural implements; no Spanish ship had visited for over thirty years. Much correspondence followed with Madrid on the urgent necessity to send a Spanish ship once every four years; then a long silence.

Trinidad's capacity to develop a productive base was crippled by the chronic weakness of Spanish shipping in the seventeenth and eighteenth centuries. Spain lacked a sound merchant marine: by the 1780s she possessed only about 500 merchant vessels, while England and Holland could deploy nearly 7,000 each. Her naval strength had declined disastrously, and by 1700 Spain was a second-rate sea power. Too much of her naval shipping was tied up in the annual flotas, or treasure fleets, to the detriment of colonies like Trinidad off the flota routes. With Spanish ships calling infrequently or not at all, the settlers had no option but to sell the little they produced to Dutch and English ships, which appeared much more frequently and charged far lower freight rates. From 1606 Madrid tried to stop this contraband trade in tobacco, and in 1612 a Spanish fleet entered the Gulf and destroyed foreign ships. But contraband trade continued, for Spanish naval power was too weak to end it, and Trinidad was remote from effective Spanish control. In the seventeenth century Dutch ships predominated, in the eighteenth French and English; yet Trinidad's trade remained small, for production was too low to justify more than a few irregular visits by foreign, or occasionally Spanish, shipping. The settlers lacked most of the amenities of European life. Don Diego Lopez, the governor, struck a note of pathos in 1640 when he told Madrid that he went around St Joseph practically naked, and that he did not own a single pair of shoes.

Spain's weakness as a colonial power was essentially economic. She failed to develop the productive industrial and commercial base necessary to maintain the empire. Spain could not, in the seventeenth and eighteenth centuries, provide the goods that the settlers in the colonies needed or wanted, yet, like every other major colonial power, she tried to exclude foreigners from trading with them. Even the great centres of Spanish colonial rule were inadequately supplied, let alone a remote outpost like Trinidad. Spain was weakened by her lack of entrepreneurial skills, her neglect of technology, her chronic shortage of capital. Despite efforts by the Crown to foster agriculture and industry, they were neglected in most parts of the empire; productivity remained low, as indeed it was in Spain itself during this period.

The weakness of Spain's productive base was not the only obstacle to Trinidad's growth. Spain could not provide the manpower for colonial development in her vast American empire. The number of Spaniards settling in Trinidad, an unpromising frontier colony, was never anything like adequate for significant economic development. After the disaster to the cocoa crop in 1725, Trinidad's non-Indian population declined to a mere 162 adult males, of whom only twenty-eight were described as 'white' or Spanish. From then on, although there was a modest recovery, the Spanish element in the population was never large enough to be the nucleus of a viable Spanish-American community. A smallpox epidemic in 1739 depleted both the Spanish and the Indian communities. By 1765 Trinidad's population was estimated at 2,503, of whom 1,277 were Christianized Indians. Many of the Spaniards abandoned St Joseph to live in the bush on their holdings; the cabildo posts could never all be filled and a handful of families controlled the affairs of the city. It was clear that Spain could not provide the colonists to develop Trinidad; by the 1770s Madrid had recognized that efforts would have to be made to attract foreign settlers.

Spain's Amerindian Policy

Further, the rapidly declining Indian population - or that part of it which was under Spanish control in organized villages - never supplied adequate labour for the cocoa industry in its period of prosperity before 1725 and for the cultivation of other crops. And the difficulty of obtaining African slaves was always an obstacle to Trinidad's development as a plantation colony. An insignificant colony like Trinidad was always neglected by the foreign and Spanish contractors granted the right to supply slaves to the Spanish empire. Until the 1780s, African slave labour was of negligible importance. Trinidad's population stagnated; the island lacked the human resources to participate in the general economic development experienced, for example, by the Venezuelan provinces in the middle decades of the eighteenth century.

It was the indigenous Indians who, up to the 1780s, supplied the labour for the Spanish-owned estates, and it was they who grew much of the island's food. But, inevitably, their numbers declined rapidly and their economic position deteriorated under Spanish colonialism. In the sixteenth century the population was probably halved (from around 30,000-40,000 in 1498 to 15,000-20,000 in 1592) as a result of slaving attacks by Spaniards, carrying the enslaved Indians to the Greater Antilles or to the pearl fisheries of Cubagua and Margarita, and raids by Kalinago, who established settlements on the north coast. To escape these attacks, some of the population moved inland during the sixteenth century.

The process by which the Amerindians were brought under the control of the Spanish authorities was slow and halting. Some of the Arawaks were granted in 'encomiendas' to a handful of privileged Spaniards (the 'encomenderos') after the founding of St Joseph in 1592. The encomendero was granted a parcel of land, with the right to exact tribute (usually in the form of labour, or crops, or both) from the Indians living on the land. In return he was expected to Christianize 'his' Indians and protect them. The encomienda was the typical method of granting lands all over the Spanish empire in the sixteenth century, but in Trinidad, only four major encomiendas were established: Acarigua (San Juan), Arauca (Arouca), Tacarigua and Cuara. The four encomenderos, up to the early eighteenth century, controlled much of the Indian labour available to the Spanish settlers. But the encomienda Indians were only a small fraction of the total Indian population: in 1712 only about 600 Indians lived in the encomiendas, cultivating food crops which they paid as tribute to the encomenderos and sold to the settlers. At the end of the seventeenth century the great majority were still living in the forest and in independent settlements, unconverted and beyond the reach of the Spaniards. Trinidad was still predominantly an Indian colony, and only slowly becoming a Christianized Indian colony. Although the encomenderos were supposed to provide priests, known as 'curas doctrineros', for each encomienda, this was largely neglected in the seventeenth century, and the 'wild' Indians living outside the encomiendas were still untouched by Christianity.

This was the situation that prompted the Spanish government to introduce Capuchin missionaries to bring the Indians under Christian organization. The first group arrived in 1687, with responsibility for evangelizing the indigenes, and in all twenty-four Capuchins served in Trinidad until the abolition of the missions in 1708. They gathered together several thousand Indians into a number of mission settlements. Some of these missions were short-lived, but four survived as Indian villages in the eighteenth century: Savana Grande (Princes Town), the largest; Guayria (Naparima); Savanetta; and Montserrate (Mayo). They were all in the southern part of the island, where much of the population had retreated in the sixteenth and seventeenth centuries. The missions had cabildos, elected by male Indians but subject to the control of the missionaries and churches. They were agricultural colonies, cultivating food crops for themselves and commercial crops for sale. The Indians worked for about two days a week on the mission estate, and under the 'mita' system of forced labour they were obliged to work outside the mission for Spanish land-owners for sixteen days in the year; the rest of their time was devoted to work on their own plots. The authority of the missionaries over the Indians was complete, and their judicial and police powers were extensive. By 1700 a few thousand Indians had been nominally Christianized and brought under Spanish control, through the two great agencies of Spanish colonization: the encomienda and the mission. This left a dwindling 'wild' population living in the forests or in independent settlements. By the end of the eighteenth century, however, the great majority of the Indians had been brought under Spanish control.

The missionaries had succeeded in gathering the majority of the Amerindians under their jurisdiction, but they encountered serious opposition from two sources: the Spanish land-owners and the Indians themselves. In 1699 the Indians at the mission of San Francisco de los Arenales (San Rafael) rose up against the Capuchins and murdered them; several Spanish soldiers headed by the governor who came to restore order were killed. It was the last Indian rebellion in Trinidad, the last flicker of resistance to the inexorable advance of colonization and Christianity. The rebels were pursued to Toco, where some were killed or captured; others preferred suicide to enslavement, leaping off a high cliff to their death in a final, mass protest.

The Spanish land-owners resented the virtual monopoly that the missionaries enjoyed over the labour of the mission inmates. This was the time when cocoa was flourishing and the need for labour correspondingly increased; the mita system never met the new demands for labour. The conflict was referred to Madrid in 1707, the settlers won, and in 1708 the missions were abolished by a royal decree: they were converted into Indian villages in which the cura doctrinero, or priest, exercised exclusively religious authority, while a corregidor, responsible to the governor, acted as magistrate and distributed the Indians' labour to Spanish land-owners. The order was implemented in 1713; the Capuchins left, the work of the missionaries was declared ended. Under the new regime the labour of the Indians in the four ex-mission villages became generally available to the settlers. As a result their population declined steadily, from 1,148 in 1722 to 649 in 1777.

In 1716, soon after the abolition of the missions, the encomiendas were ended. The Spanish government had capitulated to the demands of the settlers, who resented the fact that four highly privileged land-owners - the encomenderos - were able to control much of the available Indian labour. 'Corregidors' were appointed to control the four Indian villages that had been encomienda grants, and to regulate the labour given by the Indians to the settlers. After 1716, therefore, authority over those Indians living under Spanish control passed from the missionaries and the encomenderos to the corregidors, who became the sole dispensers of Indian labour to the settlers. By removing the twb institutions with preferential access to the Indians' labour, the mission and the encomienda, the Spanish settlers were able to exploit the Christianized Indians even more fully. The population of the former mission and encomienda villages declined slowly until the 1780s; then the rapid opening up of the island for plantation development brought about the near disappearance of the Indian villages, with the major exception being Arima.

The Weaknesses of Spanish Colonialism

The Spanish government made it its policy to separate Spaniards and Indians, to develop two distinct sets of political, ecclesiastical and judicial organizations. In theory, two 'republics', the Spanish and the Indian, coexisted within the colony. The mission and the encomienda were the institutions for the Indian republic; for the Spanish settlers the town was the major unit of colonization. Indeed, the Spanish empire was always urban; Spanish rule radiated out from formally established towns, which were administrative and ecclesiastical centres, the places of residence for officials, merchants and land-owners. The wretched state of town life in Spanish Trinidad, until the 1780s, indicates the superficiality of Spanish colonization and settlement.

St Joseph, founded in 1592, had all the trappings of Spanish 'urban' life. Its cabildo was theoretically elective, but granted the scarcity of white males (for 'pure' Spanish blood was a requirement), posts were in practice held for life and in effect became the hereditary possession of a few Spanish families. The Santa Hermandad, an ancient Spanish institution that operated like a police force, was established at St Joseph in 1644 to enforce law and order. Of course St Joseph had its church and its cabildo building. But, in reality, St Joseph was a collection of a few miserable huts, made of mud, thatched with palm leaves; its citizens with few exceptions were subsistence farmers struggling to survive with the help of a few mestizo labourers and a handful of slaves. It was not even secure: in 1637 a Dutch force sailed up the Caroni River and sacked the 'city'. Two years later St Joseph was rebuilt, but the condition of its citizens remained wretched. Governor Diego Ximenes reported in 1670 that the town was virtually deserted.

Things were even worse in the middle decades of the eighteenth century, after the failure of the cocoa industry in 1725 and the smallpox epidemic in 1739. The settlers left St Joseph and retreated to the bush, violating all the norms of civilized life in the Spanish view. In 1757 a new governor reported that St Joseph was a derelict collection of mud huts, most of them collapsed; the cabildo building had no roof. When he ordered the cabildo to build a proper municipal hall, to restore the church and repair the houses, to clean up the streets, to organize the cabildo records properly, they told him that he was asking the impossible. Their extreme destitution, their total lack of money, tools, paper and craftsmen, prevented them from complying. In disgust the governor took up residence in Port of Spain. The citizens of St Joseph were left in drunken isolation, to use V.S.Naipaul's phrase, intriguing against the governor, quarrelling with the vicar-general, passing optimistic regulations about setting up a school, calling the citizens out of the bush, building a chest for the cabildo records, and doing nothing.

Port of Spain, where the governor went to live in 1757, had existed since the early seventeenth century as a tiny fishing village and port of call for ships trading in tobacco. It had never been properly founded and it had no cabildo, but its position on the coast made it the natural commercial and shipping centre for the island. In 1757 Port of Spain had 300-400 inhabitants, Spaniards, mixed-race people, foreign settlers, a mixed community of traders, fishermen, farmers and rum distillers. When Trinidad's trade increased rapidly after 1783, Port of Spain was transformed into a bustling commercial town while St Joseph sank into disgruntled apathy.

Until the reforms of the 1770s and 1780s, Trinidad remained, in fact, neglected and undeveloped; a 'colonial slum' of the Spanish empire. The weaknesses of Spanish colonialism, combined with the relative insignificance of Trinidad within the whole American empire, made this inevitable. Trinidad was a frontier outpost far from the centres of colonial power, not worth the effort necessary to rehabilitate its economy and population. Until 1777, Trinidad was under the jurisdiction of the viceroy and audiencia (high court) of New Granada at Bogotá, two months' journey away. Trinidad was a 'ghost province'; nothing was ever done. Madrid lost its grip: a letter from the king begins, helplessly, 'To Don Juan Munoz, who it seems is, or has been, our Governor of Trinidad . . .' The king at Madrid, the viceroy at Bogotá, gave up on Trinidad, leaving the island to its fate; the Council of the Indies noted with philosophical resignation that 'the Island of Trinidad defends itself by its bad climate and the barrenness of its soil'. Despite Trinidad's proximity to the Venezuelan provinces, it was not until 1777 that the island was brought under the jurisdiction of the captain-general of Venezuela and the intendant at Caracas. During the eighteenth century, the mainland provinces of Venezuela, Cumana and Guayana developed significantly, but before the 1780s, Trinidad took no part in this economic advance; the island was increasingly isolated from the nearby continent.

Trinidad's remoteness from the centres of Spanish colonial authority accentuated what Salvador de Madariaga* considers the crucial weakness of the Spanish imperial system: a tendency to anarchy and disorder. However centralized the Spanish colonial system was in theory, in practice, in the days of the sailing ship and the horse or mule, the colonies were effectively self-governing. The Indies were left much to themselves, and in general affairs were run by local whites. The empire was so vast, communications were so slow, the terrain was often so difficult, that directions and laws from Madrid could never be fully enforced, especially in the remoter colonies like Trinidad, far from viceroys, audiencias and bishops. In these colonies the settler tended to act as he pleased, contemptuous of the law.

An example of this tendency to anarchy was the defiance by the Trinidad settlers, over a long period of time, of the laws prohibiting trade with foreign ships. In the early seventeenth century most of the settlers were engaged in illegal trade in tobacco with Dutch and English ships, with the connivance of the governor, Fernando de Berrio. De Berrio ignored several orders from the Council of the Indies to end the trade; the authorities of the mainland provinces complained against his tolerance of contraband trade. Finally, in 1611, Madrid ordered a 'residencia', an investigation into de Berrio's conduct by the governor of Venezuela, Sancho de Alquiza. He found de Berrio guilty of thirty-eight charges of trading with the enemy and of allowing the enslavement and sale of Indians. Indeed, said the judge, all the Spanish settlers were guilty, men, women and children; but since they could not all be punished, he recommended that the king issue a general pardon. The highest royal official in Trinidad had tolerated, if not encouraged, illegal practices by the whole Spanish population.

At other times the local white settlers would defy the governor as the representative of central authority. The eighteenth century was a period of increasing dissatisfaction, on the part of white Creoles in the Spanish empire, with the system of imperial government by Spanish officials. Even a small, impoverished colony like Trinidad experienced an insurrection, led by white settlers, against the royal government represented by the governor.

In 1743 the cabildo of St Joseph challenged the appointment by the governor, Esteban Simón de Lina, of an acting governor during his absence on leave. The cabildo claimed, with some legal justification, that the alcaldes or magistrates should carry on the government during a governor's absence. When de Lina returned early in 1745, the settlers rose up against him and imprisoned him; the cabildo declared him deprived of his office because of his absence without the cabildo's consent. It was a miniature coup by the settlers of St Joseph against the authority of Spain. Eight months passed before the Viceroy of New Granada, in whose jurisdiction

Trinidad was placed, directed the Governor of Cumana to send a force to the island and liberate the imprisoned governor. The governor was freed, the alcaldes were imprisoned, the leading rebels banished for ten years. The cabildo retaliated by going on strike; it held very few meetings between 1746 and 1750. Eventually it roused itself to petition the king to recall the exiles, for without them there were too few intelligent settlers to run the affairs of St Joseph. Madrid agreed, and in 1751 the decree of banishment was revoked; with the return of the exiles the intrigues and plots were revived. The settlers were naturally piqued at the governor's removal to Port of Spain in 1757, and the skirmishes continued until, at last, the cabildo accepted the inevitable and moved to the Port in 1784.

Until the era of reforms in the last quarter of the eighteenth century, Spanish Trinidad was left in the hands of the few white Creole settlers. Madrid was powerless. Trinidad lacked precious metals, its indigenous population was sparse and generally unsuitable for plantation labour, much of it was covered in tropical forest, and it was not situated on a shipping route vital to the empire. The island was not worth developing by the state, even supposing the state capable of the effort; private enterprise was not encouraged by the Spanish colonial system; foreign enterprise was absolutely excluded until the 1770s. So far from developing the island, Madrid could not even defend it. Throughout the Spanish period, Trinidad was under frequent attack by English, French and Dutch pirates or regular forces; St Joseph was sacked several times, and foreign settlements were established at various points on the coast, some of which were left undisturbed for years. As late as 1740 an English force attacked St Joseph. Spain's naval and military weakness made her incapable of defending a remote, impoverished colony like Trinidad.

The Era of Reform

Yet Trinidad's proximity to the continent made the island strategically important to the Spanish Crown, and Madrid could not abandon it altogether to the foreigners. It was clear to the government, as Governor Diego Ximinez had written in 1670, that if Trinidad was lost the adjacent mainland provinces could not be held for long. Something had to be done, particularly when British imperialism entered an aggressive and expansionist phase after 1713. At last, in the 1770s, a revitalized Spanish government roused itself: Trinidad would be populated and defended; it would cease to be a ghost province.

The Bourbon kings of Spain, and particularly Charles III (1759-88), undertook far-reaching reforms designed to make Spain and the empire stronger and more prosperous. Colonial reforms took priority, for the Spanish government was justifiably alarmed at the foreigners' success in exploiting their own colonies and tapping the wealth of the Spanish empire. Trade between Spain and the colonies was liberalized. In 1765 a decree authorized direct trade between nine Spanish ports and a number of colonial ports, including Trinidad. Duties were revised or abolished. Gradually intercolonial trade was freed: by 1789 Spain had opened up the empire to trade by all Spaniards on equal terms and from all the major Spanish and colonial ports, while still excluding foreign traders. Economic reforms were accompanied by administrative rationalization. A Secretary of State for the Indies was set up in 1714, in effect a colonial minister. In 1731 the captaincy-general of Venezuela was created to unite several provinces in modern Venezuela. Such reforms resulted in smaller units, more easily governed and defended. The French office of the 'intendant', an official with very wide financial, judicial and administrative powers, was gradually introduced in the empire after 1765. In 1776 an intendant was created for Venezuela, to reside at Caracas and have jurisdiction over all the provinces of the captaincy-general of Venezuela.

A new spirit of enterprise was galvanizing the Spanish empire. Under French influence and guidance - for France and Spain were closely allied after 1761 - Charles III's ministers sought to strengthen the empire's defences and to develop the more vulnerable and neglected provinces. No part of the empire was more neglected than Trinidad. Although the island was one of the ports opened to direct trade with Spain in the decree of 1765, no significant development had followed. Trinidad was too poor to benefit; no trade could develop until a productive base had been created. The island would have to be opened up for agriculture along the lines of the English and French colonies; it would have to be transformed into a profitable West Indian slave colony. But where would the planters, the slaves and the capital come from? Slowly, reluctantly, Madrid faced the truth: not from Spain. By 1776 the Spanish government had accepted that foreign immigration would be essential to develop Trinidad.

In that year, Manuel Falquez was appointed governor with instructions to attract to Trinidad French and other foreign Catholic settlers living in the islands that had been granted to Britain in 1763 after the Seven Years' War, especially Grenada, promising them protection and land grants. For the French Catholic planters of Grenada were subjected to severe political and social discrimination at the hands of the Protestant British. These settlers were to be given various tax incentives as well as land grants. These instructions, formalized by a 1776 decree authorizing foreign Catholic settlement in Trinidad and elsewhere, reflected Spain's anxiety to defend and develop the more vulnerable parts of the empire. The decision to admit foreigners countered Spanish tradition, but the intention was to keep Trinidad's newly developed trade firmly in Spanish hands.

In May 1777 Falquez received a visitor from Grenada, Roume de St Laurent, a French planter who became the semi-official spokesman for a group of French planters in Grenada interested in emigrating to Trinidad. These people began to arrive in the middle of 1777, along with their slaves, attracted by the promise of land grants and protection by a friendly Catholic government. In 1779 Madrid approved French and Irish (they were Catholics) emigration to Trinidad and to all the sparsely populated regions of the intendancy of Venezuela. By then at least 523 free settlers with 973 slaves had entered the island, nearly all French. St Laurent, Maurice de la Peyrouse (after whose family the Lapeyrouse Cemetery is named) and other French settlers had received land grants. By 1780 St Laurent was 'alcalde extraordinario' of the cabildo, still based at St Joseph, and exercising a strong influence on the colonial authorities. This early period of French settlement was a difficult time for the old Spanish settlers, who saw they were being superseded by the French newcomers, and who resented St Laurent's influence on the government. There were clashes and disputes between the French immigrants and the Spanish settlers and soldiers. But these were the teething troubles of a newly opening-up colony, the restlessness of a frontier communty. In 1779 St Laurent was in Caracas lobbying with the intendant; in 1782-3 he was in Madrid. He recommended greatly increased French immigration and liberal land, tax and trading concessions to the future settlers.

The Spanish government was convinced. The experiment of French immigration, begun on a small scale in 1777, would be approved and enlarged. St Laurent's reward was the Cedula of Population (November 1783), which fully accepted the principle of foreign immigration. The wave of French immigration, a mere trickle in the years between 1777 and 1783, would now become a flood engulfing the Spanish colony.

---

1. The distinguished Spanish historian.

TWO

Enter the Africans and the French, 1783-97

The Cedula of Population, 1783

By 1783, the Spanish government had fully accepted the principle of foreign immigration to Trinidad. It recognized that French planters, with their slaves, capital and expertise in the cultivation of tropical staples, would have to be attracted if the island was to be developed as a plantation colony. The result of this conviction, skilfully aided by Roume de St Laurent's energetic lobbying, was the Cedula (Decree) of Population, issued from Madrid on 24 November 1783.

The Cedula brought together two sets of problems: the failure of Spanish colonialism in Trinidad, and the difficulties experienced by French planters in the islands ceded to Britain in 1763, and in the French West Indies. The earlier efforts by Spain to develop the neglected areas of her empire had failed to benefit Trinidad to any significant extent. Now a decree applying specifically to Trinidad offered very generous terms to emigrants who were wealthy and experienced planters willing to bring in their slaves, capital and knowhow. In the 'ceded islands', and particularly in Grenada, French planters encountered severe political and social discrimination at the hands of the British planters and authorities. In the French islands, especially Martinique, problems like exhausted soils and plagues of ants made life difficult for the planters. This is why many French planters from the French islands and from the group of 'ceded islands' were prepared to emigrate to an island that offered limitless extents of virgin soil. But, St Laurent insisted as their self-appointed spokesman, Spain would have to offer them very generous incentives if they were to leave long-established, mature plantation colonies to settle in a virtual wilderness.

The principal incentive that the Cedula offered was a free grant of land to every settler who came to Trinidad with his slaves. Every white emigrant was entitled to four and two-sevenths fanegas (an old Spanish unit of measurement equivalent to 30 acres) for each member of his family and half as much for each slave he introduced. Free coloured or free black settlers who emigrated as property-owners and slave-holders were entitled to half the amount granted to the white emigrant, and a proportionate grant for each slave. Two further conditions for immigration to Trinidad were stipulated: the emigrant had to be a Roman Catholic and the subject of a nation friendly to Spain; and after five years, settlers who decided to remain permanently on the island would be entitled to all the rights and privileges of Spanish citizenship.

We can quickly note the most important results of these conditions. The settlers would be almost exclusively French, for only the French planters could fulfil the requirement of Roman Catholicism and alliance with Spain. In any case, the Cedula was specifically designed to attract wealthy French planters. Some Irish planters came in and a few Englishmen, but the immigration turned out to be overwhelmingly French. Second, the Cedula linked the ownership of land with the ownership of slaves. The more slaves the emigrant brought in, the more land he received. The more slaves the planter owned, the more land could actually be cultivated. The thirst for land and the shortage of labour interacted, and Trinidad was fated to become, in a few years, a slave colony. Third, the Cedula gave legal sanction to a coloured property-owning class. Although coloured immigrants were to receive half as much land as their white counterparts, they were nevertheless formally given land by the Spanish government as planters and slave-owners, with all the status which that implied in a plantation society. Further, the article granting the rights of citizenship to settlers after five years made no distinction between white and coloured immigrants, suggesting that the Spanish government was prepared to grant free coloured property-owners fuller civil rights than they enjoyed anywhere else in the West Indies. The free coloureds of the French colonies and the 'ceded islands', suffering economic hardships and severe social and political discrimination, responded enthusiastically to the promise of the Cedula and flocked to Trinidad in large numbers, outnumbering the white immigrants, and establishing a substantial coloured propertied class.

Tax concessions were a major incentive offered by the Cedula to the immigrants, for the burdensome Spanish taxation system, if applied to the new settlers, would have been a serious obstacle to immigration. The settlers were promised exemption for a period of ten years from the major taxes, after which time they were to pay only half the normal amount. In particular the slave trade was to be free of all duties for ten years. A decree in 1786 further liberalized these tax concessions by making the exemption from duties on the slave trade perpetual, and reducing many other levies after the ten-year grace period had expired. Trade concessions were granted to the French: trade was allowed between Trinidad and certain French ports where a Spanish consul was resident. Such a concession countered the traditions of Spanish exclusivism, but it fell far short of St Laurent's request that Spain should give France the freedom of Spanish-American ports for twenty years. France was given most favoured nation status in Trinidad's trade, but the Cedula shows the

Spanish government's anxiety not to encourage French shipping and trade at the expense of Spain's, nor to allow France to use her favoured position to gain access to the rest of the Spanish empire. In the event, ironically, it was neither France nor Spain that gained most from the opening-up of Trinidad: it was Britain, the world's leading maritime and commercial power, and the common enemy of both.

Other articles of the Cedula promised the settlers the paternal care of the Spanish government. Royal officials were instructed to supply them with livestock, flour and Spanish-manufactured goods at cost price for a period of ten years; French-speaking priests would be brought in; steps would be taken to avoid the arrival of the ants that were causing so much trouble in the Lesser Antilles; refineries would be set up in Spain to process the sugar that the settlers would produce. Such clauses represented the benevolent intentions of the Spanish government, but were incapable of immediate implementation; for the Cedula was primarily a political and diplomatic document, signalling to the French planters of the Caribbean that their welfare and interests would be the major concern of the authorities if they opted to emigrate to Trinidad. To underline the point, Madrid chose a new kind of offical to implement the Cedula. Don José Maria Chacon, who arrived in Trinidad as governor in 1784, was a representative of the Spanish Enlightenment. Well-educated, reform-minded, fluent in French and English, he was sympathetic to the French immigrants who began to enter the island, and well suited to govern what soon became a restless, cosmopolitan colony.

The immigration that resulted from the Cedula of Population transformed the size and composition of the island's population. Before 1783, Trinidad's sparse population, centred in St Joseph and the Indian villages, was predominantly Spanish-Indian. In a few years, a large influx of French planters and African slaves had changed Trinidad's demographic structure completely. The old Spanish and Indian population group gave way to a new and far more numerous African and French sector.

A Plantation Economy

We have seen that French and African immigration had begun as early as 1777 under the administration of Governor Falquez. By 1784 there were already more white French persons than Spaniards, and African slaves constituted the most numerous group. A census taken in the middle of 1784, when Chacon had just arrived, recorded 335 Spaniards and 384 French settlers, 765 'mixed' Spaniards and 633 French free coloureds (persons of mixed European and African descent) and free blacks, 260 'Spanish slaves' and 2,027 'French slaves'. By contrast, the Indian population had fallen to 1,495, and their numbers would continue to decline, slowly but steadily, in the 1780s and 1790s. As early as 1784, therefore, French planters, white and coloured, and their slaves, had outnumbered the Spanish-Indian group.

This trend was greatly accentuated after 1784, as the Cedula attracted French planters and their slaves. The table illustrates the growth of Trinidad's non-Indian population in 1784-97:

	Freemen	Slaves	Indians	Total
1784	2550	2462	1491	6503
1785	2741	3300	1405	7446
1786	3201	4430	1391	9022
1787	4110	6009	1414	11533
1788	3807	6481	1428	11716
1789	5170	6451	1432	13053
1790	5443	6396	1408	13247
1791	4695	5916	1398	12009
1792	5047	7767	1198	14012
1793	5212	8264	1268	14744
1794	5642	8733	1114	15519
1795	5257	8944	1078	15279
1797	6627*	10009	1082	17718

*Whites: 2151Coloureds: 4476

The years immediately after the Cedula, 1784-7, saw rapid growth, and a particularly large increase in the number of slaves, introduced from the Lesser Antilles with their French owners, and brought in from Africa by British slavers. Growth was slower in 1787-91 and the number of slaves had fallen by the latter year, probably the result of very high slave mortality rates as the island was rapidly opened up for plantation agriculture. After 1792 steady growth resumed, with the British slave trade flourishing. The revolutionary wars in the Caribbean brought in a new influx of Frenchmen, both white and coloured. By 1797 the total population had reached 17,718, of whom 10,009 or 56.4 per cent were slaves. Trinidad was not yet a typical slave colony, with the vast majority of its people African slaves; but the change was well under way. By contrast, in that same year the Indians numbered only 1,082, or 6 per cent of the total population. Another significant fact was that in 1797 there were 4,476 free coloureds and free blacks, and only 2,151 whites. The whites were outnumbered, not only by the slaves, but also by the free coloureds, some of whom were themselves planters and slave-owners.

After 1783 the island's plantation economy was controlled largely by the French settlers, white and coloured, who brought with them slaves, capital and long experience in the cultivation of cotton, coffee, sugar and other tropical export crops. In Trinidad, they received grants of land in proportion to their wealth and their holdings in slaves. The forest was gradually pushed back, plantations were established. Late in the day, Trinidad stepped into line as a major producer of West Indian staples and as a creator of wealth for planters and merchants.

The French immigrants settled in and around Port of Spain and in the valleys surrounding the little town. Going east, French settlers mixed with Irish and English planters, but the district around St Joseph remained predominantly Spanish. In the south nearly all the settlers were French, white and coloured, and here flourishing plantations were established. To encourage agricultural development, the Spanish authorities tried to import agricultural implements from Spain and livestock for work on the estates from Venezuela. The Treasury advanced credit for the purchase of mules and agricultural tools to new immigrants and old Spanish settlers alike. By 1795 the chronic shortage of mules, horses and oxen had been relieved, and the planters could rely on a steady supply of animal as well as human power.

Although sugar had become Trinidad's most important crop by the 1790s, it was never the only significant export staple in this period. Cocoa remained important, grown chiefly by Spanish settlers in the valleys of the Northern Range, fetching high prices because of its excellent flavour. But cotton was the crop the French settlers favoured in the 1780s, when its output expanded rapidly in many parts of the island. By 1788 cotton accounted for 70 per cent of the value of Trinidad's exports; cotton was responsible for Trinidad's initial prosperity as a plantation colony. But it declined soon after when the crop suffered from attacks of the boll-weevil, although it continued to be cultivated on a significant scale in the 1790s; by 1796, 103 cotton estates were producing 224,000 lb of cotton. The French planters also cultivated coffee, and in 1796, 130 estates were producing 330,000 lb of coffee. The estates produced food crops; for the first few years after the forest had been cleared, provisions, rice and maize were grown to support the slaves until the cotton, coffee or sugar was ready to be harvested.

But sugar was *the* West Indian staple in the eighteenth century, and most of the new settlers had owned sugar estates in their home islands. Prices were high in the 1780s, and particularly in the 1790s, and the decline of cotton production after 1788 encouraged the shift to sugar. A planter from Martinique, St Hilaire Begorrat, is said to have introduced the Otaheite (the old spelling of Tahiti) cane in 1782, and its cultivation spread rapidly. In 1787 Picot de la Peyrouse established the first sugar mill at Tragarete estate. Sugar was concentrated in the valleys near Port of Spain, along the west coast, and in the Naparimas. The yields from the rich virgin soils were high. By 1797 over 150 sugar estates had been established, with about 130 mills, mostly driven by mules, producing some 7,800 hogsheads (casks or barrels) each year. Sugar was certainly the most important export crop by the time the British captured the island in 1797, but cotton, coffee and cocoa continued to be significant, and Trinidad's economy was far from monocultural.

At last Trinidad had developed the productive base that would support an active trade. In the 1780s and 1790s the amount of shipping calling at Port of Spain increased dramatically and a flourishing export trade was established. Close trading links developed between Trinidad and the French West Indies, and between Trinidad and the British colonies, especially Grenada. St George's, the capital of Grenada, was made a free port in 1784 in order to tap Trinidad's trade.

It was the British who dominated this new trading activity. British merchants settled in Trinidad from as early as 1784, and while the French settlers concentrated on agriculture, the British established a strong hold on the island's trade. They won the privilege of using their own ships and further exemptions from duties. British merchants dominated the trade in cotton to Grenada and other British islands for eventual shipment to Britain. In 1789 seventy-three ships cleared Port of Spain with cotton, nearly all British. The export of sugar was also in the hands of British and US merchants, and the shift to sugar in the 1790s reinforced Trinidad's dependence on British ships and middlemen. The British and American firms that handled the island's sugar had agents in Port of Spain who organized the marketing of the crop and imported supplits and slaves for the planters. Because of Trinidad's proximity to the continent, and the low duties on imported goods, the island became an important entrepôt, sending British manufactured goods, foodstuffs and slaves to the continent in exchange for colonial produce.

Spain had envisaged that the economic development of Trinidad would lead to an increase in her own trade, not Britain's, the major enemy. In fact Spanish shipping did increase in the 1790s: in 1796 thirteen Spanish ships called at Port of Spain. The export of cocoa remained largely in Spanish hands, going to the Spanish market. Inter-provincial trade with the continent, in Spanish or Spanish colonial shipping, remained active, Trinidad importing animals, meat and leather, cloth and maize, and exporting slaves and money. But Trinidad's trade with Spain and the continent was far less valuable than the West Indian trade dominated by British shipping. In 1796 seventy-four foreign ships called at Port of Spain -the great majority British - clearing over three million lb of sugar and half a million lb of cotton. By contrast only thirteen Spanish ships arrived to load cocoa, while 248 small vessels called from the mainland with livestock and foodstuffs.

Trinidad's new prosperity had at last brought the island in touch with the enterprise and the bustle of the West Indian plantation

Plate 1 Riverside, St Joseph

system. By the 1790s Trinidad had become an international, frontier colony, full of foreigners preying on the island's new prosperity, anxious to make quick fortunes. They gathered at Port of Spain, which was transformed from a sleepy little fishing village into a bustling, cosmopolitan port.

With only about 632 inhabitants in 1777, the city's population had increased to 1,025 by 1784, of whom 602 were listed as 'new colonists'; by 1797 its population was 4,525, consisting of 938 whites, 1,671 free coloureds and blacks, and 1,916 slaves. The cabildo moved to the Port in 1784, and the city became a busy commercial and social centre for the French settlers and British merchants, as well as the Spanish officials who governed the colony under Chacon. Most of the houses were wooden, painted on the outside; the streets, without pavements but with a drain running down the middle, were paved with limestone from Laventille. Chacon diverted the St Ann River along the foot of the Laventille hills, and reclaimed the swampy areas along its former course. To defend the prosperous but vulnerable little port, Chacon built Fort San Andrés and a fortified mole at the former mouth of the St Ann River, and two other batteries were erected near the foot of the Laventille hills. By 1797 the city was considered one of the busiest in the Caribbean.

As Port of Spain rose, St Joseph declined; it had lost much of its former status and functions when the governor, and then the cabildo, moved to the Port. Its population was only 728 in 1797, overwhelmingly Spanish or Spanish-Indian. Some of its citizens belonged to old Spanish families resident in Trinidad since the seventeenth century, others were more recent immigrants from the mainland. St Joseph's complete decline was prevented only because a military garrison was stationed there, and because it was linked by the Eastern Main Road to Port of Spain.

The ancient capital was the refuge of the Spanish settlers, who were bewildered and resentful at the foreigners' success in transforming the island. For the old society of Trinidad, Spanish and Indian, was being destroyed, superseded by the new society which was African and French. The Spanish settlers were displaced in the cabildo; as early as 1782 three foreigners had gained seats, by 1788 six out of nine cabildo members were foreign. In fact the old pre-1783 society was shut out from influence and power; the Spanish Creoles of St Joseph, like the Farfan, Hospedales and Hernandez families, were overtaken by the wealthy newcomers.

Even more disastrous was the loss of lands that the Spanish settlers claimed to hold through ancient possession. Most of this land was uncultivated, and many Spanish Creoles hoped to sell the land they claimed at high prices to the new colonists, cashing in on the steep rise in land values. Chacon's attitude was unsympathetic. Reporting in 1785 that 'scarce is there a spot remaining that can be granted to new colonists, which is not claimed as property', he promulgated a harsh decree which declared that immemorial possession was no longer sufficient title to land. Lands claimed by Spaniards without any proper title, and which were not cultivated, would be forfeit to the Crown, unless the claimant registered the title within three months and gave evidence of his intention and ability to cultivate. Although Chacon never enforced this decree strictly, its spirit was distinctly hostile to the old settlers, who were branded in the preamble as indolent and crooked, and it was bitterly resented by them. Indeed, Chacon criticized the old Spanish settlers as if he was a foreigner himself instead of an official of the Spanish Crown. His key advisers and officials were not Frenchmen, but neither were they local Spanish Creoles: they were 'Peninsulares' from Spain or lawyers from the mainland provinces who had only recently come to Trinidad. These officials from Spain or Venezuela combined with the wealthy French planters to run the colony under Chacon. The old Spanish Creoles of St Joseph, impoverished and isolated, lost all influence over the affairs of their native island. Some of them joined the Spanish armed forces, others emigrated to the continent; a number relapsed into poverty and obscurity, and disappeared from the historical record.

This destiny was to be shared, ultimately, by the Amerindians. The opening of the island for plantation agriculture sealed the fate of the indigenous people. They could not coexist with the plantations and slave labour. The Indian population was nearly halved in 1777-97, dropping from 1,824 to 1,082 (excluding a small number still living in the forests). This steady decline was the result of many factors: miscegenation as colonists and slaves moved inland; disease; overwork on the new plantations; emigration to the continent; food shortages caused by the disruption of their traditional subsistence farming; and lower fertility because of malnutrition and poor health.

The Indians of the three surviving former encomienda villages were gathered together in 1785 and settled at Arima, for Chacon wanted to take over the extensive and largely uncultivated lands in the Tacarigua valley granted to the encomiendas, in order to allot them to new settlers. The new village was laid out in the traditional manner, and the Indians were given their mock cabildo. In the same way, the four former mission villages were amalgamated after 1783. Guayria had ceased to exist by then; by 1794 the Savanetta Indians had gone to Montserrate, while Savana Grande remained a separate village. The population of the two surviving mission villages was only 293 in 1797, and there were 495 Indians at Arima in that year. The small Indian villages on the north-east coast, mainly Kalinago settlements, also declined and most had disappeared by 1797. With the decrease in population, the disappearance of many settlements and the isolation of others, the political control of the surviving Indians became easier. Two 'Corregidores de Indios', at Arima and at Savana Grande and Montserrate, continued to carry out administrative and judicial functions, and dispensed Indian labour to those land-owners who still wanted it. The villages on the north-east coast had 'capitanes' with similar functions, appointed in the 1770s. Outside the organized villages, a dwindling few lived beyond Spanish control in the forest in the traditional way. The tragic drama that began in Trinidad with the first contact of Europeans and native Americans was nearly over; the Indians gave, way to more resiliept newcomers.

Yet the Amerindians left their indelible mark on Trinidad and Trinidadians, and large numbers of place names are of Arawakan and Kalinago origin. Because most of Trinidad's population were Amerindians until the late eighteenth century, many of the Indian toponyms (place names) remained intact, or were modified by assimilation into Spanish. Sometimes these place names derived from particular tribes: Cumana and Tamana are named after two Kalinago tribes, the Cumanagoto and the Tamanaco; while Arima is derived from Hyarima, a Nepuyo chief. Arouca is named for the Aruaca, an Arawakan tribe; Naparima means 'one hill' (Anna Parima). Many Amerindian toponyms represent names of trees, plants and animals: Guanapo (grass), Cunapo (mangrove), Chaguaramas (palmist palm), El Tucuche (humming-bird), La Seiva (silk cotton tree), Cocorite (cocorite palm), and many others. These place names are a memorial to Trinidad's first inhabitants, who also bequeathed (through Spanish) a number of words in common use today, although the Amerindian languages did not significantly influence Spanish, patois or English as spoken in the island. Many words describing plants and animals are of Amerindian origin, passed into Trinidadian English through Spanish or sometimes French: balata, cacao, maize, iguana, carata (carat palm), bachac (a kind of ant), agouti, lappe, manicou, and many others.

Techniques of preparing food were also influenced by the Amerindians. Rural folk of diverse racial origins in Trinidad adopted Amerindian foods and cooking methods. The cassava was baked on the aripo, an indigenous word for a baking-stone or griddle; the poisonous juice was extracted by the sebucan (Arawakan), a cassava presser or squeezer. The Amerindians bequeathed to Trinidad the arep, a fried pie of cornmeal with a meat filling, and the pastelle, a delicacy featuring spicy minced meat covered with corn meal, steamed in banana leaves. From the Indians, later Trinidadians learned the techniques of making bark hammocks and weaving baskets; log mortars and wooden pestles for pounding maize, cocoa or coffee, traditionally found in rural kitchens, were probably Amerindian survivals. The Indian corial, or canoe, made from a single tree trunk, continued to be used. In general, the indigenous people influenced the life-style of rural Trinidadians in the nineteenth and twentieth centuries, particularly the members of the Spanish-speaking community of Venezuelan origin, called 'peons' in the island.

But the new post-1783 society was essentially Afro-French: French planters, French free coloureds and African slaves whose cultural orientation was French West Indian. These became the nucleus of Trinidad society, replacing the old Spanish and Indian population group.

The Establishment of Slave Society

As early as 1784, after the first wave of French immigration from Grenada, Martinique, Guadeloupe, St Lucia and Cayenne, Trinidad had become virtually a French colony, dominated by a French planter elite. As James Millette has phrased it, 'the mind and heart' of Trinidad was French. The French language and the Créole patois became the most widely spoken languages. French food, dances, music and social customs spread quickly. Though these early immigrants, coming to Trinidad in 1777-90, included some shady characters and a few out-and-out rogues, the majority were well-established planters and slave-owners, conservative in politics, imbued with all the values and prejudices of slave society. These were precisely the kind of immigrants Spain wished to attract. Chacon got on well with them, and they soon came to run the affairs of Port of Spain and the countryside with his full approval.

As early as 1779, Roume de St Laurent held the office of alcalde extraordinario of the cabildo. In 1782, before the Cedula had been issued, three French planters sat on the cabildo; in 1786 seven Frenchmen and one Irishman, and two Spaniards recently arrived in the island, made up the membership. When Chacon created the post of Commissioner of Population, his first appointment was St Laurent. The Commandants of Quarters, unpaid but important officials with wide police and judicial powers in the country districts, were nearly all French land-owners during Chacon's regime. But the French settlers whom Chacon appointed to these posts, and who sat on the cabildo, were without exception wealthy white land-owners and slave-holders whose politics were royalist and conservative, men committed to the preservation of slavery and white ascendancy. Their influence in the cabildo and in the other organs of local government only reflected the preponderance of the French landed class in the society and economy of the island. So long as an identity of interests existed between them and Chacon, there was no particular danger in the extraordinary influence enjoyed by French planters in the government of a Spanish colony.

The basis of their wealth was the land, and they were essentially a plantation and slave owning group. They lived in modest wooden country houses on their estates, and if they could afford it they also had a house in Port of Spain. Intensely conscious of their elite position, they cherished their family connections and their aristocratic descent, real or imagined. They were famous for their hospitality, and most of them resided on their estates. Family life was close and formed the basis of social interaction among the French landed elite. Music and dancing were important to them, and the Carnival celebrations, which they probably introduced, lasted from Christmas to Ash Wednesday, featuring satirical sketches and jokes, and elegant masked balls. The French land-owners formed a powerful elite group; their control of slave labour, and their opening up of the island for plantation agriculture, enabled them to dominate the new Trinidadian society.

These wealthy and conservative French planters posed no threat to Chacon, for their interests by and large coincided with the objectives of the Spanish authorities. But after 1790 a different kind of Frenchman began to come to Trinidad. As the French Revolution engulfed the French West Indies, as war and rebellion ravaged all the French islands and many of the British, a wave of Frenchmen who sympathized with the revolutionary principles sought refuge in Trinidad from the reversals of civil or international war in the Caribbean. They were both white and coloured, and they ranged from committed republicans to men of no particular ideology anxious to exploit a confused situation. Fleeing the triumph of counter-revolution in some of the French islands, or the British defeat of rebellions in St Vincent, Grenada and St Lucia, they arrived in considerable numbers, especially in 1794-6. Chacon and the powerful French land-owners who ran the colony kept them out of all the institutions of local government; they exercised no political influence or power; but they were numerous and noisy, and in the threatening international situation of 1794-7, Chacon justifiably feared that he could lose his precarious control of events. After 1790, in fact, to Chacon's dismay, French immigrants brought to Trinidad all the ideological divisions of the revolution.

But the French immigrants, whether royalists or republicans, were outnumbered by the free coloureds and blacks who came from the French West Indies or from the 'ceded islands'. By 1797 there were 4,476 free coloureds and blacks as compared with 2,151 whites. The most important group within this large free coloured population consisted of planters and slave-owners who were attracted by articles 4 and 5 of the Cedula, which offered land grants and civil rights to coloured settlers. Roman Catholic in religion and French in language and culture, these families established flourishing estates, especially in the Naparimas, in the southern part of the island, and enjoyed far greater economic security and social status than their counterparts in either the French or the British colonies. In these islands, free coloureds were subject to increasingly severe restrictions on their economic activities, and humiliating regulations marked the free people of colour, however wealthy or educated, as perpetually inferior to all whites. In effect a system of apartheid was established in the British and French islands, reaching its climax in the 1770s and 1780s.

Although harsh laws against free coloureds also existed in the Spanish colonies, the practice towards them was milder. They held minor posts in the administration in many Spanish colonies by the 1780s, and they were commissioned as officers in the local militias. More significant, Chacon was a man of liberal intent, and he chose to ignore the laws that existed in the Spanish colonies against the free coloureds. As far as we know, Chacon never appointed a free coloured planter to any public post; free coloureds did not sit on the cabildo, nor serve as Commandants of Quarters, nor hold any administrative positions. They had no political power; but Chacon treated the prosperous free coloured planters with courtesy and dignity. They suffered no public humiliations; there were no apartheid regulations. In particular, and this was symbolically important to the whole free coloured community, Chacon appointed free coloured and free black land-owners to officers' commissions in the militia. The free coloured spokesmen regarded this action as tangible proof that their community enjoyed equal rights with whites under Chacon's regime, which they saw in retrospect as the 'golden age' for the free coloureds of Trinidad. Jean-Baptiste Philip, the free coloured leader in the 1820s, wrote that the coloureds of Trinidad 'have always possessed grounds for pretensions, to which no other coloured colonists could aspire. During the whole period of

Spanish administration, they were as impartially treated as the whites...' This is an exaggeration; but it is clear that free coloured land-owners enjoyed a secure legal and social status during Chacon's regime.

But the great majority of the free coloured and black population were not planters and slave-owners. The majority were smallholders in the country, and artisans or domestic servants in Port of Spain and the villages. Probably the largest single group consisted of artisans of all kinds. They built the houses and the plantation buildings in the rapidly developing island, they provided the skilled labour essential for plantation operations, and some of them managed to buy a little land and a few slaves and establish small estates. Some of the smallholders and agricultural labourers were Spanish-speaking, of Spanish-Indian or Spanish-African descent, but most of the free coloureds and blacks were from the French islands and were French- or patois-speaking.

Many of them were republicans: in other words, they sympathized with the principles of the French Revolution. Perhaps the great majority were without any clear ideology beyond a vague aspiration to equality. But the whole free coloured community came under general suspicion of cherishing revolutionary sympathies. In Saint Domingue (Haiti) the civil war had begun when free coloureds asserted their rights, and in Trinidad they were feared as a possible source of subversion and danger. The whites claimed to see the spectre of slave revolt behind every attempt by a coloured man to assert his freedom. No West Indian free coloured community had less reason to be revolutionary than that of Trinidad, but this did not prevent the whites from branding the whole class as dangerous revolutionaries. After the British capture, this myth of free coloured republicanism would be used to justify the erosion of the privileged position that this class had enjoyed under Chacon.

African slave labour was the basis of the new society created in the island in the 1780s and 1790s. Slavery had been of little importance to Trinidad's socio-economic development until the beginning of French immigration, but it soon became the only significant source of agricultural labour. The Cedula of Population, by linking the ownership of slaves with land grants, ensured that there would be a massive influx of slaves, for the larger the settler's labour force, the more extensive his land grant. The majority of the slaves came to Trinidad with their owners, and these slaves were mostly Creoles, patois-speaking and at least nominally Roman Catholics. Slaves were also bought, stolen and kidnapped from the neighbouring colonies, especially Grenada, and imported direct from Africa by British slavers.

British merchants quickly entrenched themselves in the lucrative business of supplying the newly developing colony with slaves. The Spanish government awarded contracts to British firms to supply

Trinidad and other colonies with specified numbers of slaves each year. In 1784 a contract was awarded to Edward Barry, an Irishman who settled in the island as a planter and businessman. Barry and his partner Black infuriated the Trinidad planters by importing stock in poor condition: out of forty slaves brought in early in 1785 only five or six were still alive three days later; Barry and Black regarded such losses as the normal hazards of a business operation. Other contracts were awarded, for the demand always outstripped the supply. The Liverpool firm of Baker & Dawson received a contract to supply 4,000 slaves a year to Trinidad and other Spanish colonies. Then in 1789 the Spanish government declared the slave trade to its colonies open: both Spanish and foreign merchants could sell slaves free of duties for ten years. This improved the supply, and 3,307 slaves were introduced into Trinidad from all sources between 1789 and 1791, though some of these were probably re-exported to Venezuela. Despite high mortality among slaves in Trinidad, the slave population steadily increased through immigration and purchases, and by 1797 it had reached 10,000.

Contemporary observers thought that slavery in the Spanish colonies was milder than in the British and French West Indies, and many historians agree. Spanish slave laws were generally more humane and paid more attention to the slaves as individuals with human and religious rights. P. G. L. Borde, a French Creole historian of Trinidad writing in the late nineteenth century, paints a rosy picture of slavery under the French planters after 1783. He says that the French planters treated their slaves like children entrusted to their care, and that the slaves reciprocated with a lifelong attachment to their masters and their families. No doubt paternalism was an element in the relations between master and slave, particularly on the modest, well-established estates where the slave labour force was small and the owner's family was resident. But we have no evidence that slavery in Trinidad, during the 1780s and 1790s, was 'milder' than anywhere else in the Caribbean.

For one thing, the liberal Spanish codes could never be enforced. The famous Slave Code of 1789, which may have been drafted by a French planter resident in Trinidad, Joseph de la Forest, was probably never even promulgated in the colonies. This Code has been much praised for its humanity, but when its provisions became known in the Spanish colonies, the planters of Havana, Santo Domingo, Caracas and elsewhere set up such an outcry that the Council of the Indies agreed to rescind the law, instead allowing leading planters of each colony to propose their own slave laws. Furthermore, the Spanish laws were implemented in Trinidad by French planters who had brought with them the conventions and customs of the French slave colonies, where the practice of slavery was extremely harsh. We know that the Trinidad slaves were literally worked to death in this period, when they were clearing the forest and establishing new plantations, suffering from gross overwork, primitive conditions and exposure to tropical diseases. In 1784 it was estimated that a land-owner would lose one-third of his slaves during land clearance; these were the normal, expected losses of a new plantation. In 1788 alone, nearly a thousand slaves died from diseases contracted during land clearance. These extremely high mortality rates, caused by overwork, malnutrition, disease and the absence of any medical care for the slaves, are difficult to reconcile with the notion of a mild, paternalistic kind of slavery. The myth was useful for the French planters, but the reality of slavery during the period of French immigration was far harsher.

Chacon Confronts the Revolution

The arrival of the French planters and their slaves had transformed the society and economy of Trinidad in the years 1783-97. Chacon was governing a restless, international colony. It was clear that administrative reorganization was essential to cope with the rapid development of the island.

At first Chacon governed with the aid of three or four key officials who were Spaniards either from Spain or from the neighbouring continent. The Assessor was the legal adviser to the governor, the Fiscal was Crown Attorney (roughly like the modern Attorney-General) and deputy for the Assessor. The Treasury was the department responsible for financial affairs. Chacon, the Assessor, the Fiscal and two Treasury officials formed the Junta Provincial (Provincial Council), which was subordinate to the Junta Superior in Caracas. But new agencies of local government were needed to control and supervise the influx of settlers.

In 1785 Chacon appointed three Commissioners of Population, each responsible for one of the three sections into which the island was divided. St Laurent was the first to hold this post. At first the duties were chiefly to administer land grants, but in 1787 the Commissioners were given very wide functions. They were to gather detailed information on population and agricultural production, oversee sales of land and maintain law and order; the First Commissioner was made responsible for road maintenance and the welfare of the slaves. They were also rural police officers. The three sections were further divided into twenty-eight Quarters under Commandants who helped the Commissioners to maintain law and order; eminent local land-owners resident in the Quarter were invariably appointed as Commandants. In Port of Spain the alcaldes de barrio enforced the law; the city was divided in 1786 into five barrios (districts) with two alcaldes (magistrates) for each. French planters dominated these newly created positions in local government. Now Trinidad's rapid transformation meant that Chacon was administering a colony that was essentially different from the Venezuelan provinces, and the link with Caracas became weaker during the last two decades of Spanish rule. Chacon's powers were extensive; he corresponded directly with Madrid, and his subordination to the intendant and the Junta Superior at Caracas had become a nuisance rather than an asset. Chacon's standing with the home government was high, and in 1791 he was given the title of intendant, with wider powers over agriculture, trade, taxation, Crown lands and appointments to public offices. This made him less dependent on Caracas but the links were still there. Trinidad's financial affairs came under the close scrutiny of officials in Caracas, to Chacon's irritation, and the Audiencia of Caracas, established in 1786, was the Court of Appeals for legal cases heard in Trinidad by Chacon and his Assessor. But the truth was that the frontier colony settled by powerful foreigners had little in common with the mainland provinces of the intendancy of Caracas, and Chacon felt that the administrative and judicial links were unnecessary complications. His powers were extensive, especially after he was appointed intendant, and Trinidad became increasingly isolated from the mainland provinces.

By the 1790s Trinidad had more in common with the French West Indian islands than with the provinces of the captaincy-general of Venezuela to which the island still belonged. The influx of French immigrants meant that the island was caught up in the ideological struggles of the French Revolution in the Caribbean. International war and internal rebellion ravaged the West Indies in the 1790s, and Trinidad became increasingly vulnerable to political conflict among the different population groups in the island - and to attack by an enemy power.

As the revolution engulfed the French islands, contending groups used the great principles of liberty, equality and fraternity for their own ends: royalist, conservative whites fought revolutionary whites and free coloureds; free coloureds and free blacks struggled to gain civil rights and legal equality, granted to them by the French government in 1792; the slaves rose, killing whites and burning down plantations, to gain their freedom. The French National Convention abolished slavery in all the colonies in 1794, and declared men of all colours to be French citizens with equal rights under the constitution. This generous action by the radicals in Paris terrified slave-owners and whites everywhere in the Caribbean. It was in Saint Domingue that the greatest explosion took place, but rebellion and civil war were also experienced in the French colonies of Martinique, Guadeloupe and St Lucia. Refugees flocked to Trinidad from these colonies, fleeing first the triumph of the revolution, then the re-establishment of control by counter-revolutionary forces, bringing with them their ideological conflicts and the hysteria of slave colonies in a state of turmoil.

In 1794 the radical regime in France sent out Victor Hugues to the Caribbean as its Commissioner for the French Windward Islands. His base was Guadeloupe, which he took from the British late in 1794, and he brought with him from France the two great agencies of the revolution: the guillotine and the printing press, revolutionary terror and revolutionary propaganda. His weapon was ideology. For the first time, the modern methods of total war were employed, involving whole populations and using subversion and propaganda to incite rebellions in the British colonies. Hugues's agents circulated inflammatory proclamations in the British and French islands, calling on the blacks and coloureds to rally around the banner of French liberty and overthrow the British slave-owners. Rebellions were ignited in St Lucia, Grenada, St Vincent and Dominica in 1795-6; even in faraway Jamaica Hugues's agents were active among the Maroons who rose in revolt in 1795. Hugues told the rebels in Grenada that the war had only one objective: the abolition of slavery everywhere. Slave-owners all over the West Indies trembled; in Trinidad, Chacon and the French land-owners who ran the colony watched with dismay as white and coloured Frenchmen of all shades of ideology entered the island.

If Hugues represented the revolution in its most radical stage, it was Britain that emerged as the great enemy of the revolution in Europe and in the Caribbean. The century-long struggle between Britain and France for global hegemony was accentuated by bitter ideological conflicts in the 1790s. In Europe, Britain fought to preserve monarchy and aristocracy; in the West Indies, British naval power supported slavery and white ascendancy. When revolution broke out in the French colonies, it was natural for French royalist planters to seek British protection. The planters of Saint Domingue, Martinique and Guadeloupe pledged their loyalty to the British Crown, and British troops occupied part of Saint Domingue and captured Martinique and Guadeloupe in 1794. French royalists were commissioned officers in the British army and encouraged to raise regiments to fight the revolution in Europe and in the Caribbean. Some of these renegade French officers came to Trinidad and settled as planters, like the Baron de Montalambert, who had raised a regiment in Saint Domingue to fight for the British. For these planters, British rule was infinitely preferable to the revolutionary regime in Paris, which had given civil rights to the free coloureds and freedom to the slaves. 'French today, British tomorrow,' writes C.L.R.James of these planter renegades, 'royalists, republicans, utterly without principles except in so far as these helped to preserve their plantations.'

In 1796 Britain counter-attacked against Hugues's forces in the Caribbean: the risings in Grenada and St Vincent were crushed and St Lucia was recaptured; only Guadeloupe remained in French hands. Hundreds of republicans fled, or were deported, to Trinidad;

even Julien Fédon, the leader of the Grenada rising, was thought to have escaped to Trinidad. In Trinidad they found a safe refuge, for Spain was neutral in the war until October 1796, and so the island could not fall into the hands of the British. The influx of Frenchmen who were suspected of revolutionary sympathies meant that the conflict had come to Trinidad. Chacon would now have to deal with men whose political views were diametrically opposed to his own.

He was powerless to prevent the entry of these refugees, but he made his hostility to them and their principles clear. As early as 1790, Chacon closed down Trinidad's first newspaper, the *Gazeta*, published by a new settler called Jean Villoux, because it included news of the revolution in France; Villoux was deported. In 1794-5 Chacon's letters to Madrid revealed his intense anxiety about the situation in the Caribbean and the possibility of revolution spreading among the slaves and the free coloureds in Trinidad. In 1794 he asked the cabildo to set up a committee to examine the circumstances in which 'strangers' arrived in the island, and he noted that the British capture of Martinique in the same year would put an end to the machinations of 'wicked men scattered about the islands, possessed with the daring idea of revolutionizing the West Indies'. In 1796 the cabildo refused to admit black troops under Jean Francois, who had fought for the British in Saint Domingue, stating that in Trinidad 'the seeds of revolutionary principles have not only taken root but in several instances have been seen to send forth shoots'. Indeed, it was rumoured that Jean Baptiste Richard of La Brea had organized a plot to seize Trinidad for Republican France in 1795; when a Spanish fleet arrived in the Gulf, he and his fellow conspirators fled to Venezuela. Chacon wrote home that slaves were adopting the revolutionary tri-coloured cockade introduced by the French republicans: 'the contact which our coloured people and our Negro slaves have had with the French and the Republicans, has made them dream of liberty and equality'. By 1796 Chacon was concerned that serious unrest from the slaves and free coloureds, instigated by French republicans, was imminent.

All through the 1790s Chacon pleaded for strong military reinforcements to enable him to defend the island. He organized a militia force, including coloured volunteers under coloured officers; he even armed fifty Indians with bows and arrows. He begged for Spanish warships to be stationed in the Gulf, for French privateers were operating in Trinidad waters against British shipping, while British naval vessels were virtually blockading the island, chasing and searching enemy and neutral ships and attacking the privateers. As Spain veered towards declaring war against Britain on the side of France, Chacon's fears mounted; he warned Madrid that Trinidad would be the first place to be attacked if Spain declared war on Britain. Threatened by internal unrest and external attack, Chacon knew that Spain's declaration of war against Britain in October 1796 would precipitate an immediate invasion by British forces. Yet perhaps that was not what he feared above all. For Victor Hugues, recognizing that it was in France's interests that Trinidad should remain Spanish, offered to help Chacon defend the island by sending some of his own forces from Guadeloupe. Chacon refused his offer, and wrote, prophetically: 'Should the King send me aid, I will do my duty to preserve his crown to this colony; if not, it must fall into the hands of the English, who I believe to be generous enemies, and are more to be trusted than treacherous friends.'

THREE

The British Take Over, 1797-1812

The Conquest

Chacon's 'generous enemies' had long had their eyes on Trinidad. The island was rapidly becoming prosperous, and British merchants conducted a flourishing trade with Trinidad in the 1790s. Its geographical position made it the ideal base for British commercial penetration of the Spanish-American colonies. Even more important, in the troubled international situation of the 1790s, the British were afraid that effective control of the island might pass from Spain to Republican France. As long as Spain and Britain were allies, Trinidad was safe from the British Navy which ruled the Caribbean; but this situation changed round about the middle of the decade.

In July 1795 a peace treaty between Spain and Republican France was signed; Spain was now officially neutral in the war, but the new, more moderate Paris regime pushed Spain from neutrality to alliance with France. Chacon knew what the consequences would be. In October 1795, when Spain was still neutral, he warned that if war was declared against Britain, Trinidad would be the first place to be attacked by the large British forces being prepared for a major Caribbean offensive. The defence of Trinidad was under urgent consideration in Madrid in 1796. Chacon reported that clashes between French privateers and British ships occurred almost every day in Trinidad waters; he lacked the means to make Spanish sovereignty respected. British naval vessels were chasing and searching enemy and neutral ships in Trinidad waters, and British seamen had clashed with republican French settlers on the north coast of the island. These activities climaxed in the 'Alarm' incident of May 1796, involving open fighting in Port of Spain between British sailors from the ship 'Alarm' and French inhabitants. Chacon appealed for military reinforcements and a squadron to be stationed in the Gulf of Paria until the end of the war. Then, in October 1796, the French government succeeded in forcing Spain to declare war on Britain. Trinidad was now exposed to British naval might.

The capture of the island was crucial to Britain's war strategy in the Caribbean, and plans for an attack with overwhelming land and sea forces had been elaborated long before Spain actually declared war. This Caribbean striking force was to be commanded by one of Britain's most experienced soldiers, Sir Ralph Abercromby. The British government told Abercromby that Trinidad, because of 'the Principles and Persons who have lately been introduced there', had become 'a cause of Just alarm and real danger to several of our most Valuable Islands'. By capturing Trinidad, he was told, 'even if you cannot hold it, you will remove a source of danger to our own Islands'. The island was, in fact, a threat to the security of the British West Indies and an obstacle to Britain's war strategy. The expedition that sailed to the Caribbean late in 1796 had as its first objective the capture of Trinidad, and its strength was sufficient to overcome any resistance that Chacon could offer.

A Spanish squadron commanded by Admiral Apodaca arrived in September 1796 with 740 soldiers, and Spain's determination to defend her colony seemed to be demonstrated. But Chacon's position was weak. Many of the newly arrived troops and seamen fell sick with yellow fever. Even more serious, the British captured a Spanish ship bound from Mexico to Port of Spain with a large sum of money to pay for defence works, and this was a major reason for Chacon's failure to fortify the island adequately; all kinds of military supplies were scarce or unobtainable. In February 1797 Chacon had under his command just over 2,000 armed men, many of whom were ill, and all of whom were inadequately armed and supplied. Abercromby could deploy 6,750 troops and an overwhelming naval force. Chacon surrendered on 17 February after a token resistance; Apodaca had destroyed his squadron to avoid its capture by the British. The British lost one officer, while the Spaniards suffered seven casualties.

In the busy days that followed the capitulation, signed at an old plantation house at Valsayn, Chacon co-operated with the British authorities. He was probably behind Abercromby's proclamation of 19 February which stated 'All such Frenchmen as consider themselves to be citizens of the French Republic' were to be allowed to leave and were to be given safe conduct to 'some French, Dutch, or Spanish Colony'. The ideologically committed Frenchmen left, either voluntarily or after deportation, mostly going to Guadeloupe, or to Venezuela, where they created security problems for the Spanish colonial authorities. Everyone else was to swear allegiance to the British Crown and to surrender firearms, except in the case of 'gentlemen of property who, having taken the oath of allegiance, are desirous to keep arms for their own defence' - a concession to the French and Spanish land-owners whom the British government was anxious to conciliate. The same consideration prompted Abercromby to proclaim that Spanish civil and criminal law was to be maintained, and that all officers in the judiciary and the administration were to remain in office. Abercromby left Trinidad in a few days - he had a war to fight - but before doing so he made a fateful decision: he named an officer on his staff, Thomas Picton, to remain as military governor and commander-in-chief.

Picton's Monstrous Tyranny

In six short years, Picton stamped his strong personality on the history of Trinidad, and became a colourful, controversial, almost legendary figure, hero to some, ogre to others. Until peace was signed in 1801-2, the British government left Picton almost entirely to his own devices: his mandate was to keep the island British and maintain internal security, and London showed little interest in the methods he employed. The way was open for Picton to establish an effective personal tyranny. Abercromby hinted as much when he told Picton on his assumption of the governorship:

'I have placed you in a trying and delicate situation, nor, to give you any chance of overcoming the difficulties opposed to you, can I leave you a strong garrison; but I shall give you ample powers: exercise Spanish law as well as you can: do justice according to your conscience, and that is all that can be expected from you. His Majesty's Government will be minutely informed of your situation, and, no doubt, will make all due allowances.'

An even stronger hint was given by Christoval de Robles, a strongly conservative Spanish official and land-owner with a long history of hostility against the French immigrants. De Robles advised Picton that the populace was mostly composed of desperate characters, revolutionaries and assassins:

'If you do not give an imposing character to your government before the climate diminishes the number of your soldiers, your situation will become alarming. If those men do not fear you, they will despise you ... A few acts of vigour may disconcert their projects.'

Picton, a blunt soldier for whom the governorship of Trinidad was the first real stroke of luck in a formerly fairly undistinguished career, responded enthusiastically. The result was six years of arbitrary one-man rule. Free from Spanish law, and virtually free from imperial control until 1801-2, Picton was the sole arbiter of Trinidad's fortunes.

Taking de Robles's advice only too seriously, Picton proceeded to carry out those 'acts of vigour' that would, de Robles thought, cow the population. Picton's garrison was unreliable, so he hanged fourteen alleged deserters from a German regiment in the island, without any form of trial, civil or military. De Robles had told him that the Spanish 'peons' of St Joseph were 'a set of vagabonds ... ready to join in any disorders', so he had one of them, Celestino, hanged without trial for drunkenly abusing a Spanish lady in her house. Runaway slaves were hunted down and punished; one runaway slave woman, called Present, was hanged before her owner had time to turn up and collect his property. An Irish sergeant, Hugh Gallagher, was hanged without trial when a free black woman accused him of rape and theft of a handkerchief; rumour had it that Gallagher and Picton had quarrelled over the services of a prostitute, and the woman, anxious to please Picton, made the accusation against Gallagher. To cow the French free coloureds, whom Picton regarded as dangerous republicans, he executed without trial Jean Baptiste Richard, a free coloured sea captain who had given passage to three coloured men suspected of sedition. This flurry of executions took place in the months immediately after the capitulation. Others suspected of being subversives were luckier: they were merely deported. The executions and the deportations were meant to convince the population that Picton's word was law, and that trouble-makers would be dealt with without any concern for the forms of law. Nor were the new English settlers who flocked to Trinidad after the capture treated any less severely: when they arrived, they were summoned to Picton's presence, and if he disliked their appearance or their words, he would point out the gallows opposite his house and threaten them.

It was a regime of impartial terror, with security the end. All effective power, judicial, civil and military, was combined in Picton's hands; the checks and balances of the Spanish system were gone for ever. Picton reformed the administration, making it more efficient, and his overall control was enhanced by the creation of new offices and the reorganization of old ones. Most of the new officials were completely under his thumb and could be dismissed at will. Picton introduced the regular use of torture to extort confessions from suspected criminals; torture was sanctioned by old Spanish laws but had never been employed in Trinidad. The arbitrary executions would have been impossible under Spanish rule, when all capital sentences had to confirmed by the Audiencia of Caracas; now Picton had sole jurisdiction in all criminal cases, and a man's life could be casually ended on his command. Only in civil cases involving sums of over £500 was there any appeal from Picton's ruling to the British privy council: in British colonialism the defence of property was more important than the defence of human life.

Picton's terror was impartial in the sense that European soldiers were among his victims, but the worst atrocities were inflicted on the slaves and the free coloureds. For Picton became a colonial and a slave-owner, a convert to the cause of property in human beings. The immigrants he welcomed were conservative, royalist French slave-owners, often aristocrats like the Count de Loppinot and the Baron de Montalambert, bringing thousands of 'loyal' slaves. If Trinidad was Picton's kingdom, these French planters were his barons. Under their influence he issued a Slave Code in 1800 that allowed harsh punishment of offending slaves; and he allowed them to introduce into Trinidad all the savage customs and rituals of the French West Indian slave-owners.

The French planters had a particular horror of the powerful slave obeahmen and their knowledge of poisons. In Martinique special commissions of planters – 'poisoning commissions' - were organized to deal with slaves suspected of these crimes, and Picton allowed his French cronies a free hand in Trinidad. In 1801 large numbers of slaves died mysteriously at the Montalambert estate near Port of Spain, Coblenz, and at the Diego Martin estate of St Hilaire Begorrat, a Martiniquan planter who was Picton's closest ally, to whom he habitually deferred on all matters related to slavery. Begorrat was first alcalde (chief magistrate) in 1801 and he took the matter in hand. A poisoning commission was set up; the suspects were tortured and confined in the terrible Port of Spain jail, where slave prisoners were kept for months at a time, chained flat on the floor in tiny, dark, airless cells, the notorious 'cachots brulants' (burning dungeons).

Between December 1801 and March 1802 the commission was busy sentencing the prisoners. Pierre Francois protested his innocence, but he was sentenced to be burnt alive; the sentence was carried out, and the headless corpse of a slave who had just been hanged and decapitated was burnt along with the living man, a refined Martiniquan ritual organised by Begorrat. Six other slaves, including one woman, were hanged and decapitated, with their bodies burnt and their heads displayed prominently at the entrance to their plantations. Several others were mutilated by having their ears cut off and being branded on the forehead, and then banished from the island. Most of the victims were so weakened by their months in prison and the torture during interrogation that they were unable to walk or stand when they were led out to execution. The woman slave, Thisbe, who had refused under repeated torture to implicate her husband, said as she went to be hanged that death would be 'but as a drink of water' compared to what she had already suffered. And again at the end of 1802, another outbreak of poisoning at Coblenz estate resulted in a further crop of arrests, tortures and executions. Begorrat and his friends emphasized that these punishments were normal back home in Martinique and Guadeloupe, where slaves were burnt and hanged as an awful example to the rest; Picton was so completely under their influence that he accepted their arguments and endorsed all the tortures, mutilations and barbaric executions.

Picton's regime was almost as hostile to the free coloureds as to the slaves. He pretended to believe that the French free coloureds were, to a man, rabid revolutionaries who could be kept in order only by firm government and judicious punishment; he called them 'a dangerous class which must gradually be got rid of'. His view of the free coloureds as active or passive revolutionaries, which was entirely false, justified for himself and his defenders the atrocities of his regime, that marked the start of a steady erosion of the free coloureds' rights which continued until 1826. Several of his victims were free coloureds. As for the white population, Picton identified with the wealthy, conservative land-owners, whether French, Spanish or English. Picton soon bought an estate and became a slave-owner - his enemies said that the penniless soldier made his fortune by hunting runaway slaves and selling them illegally on the mainland - and the prosperity of the slave plantations became his personal cause. The powerful slave-owners ran the government under Picton, and they decided all questions related to slaves and the free coloureds; any 'republican' whites who remained on the island after 1797 had no access to Picton. The governor had little sympathy for the English immigrants who came in after the capture, and even more after Trinidad was formally ceded to Britain in the peace negotiations (1801-2). He thought they were mostly bankrupts and adventurers, the scum of the old British colonies, and his low opinion of them was strengthened when some of them began to agitate for a 'British constitution' and 'British rights'.

For Picton's philosophy of government was a consistent argument for arbitrary rule and had no room for such notions as representative government or the liberty of Englishmen. He believed that any agitation for, or even discussion of, constitutional reform would destabilize the colony and give the malcontents, especially the free coloureds, every opportunity for trouble-making. These people could not be expected to acquiesce tamely in a new constitution that would completely exclude them, for in the British colonies with the representative system of elected assemblies, free coloured property-holders were specifically denied the vote. The free coloureds of Trinidad, who had enjoyed certain legal and customary rights under Spain, would resent a new system that ignored those rights. Better to leave the constitution alone, and avoid alienating the free coloureds and the French and Spanish whites, who rightly feared that a British constitution meant rule by the British inhabitants. Picton argued for an arbitrary, secretive government; the constitutional question should be decided without any public discussion. When a handful of British merchants in Port of Spain met at the end of 1801 to draw up a petition for an assembly and British laws, Picton was furious. Some officials and militia officers involved in the movement were abruptly dismissed, and the rest were cowed by an investigation of sixty persons who had signed the petition by the magistrates. No one had 'rights' in Picton's Trinidad; the only duty of the good subject was to obey.

Picton's regime was a 'monstrous tyranny'; government was arbitrary and capricious, designed to terrify the population, especially the slaves and free coloureds, into submission. Yet he had many defenders, both among his contemporaries and later historians of Trinidad. The defence of Picton was his own: that a strong, even severe government by a ruler untrammelled by constitutional limits was essential if Trinidad was to be preserved for Britain and if internal peace was to be maintained. Picton never denied that his government was harsh, he said that harshness was necessary: 'Surrounded with enemies, the severities I applied were fully authorized by my station and circumstances.' This argument was accepted by nineteenth-century historians like E. L. Joseph, who considered Picton to be a great governor and the 'saviour' of British Trinidad, and L.M. Fraser, who felt that the difficulties of his position more than justified his 'severities'. It is impossible to accept their view today. Picton always, deliberately, exaggerated the revolutionary tendencies of the population; in fact virtually all the committed 'republicans' left the island within a few months of the conquest, either voluntarily or after deportation. In his dealings with the slaves and the free coloureds, Picton enthusiastically endorsed all the worst prejudices and practices of his cronies from the French islands, particularly the sinister Begorrat. Picton's government was one of naked terror, unacceptable even by the standards of early nineteenth-century British imperialism.

For by the opening years of the century, important elements in British public life were beginning to question the moral justification of imperialism, and humanitarian ideas about the government of colonial peoples were beginning to emerge. The humanitarian movement had concerned itself with the issues of slavery and the slave trade since the 1780s and had succeeded in converting important people to its way of thinking. By 1802, Picton's atrocities were embarrassing to the British government; he had become a political liability as news of the executions and tortures became known in London. With the peace concluded in 1801-2, Picton's brutal government could no longer be justified. Further, the British merchants in Port of Spain who had been roughly treated when they petitioned for an assembly activated their London contacts to complain on their behalf. By 1802 the government was uneasy about Picton; but it could hardly dismiss him, since only the year before it had signalled its approval of his regime by appointing him civil governor and praising his 'ability and zeal ... in administering the affairs of Trinidad'.

Further, the British government came under attack in 1802 for allowing Picton to develop Trinidad as a slave colony at a time when the campaign against the slave trade, in and out of Parliament, was gathering momentum. The humanitarian James Stephen Senior published an influential book, *The Crisis of the Sugar Colonies*, in which he argued powerfully against the extension of slavery in Trinidad; instead, he advocated Trinidad's development by free labour. In May 1802 Trinidad was at the centre of a full-scale House of Commons debate in which the a group of MPs led by George Canning attacked the government for sanctioning the extension of the slave trade to Trinidad since the island had become British. The government decided to shelve the Trinidad issue by announcing that Picton would be superseded by a three-man governing commission, whose job it would be to investigate all the circumstances of the island, and to propose both a settlement and labour policy, and a form of government suited to its peculiar problems. The appointment of the commission was intended to take Trinidad out of the public debate, to allow the government to avoid a decision at that time. It was a concession to the humanitarians, and it was also a concession to the campaigners for a British constitution, since it recognized the dissatisfaction with Picton's arbitrary one-man rule. But, to avoid the appearance of dismissal, Picton was named Second Commissioner; William Fullarton and Samuel Hood were to serve as First and Third Commissioners respectively. Picton was thus demoted abruptly from sole governor to junior commissioner. It was, to say the least, an original tactic. Within a few weeks of Fullarton's arrival in Trinidad, early in 1803, the commission had broken up in dissension, and it failed to carry out any of the tasks entrusted to it.

Fullarton had probably heard of Picton's excesses before he left London, and it is possible that there was an unspoken understanding with the government that he was to investigate Picton's regime and report back. In any case, the two men were divided by ideology, interests and outlook. Fullarton was liberal in his attitude to the free coloureds and the slaves; Picton had adopted all the worst prejudices of the colonial slave-owner. Fullarton identified with the developing idea that colonialism should have a moral justification; Picton belonged to the old school which saw colonialism as naked economic exploitation. Fullarton was a brilliant writer, eloquent and verbose, with good contacts in London; Picton was the plain, blunt soldier and stern disciplinarian.

Above all, Fullarton was shocked at what he saw and heard of Picton's savage punishments of slaves and free coloureds. His visit to the jail, soon after he arrived, was a revelation. He saw the chained prisoners, the 'cachots brulants', and the torture chamber; the executioner presented him with a bill for money owed him for sundry hangings, multilations and floggings, all precisely detailed, which he had performed. Fullarton demanded, in the council, a full statement of all persons imprisoned, banished, mutilated, tortured or executed since the conquest, with names, dates and full details. This was Fullarton's declaration of war; the commission degenerated into a personal feud between him and Picton, with Hood, the council, the cabildo and most of the white land-owners siding with Picton. Fullarton became obsessed with his campaign against Picton; long after both had left Trinidad, in the middle of 1803, he devoted himself to securing Picton's prosecution and trial in Britain for the charge of illegally torturing a young free coloured girl, Louisa Calderon, in order to extract a confession from her.

The commission dissolved in a welter of personal dissensions, but substantive issues were also involved. For instance, Fullarton's liberalism and his traumatic experience at the jail led him to insist that magistrates and commandants, when committing slaves or free coloureds to jail, should specify the offence and the punishment. The normal procedure was to commit them with no information as to the charge, and to order corporal punishment for slaves without specifying the extent of the flogging. Fullarton's request was simple; yet his action was interpreted as undermining the proper subordination of slaves and free coloureds. Picton summed up the issue when he told the Council:

'The laws in all countries where slavery is established or tolerated allowed the master to secure the obedience of the slave by reasonable and moderate punishment. But the First Commissioner, by ordering that no punishment should be inflicted without his order, has superseded the power of masters and magistrates; and in a certain degree rendered the slave independent of both.'

That was the crux. In insisting that free coloureds should not be imprisoned without specifying their offence, Fullarton attacked the practice of casually committing free coloured 'trouble-makers' to a spell in jail 'to teach them their place'. The Commandant of Carenage, a French planter, put it clearly when he complained that Fullarton's action would 'undermine the basis of the colonial system of Government in a country where the Coloured People are so numerous and the least relaxation of subordination would produce the most serious consequences'. If free coloureds were granted simple, basic legal and human rights, the whole structure of white supremacy would be undermined.

The slave-owners could not tolerate Fullarton and made life in Trinidad impossible for him, while Picton was driven to resign his post as Second Commissioner. By July 1803 the commission had been revoked, and the British government was again faced with the problem of how to govern Trinidad.

Constitutional and Developmental Issues

All the older British colonies in the Caribbean had been granted constitutions that featured an elected assembly (elected by white male land-owners) with law-making powers, and this is what the British residents in Trinidad wanted when they agitated for a British constitution. But ever since the 1780s the British government had come to feel that it should maintain a greater degree of direct control over the colonies and that any new colony acquired by military conquest should not be granted a representative assembly, especially since a conquered colony was invariably populated by foreigners who could not be expected to be familiar with the British constitution. Instead, the colonies conquered by Britain during the Revolutionary and Napoleonic wars (1793-1815), including Trinidad, came under more direct supervision from London in a system that was later to be known as Crown Colony government.

The British government had become disillusioned with the colonial assemblies. After 1763 it had granted assemblies to several colonies with predominantly French populations - notably Quebec and Grenada - and the results had not been encouraging; many difficulties had been created for governors and for ministers in London. Furthermore, British judges had ruled that once the king had promised to establish a law-making assembly in any colony, he had given up any rights to legislate for that colony or to tax its inhabitants. The decision in the Grenada case of Campbell v. Hall (1774) established this principle: once the king had instructed the Governor of Grenada to convene an assembly, taxation could be imposed on the people only by that assembly, or by the imperial Parliament in London- not by the king. Another important ruling in 1790 stated that once an assembly had been established (in Grenada again) the king could not use his prerogative, his legal powers, to change the constitution of Grenada in any way. In other words, the king could not alter the constitution of a conquered colony once he had promised to establish a law-making assembly; he lost all his powers of legislation from the moment he instructed the governor to call an assembly. These rulings had the effect of making the British government very wary about establishing any new form of government, or divesting the Crown of its legislative rights, in a newly conquered colony. Everyone agreed that the British Parliament could legislate for a colony, whether it had an assembly or not, but after 1783 the government was extremely reluctant to use Parliament to impose laws on the colonies; ministers believed that the attempt to force parliamentary legislation on the North American colonies had led directly to the American Revolution.

As a result of these developments, the government handled the colonies it conquered in the 1790s with great caution. In 1794 Britain captured Martinique and part of Saint Domingue, and the instructions issued to the British governors of these two colonies revealed the new thinking. There was no mention of an assembly or British laws. The governors were directed to govern according to the original French laws: executive powers were to be vested solely in the governor; he was to select a small council of local residents to advise him, but it would have no law-making powers; no new taxes or laws were to be imposed unless the king (i.e. the British government) so directed. The important points in these instructions were that the king gave up none of his rights of legislation; he promised nothing to the British settlers; he undertook to govern the colony according to its old (French) laws and institutions. These were the principles followed in the government of all the Caribbean colonies conquered between 1793 and 1815, with the single exception of Tobago, a special case because it had previously been granted an assembly in 1768; and these 1794 instructions were often copied to governors of such colonies, including Trinidad. In that island, civil government was established in 1801, when Picton was appointed civil governor and directed to appoint a nominated Council of Advice consisting of prominent local residents. Spanish laws were to continue and no change of government was to be made. In 1802 the British Attorney-General ruled that since the king had not given up any of his legislative powers over Trinidad, he could impose any duty or tax he chose.

There were two other developments that made the government anxious to supervise the affairs of the new colonies, especially Trinidad, more closely than was possible with the colonies that had their own assemblies. The long war with France highlighted the obstructionist tendencies of the West Indian assemblies: they complained about contributing to the cost of defending the islands and objected to the levying of black regiments. This was annoying in any circumstances, but it was positively dangerous when Britain was fighting a global struggle in which the Caribbean was a crucial theatre of operations. The overriding needs of strategy and defence pointed to a closer imperial control over the West Indies. Second, the British slave trade was abolished in 1807, and the government felt it necessary to retain direct imperial control of Trinidad in order to prevent illegal importations of slaves from the other islands. This consideration reinforced the government's growing conviction that it should refuse to grant Trinidad an assembly.

In 1802 the government had temporarily shelved the issue by appointing a Commission of Government, but that ill-fated body failed to recommend any form of government for the island. London took up the problem again in 1804, asking the new governor, Sir Thomas Hislop, to recommend a new constitution, while making it clear that the grant of an assembly was not being considered. Hislop recommended a nominated legislative council, whose members would be chosen by the governor, not elected, and which would enjoy law-making powers. This solution would eventually be adopted by London, but not until 1831. During the years that followed Hislop's recommendation in 1804, ministers in London were too preoccupied with the war against Napoleon to take Trinidad in hand; secretaries of state for the colonies came and went, and until 1810 London seemed incapable of reaching any clear decision.

In 1809-10, however, the British government was pushed by events into a clear and authoritative statement of its policy. In 1809

George Smith was appointed Chief Justice, with a mandate to enforce Spanish law vigorously, and armed with very wide judicial powers. The extent of those powers - and Smith's peculiarly tactless and overbearing personality - brought him almost inevitably into collision with Governor Hislop and his allies in the Council of Advice. Smith had influential friends in London, and he was a strong opponent of the assembly system. Throughout 1809-10 he wrote a stream of letters to members of the government urging them to refuse, once and for all, to grant an assembly and British laws to the island, for in 1809 the campaign for an assembly gathered momentum, with new committees and petitions. Even more important, Hislop and the Council were converted to the movement for a British constitution, largely because of their common hostility to Smith. By May 1810 the Council had formally requested the king to grant a British constitution and British laws. London had no choice but to take the campaign seriously, for now the governor, the Council and the cabildo had all formally endorsed it. The Secretary of State, Lord Liverpool, said he was reluctant to grant an assembly, but he would consider the views of the governor and the leading citizens.

This gave the leaders of the campaign their opportunity. Hislop, now an enthusiastic convert to the movement, organized a 'sounding' of white opinion by asking the Commandants of Quarters (see p.27) to obtain the views of the white men in their districts. The results - after less than half of the male white population had been consulted - seemed to show a majority in favour of an assembly and British laws. A committee consisting of members of the Council and the cabildo, and a few other residents, drew up a detailed plan for an assembly, which envisaged that all white males, British or foreign-born, would enjoy the right to vote. It was generally understood that the free coloureds would not be enfranchised, though this was not made explicit; instead, the committee merely proposed that the free coloureds' rights should be safeguarded, without explaining how this could be achieved by an assembly in which they would not be represented. The committee's recommendations were sent to London in July 1810, and the movement for a British constitution seemed closer to success than ever before.

At this point the free coloureds intervened. They had been silent all along, but they recognized that with the campaign for an assembly apparently close to success, continued silence might lead to the triumph of a hostile political interest. Their leaders drew up a petition, which was signed by 236 free coloured men, asking the governor for permission to address the king that they might gain some participation in whatever new constitution might be granted. Their petition said nothing about an assembly; they merely suggested that their wealth, their loyalty and their good behaviour entitled them to *something*, to some consideration in any new form of government. In fact, they were signalling to London that they were well aware that the grant of an assembly and British laws would seriously undermine their legal and political position. They were letting the British authorities know that the free coloured leadership was justifiably afraid of government by an assembly in which they would have no representation.

Hislop was furious with the free coloureds for daring to open their mouths; he refused them permission to address the king and he cowed the leadership by appointing a committee to investigate the 'character and antecedents' of everyone who had signed the petition. But the petition itself had routinely been forwarded to London, and the Secretary of State regarded it as evidence that the free coloureds would never accept an assembly from which they were excluded. He used the petition to justify his refusal to grant an assembly. In his dispatch of November 1810 - a crucial document for the political history of Trinidad - Lord Liverpool argued that the free coloureds would have a just grievance if an assembly was granted and they were denied the vote; this constituted 'an insuperable objection' to such a policy. He did not consider the possibility of the British government granting an assembly and insisting that the free coloureds be enfranchised. He posed the issue in the following terms: either an assembly without the free coloureds, which would cause political difficulties, or no assembly at all, the option he adopted. Liverpool also cited the foreign composition of the white population and the abolition of the slave trade as important reasons for his decision. It seems clear that by 1810 British ministers had irrevocably decided not to grant the assembly system to any colony that did not possess it; the position of the free coloureds in Trinidad provided a good public justification for their decision, and this is the importance of the intervention of the free coloureds in 1810. Liverpool's dispatch stated, publicly and authoritatively, the government's position on the constitutional issue; it closed the doors to any fundamental change in the government not only of Trinidad, but of all the conquered colonies, for many years to come. The movement for an assembly was defeated, and Trinidad would continue to be a Crown Colony under the direct supervision of London and its agents in the colony.

The constitutional issue preoccupied both the British government and the local authorities during the first decade of British rule. But there was another issue that was at least as important for the future of Trinidad: the question of how the island should be developed and settled. British capitalists might be allowed to open up the island for large, slave-worked plantations, or the government might restrict the growth of large estates and the importation of slaves, and try to encourage the use of free labour. While the government in London tended to support the second strategy after 1801, the men on the spot - the planters, the capitalists and the local officials - almost invariably endorsed the first, and opposed any limitations on the growth of a slave and sugar economy.

In 1797 Trinidad was far from being a mature slave colony. It had then less than one-sixth of the slave population of Barbados. Only the western lowlands and scattered peripheral areas were settled. The true plantation colony with large estates and a massive slave labour force was still embryonic; if Trinidad was to develop along these lines, a rate of slave immigration far higher than in 1783-97 would have been necessary. At first it looked as if this would happen. British colonists and investors flocked into Trinidad after the capture (many, we saw, had settled even before 1797), anxious to develop sugar plantations at a time when sugar prices were artificially high. The number of sugar estates increased from 159 in 1797 to 193 in 1801; exports nearly doubled in quantity from 8.4 million lb in 1799 to 14.2 million in 1802. Slaves poured in. Many accompanied their owners from the British and French islands; many more came direct from Africa. The slave population rose from 10,009 in February 1797 to 19,709 in 1802: it almost doubled in five years. The fears of abolitionists like James Stephen - that the British exploitation of Trinidad would lead to a massive increase in the slave trade - appeared to be amply justified, and this led him to publish *The Crisis of the Sugar Colonies* in 1802.

The abolitionists thought that the government should intervene by preventing land grants for slave plantations and by checking the importation of slaves. This was the argument of Stephen's book. It was supported by the West India interest in Britain, anxious to protect the older British colonies from competition with the virgin soils of Trinidad. In Parliament the issue was taken up by opponents of the government, and in May 1802 the Commons debated a motion moved by Canning to suspend the importation of slaves from Africa for the purpose of cultivating new lands in the conquered colonies. Canning demanded that no new grants of lands should be made in Trinidad until regulations had been approved to prevent the extension of cultivation from causing any increase in the slave trade. He suggested that Trinidad could be developed by free labour - 'peons' from Venezuela, free blacks from the other islands, discharged soldiers of the regiments in the West Indies. It was at this point that the government got out of a tricky situation by announcing its intention to set up a commission, which would, among other things, recommend a land and settlement policy.

Pushed by abolitionist pressure both inside and outside Parliament, the government took up the notion of settlement by free labourers, and the immigration of white labourers or small farmers. Picton dismissed any such ideas; he had already told London that intelligent planters who knew Trinidad judged it to be more suitable for sugar than any other island. Picton and his planter friends saw Trinidad as another Caribbean slave colony; the abolitionists saw it as an experimental colony where European, or Chinese, or Venezuelan settlers would be encouraged; the British government tried to placate the abolitionists while doing very little to prevent the extension of the slave system and the large estates. The commission was urged to recommend schemes of white settlement, and a few British craftsmen were actually sent out early in 1803. But the more ambitious schemes for white settlement perished with the commission, and were probably never taken very seriously by the government. For in a slave-owning society where only slaves performed manual labour and only blacks were slaves, a white labourer or peasant population would have been a social embarrassment, as Picton and the planters clearly understood. The lowest acceptable position for a white man was that of plantation overseer. The existence of a large body of white labourers would undermine the principles of white supremacy on which slave society was based. With the powerful local planters and officials hostile to white settlement, and the government in London at best half-hearted, the scheme was stillborn.

But the general uncertainty about Trinidad's future as a slave colony after 1802, and particularly the strength of the movement to abolish the slave trade, combined to slow down the growth of the slave population. After the tremendous increase in 1797-1802, the rate of growth dropped considerably, with an increase of only 1,150 in 1802-11; there was the same number of sugar estates in 1834 as there had been in 1801. And in 1806 Parliament prohibited the slave trade to the newly conquered or ceded colonies, including Trinidad; next year came the general abolition of the whole British slave trade. For the Trinidad planters, grappling with a shortage of labour, this was a tremendous blow. Frenzied pleas that Trinidad should be considered a special case and should be exempted from the operation of the Abolition Act for a period of years were, of course, hopeless. After 1807 the planters faced a difficult future and a steadily declining slave population.

The question of land grants was another issue that the British government had to face. No official grants were made between 1797 and 1802, but Picton often gave new settlers verbal permission to occupy lands pending the settlement of Trinidad's political status; others bought land from established residents or land-owners leaving the colony after the conquest. British merchants invested heavily in plantation property, especially after 1802. Hislop and his Council continued to permit settlers to occupy new lands, mostly their friends or relatives, or military officers. In fact, while Picton and the commission had alienated only 1,658 acres to six persons, Hislop alienated 68,022 acres in 1803-9. He justified these unofficial grants by the claim that they were granted on condition that nothing but provisions to feed the slave population would be planted on the lands in question. But no formal grants had been made, so that these 'permissive occupancies', resting on the basis of a verbal, unofficial permission by the governor, would cause difficulties for their owners in later years. Most of these lands were probably uncultivated because of the shortage of labour. The British government failed to develop a positive land policy, Hislop and his successor Munro (1811-13) continued to grant permissive occupancies, and many of the planters who had been granted lands in this way ignored the condition that only provisions should be planted and instead cultivated export crops with slave labour.

In 1809 Hislop reported on the state of Trinidad's plantation agriculture: 739 estates were in operation, employing 18,302 slaves. Some 68.7 per cent of the total cultivated acreage was devoted to sugar, with 248 plantations and 13,219 slaves. By 1809, clearly, sugar was the dominant export crop, with English planters producing 1,292 million lb on 92 estates, while the French planters made 1,194 million lb on 143 estates; their plantations were smaller and less heavily capitalized. It was a British capitalist, Stephen Lushington, who erected the first steam-engine in Trinidad at his plantation Camden in Couva in 1804. By 1810 eight were in operation, along with nine water mills and 226 cattle mills. Cocoa and cotton each accounted for about 9.5 per cent of the total cultivated acreage, while coffee accounted for 6.4 per cent. But sugar had surged ahead to dominate the economy. Sugar exports had almost doubled in 1802-9, from 14.2 million lb in 1802 to 25.95 million lb in 1809; sugar had accounted for only 33 per cent of the total cultivated acreage in 1802, in 1809 the proportion had risen to 68.7 per cent. Whatever the intention of the British government, sugar and slavery dominated the Trinidad economy by 1810.

The Slaves and Free Coloureds

The French and British planters who came to Trinidad were given virtually a free hand to run the slave colony as they saw fit, to recreate in Trinidad all the conventions and practices of the mature slave colonies of the French and British West Indies. Picton always deferred to his planter friends on slave matters. To please them he issued the 1800 Slave Ordinance. Masters were allowed discretionary powers to inflict corporal punishment on their slaves, up to thirty-nine strokes, and even more severe penalties were imposed for offences considered serious. The custom of giving Saturday to the slaves to work on their own plots was abolished, and a planter who did not work his slaves on Saturdays was fined $50.* The Code emphasized strict security regulations; the few clauses dealing with diet, religious instruction and care of the slaves were half-hearted and probably never seriously intended. Picton allowed the planters to use the judicial system of the colony to terrorize the slaves. The famous Port of Spain jail, which so horrified Fullarton in 1803, was essentially a centre for slave discipline rather than an institution for punishing convicted criminals. The slave-owners, in effect, paid to have errant slaves disciplined, for they paid jail fees for each slave in prison; in return the jailer chained, flogged and tortured the prisoners, at his sole discretion. This is why Fullarton's 'interference' in jail procedures alarmed the planters; it threatened to make the prison useless as a disciplinary agency.

Yet the slaves resisted. They practised their own religious rites, and the obeahmen were powerful in slave quarters. Poisoning, we have seen, could be a terrible instrument for revenge and destruction, even if the frequency of its use was exaggerated by fearful Frenchmen, and the atrocious punishment meted out to all who were accused of complicity never stamped it out. In 1804 Dominique Dert, a French planter, mysteriously lost several slaves on his Bel-Air estate. Then an infant slave who was probably Dert's own child died suddenly, during the same month as the others, with symptoms recognized generally as being due to poison. The child had been the pet of the whole estate. Jacquet, the headman, a trusted senior slave who at the age of 66 was very old for a slave, confessed to all the poisonings. He said he would eventually have poisoned Dert and all his family. Revenge on his owner took the form of destroying his property, including the baby. Soon after Jacquet was himself found poisoned, perhaps by his own hand, perhaps murdered.

In 1805 evidence emerged of a whole black underground, a network of secret societies through which the slaves created an existence entirely separate from the world of the plantation. Two French planters with estates in the Diego Martin valley heard blacks singing a subversive song in patois:

Pain c'est viande bequé, San Domingo!
Vin c'est sang bequé, San Domingo!
Nous va boire sang bequé, San Domingo!
Pain nous mangé est viande bequé
Vin nous boire c'est sang bequé. +

Interrogations revealed that a great gathering would soon be held at Carenage of black regiments ('convois') with their kings. Hislop got out the troops and arrested the slaves named by the informers as kings, queens, princes, dauphins and dauphines. The arrested slaves talked freely at first, only later realizing that they were betraying themselves and their comrades.

The kings had flags and elaborate uniforms which mocked European military dress. King Samson was a powerful obeahman, but by day he pretended to be just a foolish old Ibo. Some of the regiments were Creole, some were African, some were based on a common origin in Martinique, or Guadeloupe, or Grenada. Everyone had a title. The kings exchanged messages and visited each other; they could only be approached with ceremony. The judges punished offenders; ceremonial feasts were held, and (perhaps) mock communion services, with secret songs and slogans. Under torture the prisoners 'confessed' that a rising was planned for Christmas Day 1805, with two prominent and presumably much-hated planters to be the victims; their murder was to be followed by a feast and dance at Mr Shand's new windmill at Diego Martin. Four kings were hanged and decapitated, many more lost their ears, or were flogged and banished. Samson's queen was sentenced to wear chains and a ten pound iron ring on her leg for the rest of her life. All the women involved, however marginally, were given severe floggings. The 'plot' grew in local white gossip: the rebels planned to massacre every white man by grinding them up in Mr Shand's mill, 'while lots were to be cast for the white ladies. Not a child was to have escaped their fury.' The planters, especially the French, were haunted by their fears of riot and massacre, and were convinced that only the severest punishment could terrorize the slaves into submission.

They were no less afraid of free coloureds, who outnumbered the whites; in 1802 there were 5,275 free coloureds as compared with only 2,261 whites, and the great majority of the free coloureds (2,925) were French. The planters never could forget that in Haiti it was the free coloured struggle for civil rights that led to the great rebellion and the ruin of the whites; and we have seen that Picton pretended to believe that the free coloureds of Trinidad were dangerous revolutionaries. He used their alleged republicanism as a pretext to undermine their position. Under Chacon the free coloureds, although excluded from public life or administrative posts, enjoyed legal equality with the whites and were treated in general with courtesy and consideration. Picton's regime marked the beginning of a steady erosion of their rights, in violation of the spirit if not the letter of the capitulation, which had promised to respect their legal rights.

The coloured militia officers whom Chacon had appointed were stripped of their rank, the troops were racially segregated with the coloured militiamen, including the ex-officers, put under a white sergeant. Free coloureds, even respectable land-owners, were forced to serve as 'alguaciles' or constables, performing the humiliating duty of guard service at officials' houses. They had to get police permission to hold a ball and pay a discriminatory tax of $16. When challenged they were obliged to show proof that they were free and that they had taken the oath of allegiance. A curfew at 9.30 p.m. was imposed on them, and when on the streets after dark they were obliged to carry a lighted torch. They could be arrested if found carrying a stick on the streets. In fact the free coloureds were subjected to a whole battery of discriminatory laws designed to humiliate them and cow them into submission, although their position was not yet as bad as in the older British colonies. The whole tone of the administration had changed with respect to the free coloured community; while Chacon had treated free coloured land-owners with sympathy and courtesy, Picton dealt with all coloureds, of whatever rank or education, with contempt. The dismissal of coloured officers symbolised a blow at the entire class.

When Fullarton came to Trinidad, he tried to secure a few basic human rights for the free coloureds. He and his wife treated the people of colour with consideration, and he tried to stop the common practice of keeping coloured 'trouble-makers' in jail for no specific offence. A coloured slave-owner named Durand had been committed to jail by the Commandant of Carenage because he had refused to send his slaves to work on the roads; it was not the first time that he had offended powerful local whites. But the Commandant had not specified his offence, and Fullarton ordered his release. The Commandant was outraged: he claimed that the coloureds were jubilant, that they were saying that whites and coloureds were now equal, that insurrection was imminent. For the whites feared that the extension of the most minimal legal rights to the people of colour would undermine the structure of race supremacy. A rumour made the rounds that Mrs Fullarton had seated a 'dark mulatto' next to the Baron de Montalambert at her table, and this rumour was said to have 'dangerously excited' the coloureds; but the Baron scotched the story by making it clear that he would have immediately left the room if she had done any such thing. In any case, Fullarton's sympathy for the free coloureds was felt by the planters to be dangerous, and in 1804 the Council of Advice extended the 9.30 curfew, previously applicable only to slaves, to the whole free coloured class.

The free coloureds had not played an open role in political life before 1810. Custom dictated that they had no political rights, and the penal laws were intended to intimidate them. But they had always been an important element in the constitutional issue. Picton had opposed an assembly because he felt their exclusion would make them even more dangerous. George Smith, the Chief Justice in 1810, opposed the assembly system, partly because of the free coloureds, with whom he strongly sympathized. When they finally intervened with their petition in 1810, Hislop's reaction indicates how dangerous any open political activity was. Not content with refusing them leave to address the king, he established a committee of the Council to investigate everyone who signed, to distinguish between the British-born subjects and the foreigners, and to investigate thoroughly the 'antecedents' of the latter. There was a rumour that some 'republican' coloured men from the French islands were coming to Trinidad in a few months. Then a coloured man publicly threatened to assault a Frenchman; he was said to have a revolutionary past, and he had signed the petition. When he escaped from jail, and posters offering rewards for his recapture were torn down, many felt sure that a dangerous plot was in the making. So Hislop swung into action. A census of all coloured males over the age of twelve was taken, many were interrogated, a few were imprisoned or banished. This was the official reaction to a petition that was couched in the most obsequious language and which merely asked for some consideration in the decision to grant a new constitution. Hislop was convinced that he had nipped a dangerous conspiracy in the bud; he referred to the revolutionary upheavals ('Robespierrean terror') in Venezuela at the time, and reminded the Secretary of State that revolution had started in Haiti in just this way. No wonder that the coloureds were again cowed into silence. A prominent absentee Trinidad planter drove the point home when he told the House of Commons in 1811 that the free coloureds were 'a vile and infamous race', and that serious mischief had been done 'from setting the doctrines of the Rights of Man afloat in the minds of these people. I can only compare the conduct of Mr Smith [the Chief Justice who sympathized with them] in stirring them up to that of a madman who scattered firebrands.'

In the years after 1810, the position of the free coloureds would deteriorate, with vicious laws designed to persecute and humiliate them, until they began to organize a campaign for civil rights and political equality, taking advantage of the new humanitarian leanings of the British government. In the same years, London began, at last, to devise new slave policies to prepare the way for eventual emancipation, and Trinidad would be the experimental colony for these new policies.

---

1. In Trinidad, sums of money were commonly quoted either in pounds sterling, or in local dollars; smaller sums were generally given in dollars, larger sums in sterling. The pound sterling was the equivalent of 4.80 Trinidad dollars.

2. The bread is the flesh of the white man, San Domingo! [Haiti]
The wine is the blood of the white man, San Domingo!
We will drink the white man's blood, San Domingo!
The bread we eat is the white man's flesh
The wine we drink is the white man's blood.

FOUR

The Experimental Colony 1812-38

Slave Registration, Amelioration and Emancipation

A wit in the Colonial Office (in London) wrote in 1812: 'Trinidad is a subject for an anatomy school or rather a poor patient in a county hospital on which all sorts of surgical experiments are tried, to be given up if they fail and to be practised on others if they succeed.' For in the twenty or so years before the passing of the Act of Emancipation in 1833, Trinidad's role was to be the model British slave colony, the Crown Colony in which new policies for improving the status of the slaves and giving rights to the free coloureds were to be tried out. If these policies - imposed on Trinidad because the island had no elected assembly that could resist legislation unpopular with the slave-owners - succeeded in the judgement of the Colonial Office, then efforts would be made to persuade the old colonies that did have assemblies to follow Trinidad's example. These were years in which humanitanians became increasingly influential in Britain, and as a result the Colonial Office moved slowly to develop new policies for ameliorating, or improving, the slaves' situation and, finally, for emancipation. Trinidad played a central role in this development

After the abolition of the British slave trade in 1807, the abolitionists concentrated on the illegal inter-island slave trade. Slaves were brought from the older British colonies and the foreign islands to be sold in Trinidad. The abolitionists became convinced that large-scale illegal importations into Trinidad were taking place, and led by James Stephen, they pressed for compulsory registration of all slaves already in the British colonies as a check against illegal entries. The government was persuaded, in 1812, to establish a registry of slaves in Trinidad as an experiment; if it worked well the other colonies would be urged to adopt a similar measure. 'The poor patient has to go through some very severe operations,' continued the writer quoted above. 'She is now actually bound down for a most painful one - a registry of slaves, prescribed by Dr Stephen . . .'

An Order in Council in March 1812 introduced a system for the compulsory registration of all slaves in Trinidad. The abolitionists hoped to prevent illegal importations by making it dangerous to possess a slave who had not been legally acquired, for the Order stipulated that the ownership of a slave depended on his/her being duly registered. In other words, only registered slaves could be held in bondage; an owner's title depended on registration, and any person not so registered would be deemed free. After the original registration, all changes in the slave population (by death, birth, manumission or sale) were to be periodically recorded, so that it would be very difficult for an owner to hold in slavery a person who had not been legally acquired. Further, the abolitionists hoped that the system would prevent gross ill-treatment of slaves. The owner had to record each year such things as births, deaths, casualties, mutilations, runaways and recaptures, and this publicity would, they expected, prevent atrocities and the worse forms of abuse; perhaps it would also encourage owners to improve living conditions so that more slave infants would survive to maturity.

The Order stipulated that the first registration should be completed in one month, and that it should be followed by annual registrations to be completed in ten days. After the first registration, no unregistered person could be held as a slave, and it would be illegal to transact business involving slaves or slave-worked estates unless they were registered. The registrar was not to be a slaveowner.

But the actual enforcement of the Order departed radically from these provisions. In the first place, Henry Murray, the registrar, was a local land-owner who had merely transferred his slaves to a relative to comply with the requirement. If he was not technically the owner of plantation slaves, he was a fully paid-up member of the local oligarchy. Further, he held several other offices and never devoted much of his time to the registry. Even more serious, Murray agreed to extend the deadline far beyond the one month that the Order stipulated. In fact the first registration was not completed until the end of 1813. These delays meant that slave-owners had a period of several months in 1813 in which to make last-minute arrangements for purchasing slaves illegally imported into the island before the registration was closed. Both Murray and the new governor, Sir Ralph Woodford, were less than enthusiastic about the scheme, and their negligence and willingness to compromise with the slave-owners prevented the efficient implementation of the law. Of course the planters were furious; any 'interference' in the way they managed their slaves was intolerable to them, and they did what they could to sabotage the scheme. One planter told a friend in Britain that:

'The establishment of the registry took place, to some extent, amid all the imprecations against it; and a great number of the inhabitants registered, to avoid giving an example of disobedience and causing trouble. No measure was ever more unpopular or excited more discontent, even among the ignorant coloured classes who this kind of imposition affects more severely; for he who has only one slave pays two gourdes [a local currency] for his return in the same way as he who has a hundred.'

When the final returns were in at the end of 1813, a total of 25,717 slaves had been recorded. This represented an increase of 4,429 or 14 per cent over the census of the slave population taken in 1811; and Woodford admitted that as many as 4,441 slaves had been registered after the first deadline had passed, that is, between 22 April and 31 December 1813. These figures were regarded by the abolitionists as proof that extensive illegal entries had taken place, for the apparent increase of over 4,000 slaves in 1811-13 could not possibly have been due to natural causes; deaths always outnumbered births in the Trinidad slave population. Nor could many have come in legally with their owners from the other islands, for such arrivals would have been entered in the Customs records. Even if the 1811 returns were inaccurate and underestimated the number of slaves (because they had been compiled for tax purposes), as the slave-owners and their defenders argued, there can be no real doubt that extensive smuggling of slaves into Trinidad had taken place since 1808 when the general abolition of the slave trade became effective, and particularly between the arrival of the Registration Order in August 1812 and the end of the first registration in December 1813.

Local opposition and official negligence combined to ensure that the registration scheme never worked as Stephen and the abolitionists had hoped. Although the law was changed to allow triennial instead of annual returns, the returns were always delayed. The triennial returns for 1831 were not transmitted to London until 1834. The returns were often defective, and it was difficult to detect cases of flagrant ill-treatment from them, or to determine accurately the causes of slave mortality. The inefficiency of the whole scheme meant its failure to improve slave conditions, although the abolitionists insisted that the other colonies should pass Registration Acts based on the Trinidad law, and in 1819 Parliament centralized the registry of slaves for the whole British West Indies in London and forbade British subjects to purchase unregistered slaves.

Yet for historians the returns provide invaluable data about the slave population in the last twenty years of slavery. Because Trinidad had begun its development as a slave colony so late, its demographic structure was not yet that of a mature slave society: in 1810 only 67 per cent of the total population were slaves; in the older colonies the proportion was at least 90 per cent. Slaves were much more frequently the property of coloured or even black slave-owners than in the other colonies; sometimes their owners may have been relatives. Slaves were concentrated in relatively small holdings. In 1813, 60 per cent belonged to units of under fifty slaves (in Jamaica the proportion was only 24 per cent), and only 8 per cent lived in units of over 150 slaves. As late as 1834, the average owner had only seven slaves; 80 per cent owned less than ten, while only one per cent held over 100 slaves. An unusually high proportion of Trinidad slaves were urban: almost 25 per cent lived in Port of Spain in 1813, and this pronounced urban orientation was to be important for the development of post-emancipation society. Another 20 per cent lived on estates growing coffee, cocoa or provisions, so that only just over 50 per cent lived on sugar plantations.

Again unlike the older colonies, in 1813 the majority of the Trinidad slaves were African-born: there were 13,980 natives of Africa and 11,629 Creoles (born in the West Indies, not necessarily in Trinidad). Just over 60 per cent of the Creoles were Trinidad-born, while the rest had come from the other British colonies, or from the French and Spanish Caribbean. The African slaves came from a very wide geographical spread, with slaves from the Bight of Biafra forming the largest single group (39.4 per cent). In Trinidad, the 1813 returns show that Africans tended to marry (that is, form stable unions with) fellow Africans: only ten per cent of the married African men had Creole wives. There was considerable intermarriage between Africans from different regions, and as a result the distinct African ethnic or regional groups soon lost their individual identities. Stable family units, headed by a husband and wife who both belonged to the same master and therefore were able to live together with their children, were quite common in 1813, especially on the larger plantations where it was easier to find a mate on the same estate. (Husbands and wives belonging to different owners could not live together and so the children would be registered with the mother as belonging to a family unit headed by the woman.) In these nuclear family units the husband was often a privileged slave, a skilled tradesman or a driver, and this has led one historian to conclude that the male heads of slave families in Trinidad were not always economically marginal to the family's existence, and that the authority of slave husbands in these units was probably greater than many historians have thought.

Although nuclear family units headed by the husband were quite common in 1813, overall the majority of the slave children lived in units headed by their mother, and these 'matrifocal' units were especially common in urban slave families. In fact it seems that the matrifocal tendency in slave family structure became stronger as the Creole population grew and urbanization developed. For the Africans the nuclear family, or better yet, the extended family containing several generations of kin, remained the norm, but it was very difficult to achieve in Trinidad, except for those few slaves living on plantations with a large stable slave population. And the formation of stable families was constantly interrupted by mortality. Deaths always greatly outnumbered births, and in 1816-34 the population declined by 32 per cent. The 1816 returns showed a slave population of 25,287; by 1834, the last year of slavery, the figure was only 17,539. Severe mortality and low fertility combined to cause a steady decline in the slave population, and this fact alone points to the failure of the amelioration policies of 1812-34.

The Registration Order had been expected to check the illegal inter-island slave trade to Trinidad, but in fact this traffic continued. Up to 1825 it was legal for planters who intended to settle in Trinidad to bring in their slaves, and Woodford encouraged the importation of slaves with their owners after 1813. The authorities were very reluctant to enforce the laws against illegal importation. Between 1813 and 1824 over 4,000 slaves were imported legally, accompanying their owners who were, ostensibly, settling in the island; but of course there was room for all kinds of abuses, and slaves supposed to be accompanying their owners were often being imported for sale on arrival, for slaves fetched very high prices in Trinidad because of their scarcity. Burton Williams, a planter from the Bahamas, brought in at least 324 slaves in 1821-3. Large planters from the older British colonies, like Williams, received every encouragement from Woodford to settle with their slaves; they were given land grants and often the import tax was remitted on the slaves they brought in.

But the British government, under abolitionist pressure, became aware that extensive smuggling was taking place under the cover of slaves accompanying their owners, and in 1824 an Act that became effective in Trinidad in January 1825 prohibited the removal of slaves (other than personal domestics in actual attendance on their masters) from one colony to another, except with the specific approval of the Secretary of State. And it was made clear that such approval would only be granted under stringent conditions: the slaves involved should not be employed on sugar estates, they should be moved with their consent and in family groups, and all female infants born after arrival in the new colony should be automatically freed. Of course these conditions were quite unacceptable to the larger slave-owners interested in settling in Trinidad. This law, therefore, effectively ended the settlement of planters from the old colonies in Trinidad, since they would hardly emigrate without their slaves. Several slave-owners from the older colonies applied to transport their slaves to Trinidad between 1825 and 1829, but the conditions laid down by the Colonial Office discouraged them from going further; in 1828 alone eleven slave-owners with over 2,000 slaves from seven different colonies were prevented from settling in Trinidad.

After January 1825 the only slaves who could be legally brought into the island were domestics in actual attendance on their owners, and this loophole was used to develop a well-organized system of illegal importation. Owners brought field slaves from Barbados and other colonies, took them to Trinidad ostensibly as domestics, and then sold them for plantation labour. At least 1,109 slaves entered Trinidad as 'domestics' between 1825 and 1830. This illegal traffic was carried on with the connivance of Woodford and other officials. When Sir Lewis Grant became governor in 1829, he began an investigation which soon convinced him that the local authorities had ignored flagrant examples of illegal entries since the beginning of 1825, and that many local slave-owners had knowingly purchased illegally imported slaves. For instance, in 1829 Charles Hobson brought in seventeen 'domestics' and was not even questioned by the appropriate authorities. From Barbados alone 266 'domestics' were imported in 1827-8, of whom 204 had been sold by 1829, a clear indication that they were not genuine domestics accompanying their owners. One boat made seven different trips to Trinidad in 1827, landing a total of sixty-one 'domestics'. The evidence for a systematic illegal traffic with the connivance of the local authorities was overwhelming, and Grant decided to act.

Early in 1832 he issued a Proclamation that declared that all slaves who had been illegally imported were forfeit to the Crown, and their owners were liable to criminal prosecution; but they were given a six-week grace period to voluntarily manumit these slaves and escape prosecution. This entirely justifiable law outraged the slave-owners, who were already agitated about the tough amelioration Order in Council of November 1831. They claimed that the law would cause hardships to the 'innocent purchasers' of illegally imported slaves. They formed a committee to represent the owners of slaves imported since January 1825 and petitioned for the revocation, or at least suspension, of the Proclamation. Grant of course refused; in his view every slave introduced since January 1825 who was not in actuality a domestic in attendance on his/her owner's family had been illegally imported and therefore should be set free. When the owners involved failed to use the grace period to manumit the slaves, he ordered the Attorney-General to begin prosecutions. By August 1832, 480 cases had been sent up for trial, and Grant rejected a petition calling for compensation to the owners for the loss of the illegally imported slaves.

Grant's firmness infuriated the planters. The cabildo, whose members were all slave-owners, voted funds to help pay the legal expenses of the planters being prosecuted; Grant as president of the cabildo vetoed the vote. Undaunted, the cabildo ordered the Alcalde (keeper) of the Jail not to feed the unfortunate slaves being held as the subjects of the cases; Grant vetoed that too. Finally, documents needed for the trials were stolen in November 1832 from the office of the court that was to hear the cases. The leading newspaper, the *Port of Spain Gazette*, rejoiced over the theft, and no one was ever arrested; the thieves were almost certainly prominent slave-owners. Their action delayed but did not prevent the trials being held, despite hysterical opposition from the planters and their allies. Up to the beginning of 1834 at least 579 slaves were freed as a result; then the Secretary of State directed that the trials should be shelved as emancipation was to take effect in August 1834. The history of the illegal slave trade to Trinidad since 1813 illustrated how easily the policy of the imperial government could be frustrated by determined resistance by the slave-owners and the connivance of the local authorities.

Precisely the same fate befell the amelioration policy in Trinidad. In 1823, under pressure from the humanitarians, the British government undertook a new policy for the amelioration of the condition of the slaves in the British West Indies. Trinidad was again cast in the role of the experimental colony: the reforms would first be applied to Trinidad in an Order in Council, and then extended to the other Crown Colonies; finally the colonies with assemblies would be persuaded to pass laws embodying the Trinidad reforms. Trinidad was chosen rather than the other Crown Colonies of St Lucia and British Guiana because it was thought that the Spanish legal heritage had made slavery there milder than in those territories where the legal tradition was French or Dutch.

The Secretary of State, Lord Bathurst, started the ball rolling in the middle of 1823 by asking Woodford to discuss with the Council of Advice the reform proposals, which had been agreed on after negotiations with the West India interest in London; the reforms were a compromise between the anti-slavery party and the West Indian representatives in Britain. Bathurst's proposals included limitations on corporal punishment, the encouragement of slave marriages and manumission, the abolition of Sunday markets and Sunday work, the admission of slave evidence in the courts, the appointment of a Protector of Slaves, and other reforms designed to give the slave legal rights while remaining property.

Predictably, these proposals, despite their studied moderation, provoked alarm and apprehension among the Trinidad slaveowners. The Council of Advice, under the leadership of W. H. Burnley, protested strongly; meetings of slave-owners were organized in the districts to abuse the British government and its daring new policy. The planters of Arima resolved 'to deprive the master of the power of inflicting corporal punishment on any slave, male or female, would subvert the discipline of his estate. Deprivation of the Sunday market would produce the loss of one day per week to the owner of the slave and would not produce the religious effect desired . . .' The slave-owners of North Naparima declared that 'the abolition of whipping ... is virtually a deprivation of property' and 'to enforce marriage among slaves would if carried into effect add the sin of perjury to that of adultery'; and the planters of Pointe-à-Pierre proved to their own satisfaction that 'flogging is the most humane, prompt and efficacious mode to c rush disorderly behaviour'.

Woodford was sympathetic to the planters, and he relayed many of their objections to the Colonial Office. His representations delayed the hour of decision; not until March 1824 was the Amelioration Order in Council finally promulgated. Ironically, although Woodford's commitment to amelioration was lukewarm, and although he sympathized with the owners' fears of interference in their authority over the slaves, he was principally responsible for drafting the Order. The Colonial Office modified his draft, which was itself based on Bathurst's original proposals, but the details were largely Woodford's work.

The Trinidad Order in Council of March 1824 attempted to restrict the owner's right to discipline his slave, and to give the slave certain legal, religious and human rights, while not affecting his/her status as chattel property. It was illegal to carry the whip in the field to coerce the slaves to work; corporal punishment of females was absolutely forbidden; male slaves could only be flogged twenty-four hours after the offence, in the presence of a free person other than the owner or manager who ordered the punishment, and such floggings were limited to twenty-five blows. All punishments were to be recorded in books that were to be presented quarterly to the Commandants. Sunday markets and Sunday labour for the owner were prohibited. Marriages were to be encouraged, even without the owner's permission; no families were to be split up through sales. Slaves could possess and bequeath property. Manumission was to be facilitated, even without the owner's consent, and regulations stipulated how a slave wishing to manumit himself should be appraised. Savings banks were to be set up to safeguard the slaves' property and encourage thrift. Finally, slave evidence could be admitted in court, if a clergyman had certified that the slave had sufficient religious instruction to understand the nature of an oath and to be a competent witness. A Protector of Slaves, who could not be the owner of plantation slaves, was to act on behalf of the slaves. The Secretary of State instructed Woodford that the Order was to be strictly enforced; if the Commandants or other local officials refused to co-operate he was to dismiss them.

The Trinidad slave-owners might not have had an assembly, but they made their opinion of the Order very clear. Led vigorously by Burnley, the Council criticized the Order and asked Woodford not to put it into effect until further time had been given the planters to petition London. In May 1824 Burnley organized an indignation meeting in Port of Spain. The cabildo issued a formal protest, claiming that the order would injure the slaves, jeopardize the colony's safety, ruin the slave-owners, and subvert the sacred rights of property. If it was enforced, compensation should be given the slave-owners for their 'losses'. Even a group of coloured slaveowners petitioned against the Order. Woodford was sympathetic, and supported many of the planters' claims: he told Bathurst that the slave-owners were in some danger, he suggested that compensation might be appropriate, and he particularly criticized Clause 42 which allowed the government to confiscate the slaves of any owner twice convicted of offences against the Order. Woodford thought this hard since it had only just been made illegal to punish female slaves, who were 'allowed by all to be the most prone to give offence'. Bathurst insisted that the Order must be implemented as it stood, and it became law in Trinidad on 25 June 1824; but he agreed that the confiscation clause would not be enforced until the case in question had been reviewed by the Colonial Office.

Like the Registration Order, the 1824 Amelioration Order was largely sabotaged by the slave-owners and the local officials. The Protector of Slaves was Henry Gloster, a barrister closely connected to the slave-owning interests, and a pluralist who held two other major offices. Other high officials involved in the implementation of the Order were mainly slave-owners, including the Commandants and the assistant Protectors. James Stephen criticized the policy of 'referring the work in its form and practical details at least, to its known and irreconcilable enemies'; in particular he thought it wrong that office holders, and especially the Protector, should merely be required not to own plantation slaves, while being allowed to own domestics. In his view slave ownership inevitably predisposed officials to connive at abuses. Further, Woodford himself was less than enthusiastic, and he wrote in 1824 that he regretted that the Order had been promulgated as it stood. Under these circumstances, the Order failed almost completely to achieve its objectives.

Between 1824 and 1829, only two slaves were certified as being competent in court; presumably Catholic and Anglican clergymen failed to co-operate. In the same period only four slave marriages took place. Manumissions by purchase did increase after the order became law; 409 slaves bought their freedom betwen 1824 and 1827. But prohibitively high prices were often demanded by the owners, and then the slave was appraised by officials who were themselves slave-owners. In 1826 Pamela Munro, a domestic, was appraised at £261, a sum three times that paid for the same slave shortly before. Yet the slave had no redress against flagrant injustice; neither governor, nor Chief Justice, nor Protector was empowered to intervene. In 1829 three slaves, of widely different values, were appraised by one umpire at exactly the same price, £216 13s 14d, which none of them could pay; one of the slaves belonged to the Chief Justice who had appointed the umpire. The Order and subsequent proclamations authorized other forms of punishment for female slaves, since flogging had been prohibited, including solitary confinement, confinement in stocks, and the punishment of being forced to work the treadmill in jail; girls under ten years of age could be flogged. Although Sunday labour had been prohibited, the

Secretary of State authorized owners to force domestics and watchmen to work on Sundays. Very few slave-owners were ever prosecuted for breaches of the Order. It was extremely risky for a slave to make a complaint, and difficult for her to substantiate her case if she had the courage to proceed. The weakness of the Order is well illustrated by an 1826 case: a slave complained of rape, but she was the only witness, she had no certificate of competence to give evidence, therefore the accused had to be discharged. Clause 42, which provided for confiscation of an owner's slaves after a second offence against the Order, was never enforced between 1824 and 1834. The Order had no teeth, and in the face of opposition and indifference, the amelioration policy had little real success between 1824 and 1831.

Yet the planters' hostility remained strong, and the slave-owners dreaded any legislative interference in their authority over their slaves. For slavery depended on their absolute and unchallenged right to punish and discipline the slave, short of actual murder. This authority was undermined as soon as a third party - the Protector, the law, the courts - was allowed to stand between the master and the slave. The historian L.M. Fraser, always sympathetic to the slave-owners, explained that they believed that the Order would destroy the friendly and kindly feelings between owner and slave in patriarchal Trinidad. Now the slaves had 'rights'; acts of kindness that the masters had always performed were put on a legal and formal basis, and the absolute property right of the owner was undermined. This was also the view of Mrs A. C. Carmichael, the wife of a British slave-owner who owned Laurel Hill estate in the 1820s. She argued that the Order eliminated the slave's 'respect' for his master and destroyed the affection that existed between master and slave in Trinidad. Although the 'good Negroes' remained loyal and well-behaved, the 'bad characters' became restless and insubordinate; the master's ability to control his slaves was undermined. Yet when the slave-owners refused to co-operate with the British government in carrying out the very moderate reforms of 1824, they strengthened the case of the anti-slavery party and hastened the coming of emancipation.

By 1830 the government recognized that the 1824 Order had not been effectively implemented, and it tried to make the law more specific and less ambiguous. At the end of 1831 a comprehensive new slave law was issued for the Crown Colonies. This Order, called by the planters the '121-pronged scourge' because it had 121 clauses, strengthened the previous amelioration laws and introduced new and tougher regulations. For instance, it stated that neither the Protector nor any of his family was to hire domestic slaves; persons could be prosecuted for intimidating slaves who complained to the Protector; inquests were to held when slaves died suddenly or mysteriously; all field labour for the owner on Sunday was absolutely forbidden; male slaves could receive only fifteen lashes; slave evidence was to be admitted in all cases equally with that of free persons. In addition, very precise regulations on food, clothes and hours of work were laid down. The Order of November 1831 was by far the toughest and the most comprehensive of all the amelioration laws.

Its publication in Trinidad at the beginning of 1832 led to a hysterical outburst from the slave-owners, whose tempers got worse as emancipation loomed ahead. The cabildo issued a formal protest and asked Governor Grant to suspend the Order, invoking an ancient Spanish law to the effect that Ordinances that encroached on property rights had to be suspended until the king's pleasure was known. A public meeting was held in Port of Spain which set up a standing Committee of Slave Owners to fight for the cause. Petitions were fired off to the king, to the Lords and to the Commons, calling the Order 'a vexatious and most injurious interference with the authority of the master over his slave', and threatening that if the planters were not compensated for the 'losses' they would incur as a result of the Order, they would have to request the king to 'dissolve the connection with the British Crown': a notable example of Trinidadian 'robber-talk'. The planters tried to involve free coloured slave-owners in their campaign, and they nominated four coloured planters (in their absence) to the Committee of Slave Owners, but they declined to serve; their tactic was to disassociate themselves from the white planters and emphasize their co-operation with the British government.

Throughout 1832-3 the planters' bitterness mounted. The columns of the *Port of Spain Gazette* were filled with hysterical articles and letters. In May 1832, resistance took the form of sabotaging the trial of slave-owners prosecuted for breaches of the new Order. Such offences were tried in the new Supreme Court, which consisted of three professional judges and three 'assessors' who were to be chosen from the cabildo. Of course cabildo members were all slave-owners. The two alcaldes of the cabildo who were supposed to serve as assessors refused to attend the trial of a slave-owner who had struck her female slave in breach of the Order: they argued that the offence was trivial and the slave's complaint frivolous, that the trials encouraged the slaves to defy their owners' authority, and that such trivial cases should not be heard in the Supreme Court. These cases were brought to a standstill for several months by the alcaldes' action. The *Port of Spain Gazette* hailed them as heroes. Although numerous prosecutions were made for breaches of the Order, the majority were dismissed or the accused was acquitted. Further, the clauses on food, holidays and hours of work were systematically ignored. In fact, the 1831 Order was largely defeated by the resistance of the slave-owners and their allies holding strategic positions - like the alcaldes. No wonder that the abolitionists, and finally the British government, decided at last that the time had come to stop tinkering with slavery, and to use the authority of the imperial Parliament to legislate for the end of slavery in the British empire.

The Act of Emancipation was passed in August 1833, and became law on 1 August 1834. While children under six were immediately free, all other slaves had to serve an 'apprenticeship' of six years for field slaves and four years for other slaves, during which they would be obliged to labour for their former owners for three-quarters of the working week, without wages. For the rest of the week they were free to seek paid work. Special Magistrates appointed and paid by the British government were to enforce the system and protect the apprentices' rights. Twenty million pounds were voted to compensate slave-owners for the loss of their property. The Act represented a compromise between the anti-slavery party and the West Indian interests; if anything it gave the West Indians more than the abolitionists.

In Trinidad, Governor Hill reported at the end of 1833 that the public was prepared to receive the act 'with serenity, and to give it fair play'. He was being optimistic, but the slave-owners' protests began to die down as the futility of resistance became clear. A local commission was set up to determine compensation, based on the average value of each slave in the eight years before 1830. Payments ranged from £25 for aged or ill slaves to £170 for drivers and £150 for skilled tradesmen. Hill made strenuous efforts in 1833-4 to ensure that both slaves and owners understood the provisions of the Act, and stringent regulations were enacted to keep the apprentices under control and to prevent insubordination or wilful disobedience. Since the British Special Magistrates had not arrived by the end of July 1834, Hill appointed Commandants and other local land-owners to act temporarily, in violation of the Act, and prepared the militia for possible trouble.

Emancipation day - 1 August 1834 - was calm; but a crowd of apprentices gathered in Port of Spain near Government House shouting 'Point de six ans!' ('Not six years more!') and complaining that absolute freedom had been denied them. On the next day the crowd reappeared. Some were arrested for breaches of order, and twenty-three were publicly flogged, but Hill resisted pressure to declare martial law and removed the regular troops from the city to avoid provoking trouble. There was no disorder anywhere else in the island. By 12 August Hill reported that the great majority of the apprentices were working peacefully. Four long years would pass before full freedom would be won by the slaves of Trinidad, but, at least, after years of futile efforts to 'ameliorate' slavery, liberty was in sight.

The Free Coloureds and Civil Rights

In 1810 at least twenty per cent of the population of Trinidad were free coloureds and free blacks, and they had been an important element in the island's society since the 1780s. Their legal and political situation had worsened since the British capture in 1797, and in the early 1820s their leaders began a campaign for legal equality and civil rights, reacting both to the British government's new humanitarian leanings and to Woodford's regime, which was particularly hostile to their interests.

In 1813 free coloured land-owners were numerous, especially in the southern part of the island. They owned 37.3 per cent of the estates, and 31.5 per cent of the slaves, in the Naparimas. But they tended not to be owners of large sugar estates or many slaves. Only two coloured planters owned sugar estates with over 100 slaves, and the only coloured planter in the 1820s who was a man of considerable wealth was Louis Philip, who owned large plantations and many slaves. On the whole, free coloureds were less significant slave-owners than land-owners: land was cheaper, and easier to obtain, than slaves. Very few coloureds were large merchants, so the coloured planters depended on white merchants for capital and supplies, although there were many small-scale coloured traders in Port of Spain and San Fernando. Most coloured sugar planters were seriously in debt to white merchants, but probably those planters who grew cocoa, coffee or provisions managed to keep free of debts.

The Trinidad free coloured community differed from that in the other British and French islands in that it was not particularly urban. Between 1811 and 1834, probably as many free coloureds lived in the country as in Port of Spain, St Joseph or San Fernando. There were many hundreds of coloured or black land-owners, often owning just a few acres and a handful of slaves, growing cocoa, coffee and provisions. In fact, free coloureds formed a class of small farmers all over the island. The 'Spaniards', people of Spanish-Indian or Spanish-African descent who had originally come from Venezuela and lived around St Joseph and Arima cultivating coffee and cocoa, were Spanish-speaking, and often isolated by poor roads. Free coloured smallholders abounded in remote areas like Toco, Mayaro and Icacos, where they were probably a majority, farming and fishing. Many of these people were very poor and their life-style was similar to that of the slaves. At the opposite end of the scale were the prosperous coloured planters of the Naparimas and those free coloureds who owned property in Port of Spain and San Fernando.

In the 1820s the leading free coloured family, the Philips, was well established. Of Grenadian origin, settled in Trinidad since the 1790s, they owned considerable property in the Naparimas. Louis Philip owned the Concorde and Phillipine sugar estates, as well as land in Port of Spain, San Fernando and Grenada. Two of his sons became medical doctors and public men; Jean-Baptiste led the free coloured campaign in the 1820s, St Luce became the first coloured member of the new Council in the 1830s.

Men like these, well-educated professionals with a solid background in coloured landed society, felt they had strong claims to equality with the whites.

For these men, the legal discrimination and social humiliations with which they had to contend became increasingly intolerable. We saw in Chapter 3 that under Picton and Hislop their legal and political situation had deteriorated markedly. Woodford's regime was a new period of oppression for the free coloureds, marked by deep-seated personal prejudices. In 1822 an Order in Council was introduced at Woodford's instigation which allowed the alcaldes to order imprisonment or corporal punishment for free coloureds/blacks (not whites) convicted on summary conviction of petty misdemeanours or trivial infractions of municipal or police regulations. The alcaldes were, of course, invariably white slave-owners, anxious to subordinate the free coloureds in every possible way. This law, which allowed the alcaldes to order free coloureds to be flogged virtually at will for petty offences, outraged their leadership; for them corporal punishment was the symbol of all the degradations of slavery from which they had escaped. Woodford's efforts to explain away the objectionable clause were a failure, and the law galvanized the coloured leaders into action.

Social humiliations rankled almost as much as legal discrimination. No legal documents could be presented that did not state the writer's status as a free coloured. Woodford deliberately encouraged officials and whites in general to address free coloureds, even prosperous and respectable persons, without the courtesy titles of Mr, Madame, and so on. He was hostile to the numerous unions of white men and coloured women, because he believed that free coloureds were acquiring property and wealth by inheriting land from their natural white fathers, and he did what he could to prevent legal marriages between white men and coloured women. He wrote in 1817 that he had never received an application for such a marriage, but if he did he thought 'it would be proper to decline sanctioning the same'. Jean-Baptiste Philip claimed that a French planter had been forced to go to Grenada to marry a coloured woman.

Coloured doctors had to pay for a licence to practise while whites were granted them freely. Dr Francis Williams, who had been born in slavery and whose mother was still a slave, was denied a licence from the Medical Board, although he had graduated from a British university, simply because of his slave birth. This decision was only reversed after the intervention of the Colonial Office. St Luce Philip, the only doctor with a university degree in the whole southern district, was forced to serve in the militia as a private, while white 'doctors' without degrees were commissioned as surgeon or lieutenant. In 1821 Woodford issued a schedule of fees for doctors that discriminated between the fees to be paid for the same kinds of medical care for whites, free coloureds and slaves.

Public institutions were segregated formally or informally. A steam launch paid for by public subscription to ply between Port of Spain and the districts was divided into exclusive sections for whites and for coloureds. Woodford had to rescind this decision when the coloureds refused to use the boat. When the new Anglican church was opened in 1823, a section at the back, separated from the rest of the church by a wooden partition, and filled with plain board benches, was reserved for slaves and free coloureds; an act of discrimination that, naturally, greatly offended the whole free coloured community. Woodford did what he could to prevent social meetings among the free coloureds. A small literary and debating society organized by young coloured men was broken up, and a scheme for a secondary school for coloured children had to be abandoned because the government would not authorize a large meeting to collect subscriptions. It is hardly surprising that the coloured leaders concluded that Woodford was their worst enemy.

They launched their campaign for civil rights in 1823. The timing was, of course, due to the inauguration of the amelioration policy, for although the policy was concerned with the slaves, the free coloureds wanted to take advantage of the new humanitarian leanings of the British government. And it is no coincidence that the free coloureds of several other colonies - Jamaica, Barbados, Grenada - also presented petitions in 1823. In Trinidad, the memorial of the free people of colour asked for 'admission without respect of colour to the full enjoyment of all those rights ... enjoyed previous to the capitulation of 1797'. In particular, they wanted admission to civil offices and commissions in the militia, and the removal of all restrictions on their meeting together. In effect, the 1823 petition asked for legal equality with the whites, the removal of all the discriminatory legislation enacted since 1797. In 1824 Jean-Baptiste Philip published in London, under the pseudonym 'A Free Mulatto', a brilliant statement of the free coloured case which was addressed to Secretary of State Bathhurst. This document has an important place in the history of political protest in the West Indies, and it enables us to grasp the legal, social and psychological humiliations that confronted the free coloureds at that time.

The British government was sympathetic to the free coloured case, and in 1825 the Colonial Office instructed Woodford to repeal some of the more obnoxious legislation. By a Proclamation in January 1826, many of the vexatious police regulations against the free coloureds were revoked: for instance, the law forcing coloureds to serve as 'alguaciles' (police constables), and the regulations imposing a $16 tax on balls, the 9.30 p.m. curfew, the obligation to carry a lighted torch at night, the necessity to identify status as a free coloured in legal documents, and the discriminatory schedule of medical fees. Another Proclamation of the same date stated that the rights and privileges of citizenship that had been guaranteed by the 1783 Cedula were to be enjoyed by all those coloured inhabitants whose ancestors had been granted land under the Cedula, and by those who had got land other than by grants under the Cedula, provided that they had resided in Trinidad for a specific period. In other words, coloured land-owners were to have the right to civil and military offices. This was a considerable victory, but it was not until 1829 that full legal equality was won. An Order in Council of March 1829 removed all legal disabilities against the free coloureds.

But legal equality in itself was not enough; after 1829 the coloured leaders concentrated on converting this 'paper equality' into a right to occupy important civil offices. Both the Colonial Office and the governor felt that it was necessary to move slowly in making appointments in order to avoid offending the whites. In 1833 some coloured land-owners were appointed to officers' commissions in the militia, to the great joy of the free coloureds; but it was a short-lived triumph, for the militia itself was soon to be abolished. Appointments to civil posts were rare, and the posts involved tended to be minor. The first coloured to be appointed to a civil service post after the 1829 Order was John O'Brien, who was made clerk in the Attorney-General's office. In 1838 a coloured planter, André David, was appointed to the prestigious position of Stipendiary Magistrate. But appointments were few and far between, and a group of educated coloured men with political interests agitated all through the 1830s for a fairer share of public posts. A petition in 1839 complained that coloured men were excluded from posts of 'trust, dignity, and emolument and only admitted to some petty stations and subordinate government clerkships in order to keep up appearances'. The same complaint was to be made all through the nineteenth century and beyond, but at least the flagrant legal and political discrimination of the early years of the century was impossible after 1829.

Before emancipation the term 'free coloured' included everyone who was not a slave and was not white. There were many freed slaves, black and coloured, in Trinidad society, particularly in Port of Spain, and there were three settlements of former slaves which are of special interest.

In Port of Spain, just before emancipation, lived a community of Mandingo ex-slaves. These were people who had originally come from the area of West Africa between the rivers Senegal and Gambia; they were Muslims and a few of them were literate in Arabic. Under the leadership of Jonas Mohammed Bath, a Muslim priest who had arrived in Trinidad as a slave in 1804 or 1805 and had bought his freedom for $500, this community pooled its resources to buy the liberty of Mandingo slaves. They formed a kind of self-help association, with about 140 members in 1838, involved in trade, money-lending and planting: they owned cocoa estates, slaves and houses in the city. By August 1838 Bath was able to boast that 'very few, if any' members of the 'tribe' were still apprentices. To free a fellow Mandingo cost, on average, $500, a considerable investment, and a freed Mandingo had to repay this sum by instalments or perhaps by working for the association until the debt was repaid. They owned slaves, probably not Muslims, whose status may have been close to that of slaves held in Africa, where they were treated as inferior members of the household.

This community retained its African identity and its religion. Islam was the bond that kept them together. They retained their Muslim names along with their new Creole ones, and, even more significantly, they were determined to go back to Africa. They sent three petitions to the governor or the British government asking for help in securing passages to Africa. These petitions were rejected, and Bath died in 1838 without ever seeing his beloved homeland again. But a few individual members of the community did succeed in getting to Africa on their own. In 1837 Mohammed Hausa (Philip Findlay) and Jackson Harvey got back to Benin through the help of the Royal Geographical Society in London and the Colonial Office. The next year Mohammedu Sisei (Felix Ditt) went from Britain to his birthplace on the River Gambia with his Creole wife and child. But the group as a whole remained in Trinidad, and Mohammedou Maguina succeeded Bath as the 'patriarch' or leader of the Mandingo of Port of Spain. And there were Mandingo and Muslims among the free African immigrants who came to Trinidad in the 1840s and 1850s. The Mandingo were uniquely successful in maintaining their African religion, culture and language in a slave society.

Another settlement of former slaves was composed of American ex-slaves, some of whom had fought for Britain in the war of 181214 in the Corps of Colonial Marines, while others had been liberated by British officers during the course of the war. After 1816 some of these men with their families were settled in Trinidad in eight 'Company villages' in the southern part of the island near Princes Town. Each refugee was allotted 16 acres of land, and the villages were put under the control of unpaid sergeants and corporals who were to have minor disciplinary powers, and a white superintendent. The 'Americans', as they were called, were expected to maintain road communications between San Fernando and the southern and eastern coasts, and to open up a district that was still largely uncleared in the 1820s. These people were mainly Baptists, practising the exuberant forms of worship to be found in the slave states of America. After 1831 the Company villages ceased to be separate settlements under the special control of the government, and gradually, as sugar cultivation spread into the southern district, they were more and more integrated into the general economic and social life of the island. Yet as late as the end of the nineteenth century the descendants of the Americans were still proud of their separate identity and their history.

Around the same time that the Company villages were established, a number of demobilized soldiers of the West India Regiments were settled in villages between Arima and Manzanilla. Many of these ex-soldiers were of African birth. Seven villages were set up at Manzanilla, Quare, Turure, Hondo River and La Seiva between 1818 and 1825. The villagers were expected to build and maintain a road from Arima to Manzanilla to facilitate communications with the east coast; they were given land and pensions and put under the control of sergeants and corporals. The expectations about the road were not fulfilled, for the good reason that, as the ex-soldiers explained, 'they did not want a road or bridge; it might be very well to enable the white men to ride, but they always walked and could find their way through the forest'. Besides, they were not paid wages for their work on the road. The east coast settlements were very isolated in the 1830s, and Christian clergymen rarely visited; as a result a few Mandingo Muslim ex-sergeants converted many of the settlers to Islam. By 1840 Quare was predominantly Muslim, and the language spoken at these settlements was said to be 'Manzanillan', a mixture of English, French and African words. In the 1840s schools were established at Manzanilla and Turure and clergymen began to make occasional visits.

But in the years that followed many of the villagers settled elsewhere; others stayed on as small farmers, becoming almost wholly isolated from the rest of the island until the late 1860s, when a permanent road from Arima to the coast was built, and the settlements began to lose their separate identity.

Economic, Constitutional and Legal Changes

Amelioration, emancipation and free coloured rights were the principal issues that agitated the society in the years between 1812 and 1834, but they were not the only ones. Planters were concerned about the shortage of field labour that Trinidad felt so acutely since the abolition of the British slave trade in 1807; this is why they were so indignant when the British government refused to allow slave-owners from the older colonies to settle in the island with their slaves after 1825. Further, an unusually high proportion of the Trinidad slaves were not field hands; in 1834 one slave in three was a domestic. There can be no doubt that the shortage of field labour slowed down Trinidad's development as a plantation colony in these years. Planters were also faced with falling sugar prices in the 1820s, and most of them were seriously in debt to merchants in Port of Spain or in Britain. Despite the difficulties, sugar production increased steadily: from 18.5 million lb in 1813 it had doubled to 37.7 million in 1833, and by then 2,500 acres were in sugar.

For Trinidad still offered vast amounts of virgin soil to the sugar capitalists at a time when yields were declining in the older colonies.

Port of Spain grew into a flourishing commercial centre in these years. Its population increased from 7,151 in 1801 to 11,701 in 1838. In 1838 'coloureds' made up 58.5 per cent of the city's population, while 'blacks' (ex-slaves) and whites comprised only 25 per cent and 16 per cent respectively. Port of Spain was the home of British officials and businessmen and French and Spanish Creole merchants and planters, but the coloureds were numerically the dominant group in the city. Port of Spain's economy was based on its function as a port, with its fine harbour and its geographical position which made it a possible entrepot for British trade with South America. As trade developed in the early years of the century, the wharf district was built up with markets, warehouses, offices and banks to facilitate the collecting, handling and exporting of produce. This was the city's business heart. The cabildo market on George Street was built in 1818, along with a butchers' market and a fish market. In this busy district, shops and stores proliferated, with the owner usually living above, or at the back of, his store. The land south of King Street (now the northern side of Independence Square) was reclaimed, and in the 1820s Woodford laid out South Quay between King Street and the muddy shoreline on what is now the southern street of Independence Square.

But the city began to expand beyond the old commercial core. The sugar estates around the old town were bought up, and settlement spread to the north and north-west of the old centre. Ex-slaves and free blacks settled on the Ariapita lands and took up work on the wharves, forming the lower-class settlement of Corbeau Town on the marshy shorelands. Ex-slaves and other poorer people also settled in East Dry River, Laventille and Belmont, and the area along the old St Joseph road became an adjunct to the increasingly poor and overcrowded old town centred on Nelson and Duncan Streets. Better-off citizens moved to the west and north of the centre to settle on the Tragarete lands and other former estate lands. Woodford was responsible for converting the Paradise estate, which the cabildo bought, into the Savanna. So the city was expanding rapidly, but before emancipation the majority of its inhabitants still lived within the original old town.

One of the major issues agitating the more prosperous citizens of Port of Spain and the planters in the country was the question of what kind of laws, and what form of government, should be established for Trinidad. We saw that in 1810 the British government ruled that Trinidad would not be given an elected assembly, and that the constitution established in 1801 would continue: rule by the governor assisted by a Council of Advice which was not elected and which had no law-making powers. Although demands for an elected assembly continued to be made after 1810, the focus of attention shifted to the issue of laws, which the British government had shelved in 1810. Should the existing Spanish laws, greatly modified in practice since 1797, continue to form the island's legal code? Or should British laws be introduced, gradually or immediately? On the whole the British merchants and professional men favoured the second alternative, while most of the French and Spanish Creoles had grave reservations about the wholesale introduction of British laws.

There were a number of issues involved. Spanish civil law was thought to protect planters who owed money to merchants to a far greater extent than British law. The Spanish system made the recovery of debts secured on plantation property extremely difficult, costly and protracted, and the retention of Spanish laws after the formal cession to Britain in 1802 was a severe blow to the British merchants and their principals in Britain who were investing heavily in Trinidad sugar plantations. They saw the retention of Spanish law as a device calculated to ruin themselves and shield the planter-debtors, who tended to be French or Spanish, though there were British planters too. So one of the strongest arguments made for the introduction of British civil law was that it would free credit for plantation agriculture and thus advance the island's economic development, while the retention of the Spanish civil code would retard investment and production. This was the theme of an 1805 petition for British laws: the existence of the Spanish code, it stated, was calculated to shield the fraudulent debtor from the just claims of his creditor; it had cramped the island's economy and destroyed good faith in business transactions. The planter interest and its allies countered that the introduction of British laws would simply allow greedy merchants, often not resident in Trinidad, to wrest ownership of the island's estates from the resident proprietors who really had its interests at heart. Chief Justice Smith expressed this view when he argued for the retention of Spanish law in 1810. He said that in the other colonies, British law had resulted in merchants coming to own half the landed property. He thought that Spanish law was of great value to Trinidad's long-term prosperity: it lessened the credit available to the planter, forcing him to be frugal and independent, while British law, facilitating easy credit, led to extravagance and often transformed the estate of a respectable resident owner into a mere farm worked for an absentee owner. Economic conflict, in fact, lay behind the campaign for and against British law.

By about 1812 the British government had become convinced that reforms were necessary, for the legal system in Trinidad by then was a confusing and uneasy mixture of Spanish law and British procedures. Spanish law had been greatly modified, partly through ignorance, and partly through the hostility of British judges and officials to laws that they tended to regard as unnecessarily complex and often obsolete. The chance for a systematic programme for legal reform was improved by the long tenure of office by Woodford, and by his close co-operation with Chief Justices Bigge and Warner. Woodford's programme was to make plantation property safer, and to create a better investment climate, without eliminating Spanish law. This could be done by reorganizing the two superior courts to make procedure more English, and by introducing certain reforms in Spanish civil laws, especially those dealing with the collection of debts. Under Spanish law, a plantation could not be sold for debts unless they equalled the whole value of the estate; this made recovery of debts on plantation property very difficult. By an Order in Council in 1822, plantations could be sold for debts without reference to the value of the property or the size of the debt. Although the special property rights of married women or widows allowed by Spanish laws (called ganancial rights) were not abolished, the Order made the property of married women more liable to seizure for debts. A Complaint Court was set up with the Chief Justice exercising summary jurisdiction over all civil cases involving sums of less than $1,000, while the Provost-Marshall was empowered to enforce writs of seizure. These reforms, the work of Woodford and Bigge, made it easier to collect debts, especially those on landed property.

In 1827 a Commission of Legal Enquiry, set up to investigate the complex legal situation of the island and make recommendations, published its report. It announced that Spanish law was still the common and statute law of Trinidad, binding in all cases not specially provided for; English laws were not binding, except for laws on trade and navigation and laws in which Trinidad was specifically mentioned. The commissioners noted that the major grievances against the Spanish code were: the testamentary laws that restricted the individual's right to dispose freely of his property by will, in order to protect the rights of widows and children; the age of majority, which was 25 in Spanish law while it was 21 in English law; and the ganancial rights that protected the wife's rights to a share in all property acquired during the marriage (this was said to damage the claims of legitimate creditors). In general, the commissioners agreed that Spanish civil law was minute, complex and 'often vexatious'. So far as criminal law was concerned, they found the inhabitants generally in favour of introducing English criminal laws and procedures. They recommended the gradual removal of the defects in the Spanish laws, and the introduction of those English laws considered suitable for the special situation of the island. In particular, they recommended the abolition of ganancial rights, the removal of restrictions in the disposing of property by will, the reduction of the age of majority to 21, the abolition of the cabildo, and the introduction of English procedures in criminal cases. Their report was accepted by the British government.

The Commission had also recommended the establishment of a council with law-making powers restricted to local matters and including some representatives (not elected) of the local property-owners. Such a council, with legislative powers, could enact Ordinances that could gradually reform the laws and introduce parts of the English legal system as the Commission had advised. At the beginning of 1832, therefore, a Council of Government was established, consisting of the governor as president, six officials, and six 'Unofficials' - prominent local residents nominated by the governor to 'represent' the whole taxpaying community. The Council was empowered to enact Ordinances that would have the force of law in Trinidad; these had to be assented to both by the governor and by the king, or in other words by the Colonial Office. The Council of Government, later renamed the Legislative Council, could be charged with the reform of the island's legal system.

Changes in the civil law were made first. In 1832 the age of majority was lowered to 21, in 1833 habeas corpus was introduced, and in 1837 English laws on bills of exchange and promissory notes were made binding. But the Council failed to agree on a new law on the disposal of property by will, and the issue was shelved until after 1838. Criminal law seemed easier to deal with. By 1834 most of the propertied classes favoured the adoption of English criminal law. Spanish laws were felt to define offences ambiguously, to enable the guilty to escape on petty technicalities, and above all to be too lenient to offenders. As full emancipation approached, the upper classes began to get nervous about the safety of their property and their persons. In opting for English criminal law, they were deliberately opting for a harsher system: a sharper definition of crimes and heavier penalties. In 1834-6 the Council of Government enacted Ordinances that introduced English criminal laws on fraud, larceny and offences against the person. But the Colonial Office disapproved and they were not given the royal assent; the Colonial Office wanted to delay any wholesale introduction of English laws until emancipation had been completed. The issue was shelved until the 1840s. In that decade a 'legal revolution' was carried out that saw the assimilation of Trinidad's legal system to that of England.

One ancient Spanish institution failed to survive into the 1840s: the cabildo. This municipal body, whose members were elected by the male property-holding residents of Port of Spain, had considerable powers of jurisdiction and administration over the city, and its magistrates, the alcaldes, heard minor criminal cases in the city. It also claimed vague rights to uphold the interests of the community against arbitrary actions by the local government, rights that had their origin in the old Spanish constitution which no one really understood by the 1820s. By the early 1830s the cabildo was probably doomed. The establishment of the Council of Government early in 1832 meant that the cabildo had been relegated to the status of a secondary assembly. By then, too, a movement to 'anglicize' (make English) the laws and institutions of the colony had begun; a peculiarly Spanish institution like the cabildo would not be allowed to survive indefinitely. Even more important, the cabildo, whose members were all slave-owners, took a vigorous part in the opposition to amelioration and emancipation. It came to be seen as a nuisance, as a source of trouble and opposition, by both the British and the local governments. When the Council of Government was set up, the Colonial Office decided not to abolish the cabildo (as the Commission of Legal Enquiry had recommended) on the mistaken belief that it was a genuinely popular body. But the new Council was to be the instrument to effect changes in Trinidad's laws and institutions, and the cabildo - a Spanish body that invoked Spanish laws and concepts of municipal government in crises - was not likely to escape. The conflict with the governor over the slave question hastened its end.

When the 1831 Amelioration Order was published in Trinidad, the cabildo issued a strong protest, and asked Grant to suspend it, claiming to act as 'guardian of the welfare and protector of the rights of the community over which we are appointed to preside'. It invoked an ancient Spanish law to the effect that laws which invaded property rights were to be suspended until the king's decision was known. We have seen that the alcaldes, who were officers of the cabildo, sabotaged the court cases against slave-owners for breaches of the Order by refusing to sit as assessors. The cabildo also took an active part in the campaign against the prosecution of slave-owners who had bought slaves illegally imported since 1825. Another conflict with the governor centred on the Royal Gaol (Jail). The cabildo cited Spanish laws to show that they had the right to elect or dismiss such officers as the Alcalde (Keeper) of the Gaol, and they warned the governor not to bring the government 'directly in collision with the only semblance of a freely elected body in the Colony'. The cabildo was challenging the authority of a British governor in a Crown Colony, and invoking Spanish law to do so. Its survival was only a matter of time.

In 1840 the Council of Government abolished the cabildo, and replaced it with a town council, modelled on English municipal bodies. The new town council was to be strictly subordinate to the local government. All its acts were subject to the governor's ratification; its powers were far less extensive than the cabildo's and they specifically excluded control over the municipal police, and the Gaol; none of its officers was to exercise any judicial functions. It was to be an elected body, but the franchise was only to be given to male property-holders; perhaps 300 out of a city population of around 14,000 would have qualified to vote in 1840. On 6 June 1840 the cabildo ceased to exist. Its passing provoked virtually no protest. Its abolition was inevitable at a time when the movement to anglicize

Trinidad had begun, and when it was engaged in conflicts with the local government which it could not possibly win.

The 1820s and 1830s were anxious years for the Caribbean; in Trinidad especially change and uncertainty seemed all around. For the white ruling class, it seemed that the props of their privileged social and economic position were being knocked away one by one: the cabildo had gone; free coloureds had won their rights; the imperial government was intervening with increasing vigour in their management of their slave labour. Finally, in 1834, slavery itself was abolished. The short reprieve that the apprenticeship represented for the planters was ended abruptly in 1838. The former slaveowners and the former slaves, as well as the large intermediate class of free coloureds, would be faced with the challenge of adjusting to full freedom after 1 August 1838.

FIVE

The Ordeal of Free Labour and the Colonial Economy, 1838-1900

Labour Problems following Emancipation

Complete emancipation in 1838 marked a legal revolution for Trinidad, as for the other British West Indian colonies. It meant the end of a period when social relations between the races were clear and unambiguous, the end of a system of well-defined labour relations. The ex-slaves were not about to enter into anything like social or racial equality with their former owners, still less were they about to be granted political rights; it meant a legal or nominal freedom, and, perhaps, nothing more. The planters after 1838 wanted to make freedom merely a nominal change in status, while the ex-slaves wanted to win a real economic independence of the planter and his operations; this clash would shape post-emancipation developments in the island. Both sides had some advantages: the planters had political influence, unquestioned social superiority, the ownership and control of the major economic activities; the ex-slaves could exploit a labour market in which labour was scarce and planters had to compete for what was available, and they could take advantage of the abundance of land. In these respects the ex-slaves of Trinidad were in a stronger position than their counterparts in Barbados and the Leeward Islands.

The Apprenticeship ended early, in August 1838, two years before the Act of Emancipation had provided. This was the result of the campaign by the abolitionists for its early end, and the effect of that campaign on British public opinion. The Colonial Office put pressure on the assemblies of the older colonies to pass Acts ending the Apprenticeship on 1 August 1838, and by June of that year most of the smaller colonies had complied. In Trinidad, a Crown Colony, there was no real hope for a successful resistance, but the planters protested and the legislative council grumbled; the apprentices for their part told Governor Hill that on no account would they work after 1 August. Hill appealed to the Colonial Office to send out an Order in Council ending the Apprenticeship (since London could legislate directly for colonies like Trinidad which did not have an assembly), but it was not needed. In all the circumstances, the planters had to accept defeat, and at the eleventh hour, the last week in July, the legislative council enacted a measure to end the Apprenticeship on 1 August.

The great day passed peacefully. Governor Hill was able to report 'perfect tranquillity' in Trinidad by the end of August. Riot, revolution and massacre - the fears of many whites, who could never forget Haiti - did not materialize; but the problem of labour immediately became acute.

Trinidad had always had a 'labour problem'. It was an island newly opened up for sugar cultivation. It became British only ten years before the abolition of the British slave trade, and even before 1807 restrictions had been placed on the importation of Africans into the island. After 1807 the efforts of the anti-slavery lobby and the British government were concentrated on preventing an illegal trade of slaves from the older colonies of the eastern Caribbean, and these efforts were increasingly successful after 1825. For a relatively large island, with considerable potential as a producer of sugar, its slave population was small. In 1838 only 20,656 apprentices were freed, and a high proportion of them were domestics, women and children. A small force of field labourers contrasted with an abundance of land. In 1838 only 43,000 acres were cultivated out of a total acreage of 1.25 million acres. Furthermore, Trinidad's potential as a major producer of sugar was clear: the Surveyor-General said in 1841 that four-fifths of the land was suited to sugar, and W.H. Burnley thought that if only one-seventh of the Crown lands was opened for sugar, the island could provide enough of this commodity to satisfy the demands of the British market. However exaggerated these opinions may have been, the situation was clear enough: in 1838 Trinidad's potential for the expansion of cultivation was tremendous, while the field labour force was small even in relation to the existing cultivation.

To this basic situation was added, after August 1838, the problem of inducing free people to labour steadily, continuously during crop, and cheaply, on their former estates. During slavery the labourers could be, and were, compelled to work scandalously long hours; now they would work as long as they thought necessary to meet their cash needs, even if they continued to reside on the estates. Planters complained both of an absolute shortage of labourers, and of a decline in the work done by the labour that they could obtain. Burnley, still the leading spokesman for the Trinidad plantocracy after 1838, stated to the 1842 Select Committee of the House of Commons that the chief cause of distress (he meant planter distress, of course) in Trinidad was 'the want of a sufficient labouring population to enable them to keep the large capital invested in sugar estates in profitable employment'. On the other hand, Robert Bushe, an estate owner and manager, told the Committee he had as many labourers on his estate as during slavery, but they did much less work. During crop, the same numbers as were employed during slavery could not provide adequate labour, for in those times they had worked up to eighteen hours a day, while after freedom they never worked more than nine hours. The manager of Orange Grove estate stated in 1841 that the 300 resident labourers on the plantation did about the same amount of work as the 200 slaves employed before 1834. In the factory the labourers did at least one-third less work than the slaves, and this manager stated that he suffered great losses from negligence and wilful misbehaviour by his workers. Bushe thought that if the labourers would work twelve hours a day, six days a week, during crop, the estates could maintain pre-1838 production levels with the existing labour force. But why should a free person work such hours?

The planters adopted strategies to meet the situation that were much like those tried out by their counterparts in other colonies. First of all they tried to offer inducements for the ex-slaves to work regularly on the estates. One important inducement was that field work in Trinidad was mainly assigned by the task, except during crop, and the average task, which was a specified job of work on a defined area of land, took between four and five hours for the 'able-bodied' man. The industrious worker could do two or even three tasks a day, with much higher earnings than if day work was the system. Disputes could and did arise over the size of the task, but up to 1846 the tendency was to be lenient in fixing the dimension of the task because planters were competing for labourers.

But the major inducement that the Trinidad planters offered was a rate of wages far higher than in any other British West Indian colony, a reflection of the shortage of labour. In 1838 the average wage was 30 cents per task. Burnley stated that in May 1841 the average wage had risen to 50 cents; some estates paid between 60 and 65 cents per task for field labour, and skilled men earned more. In crop, when payment was by the day, labourers could earn well over 50 cents. Since a task took about four or five hours for an industrious man, said Burnley, a labourer could easily earn over a dollar a day at task work. These wages for field labour - between 50 and 65 cents per task or per day - were higher than any paid in Trinidad for a century to come. In 1938 unskilled labourers in sugar were earning 35 cents per day, and the weekly wage for field labourers ranged between $1.20 and $3.00. For a short period, the planters were forced by the pressures of labour shortages to pay competitive wages to their workers. But not for long. In 1841 a meeting of planters decided to reduce wages during the 1842 crop to 30 cents per day; the workers refused to accept the reduction and the pressures of crop forced the planters to back down, and by February 1842 the wage on most estates was back to 50 cents. At the end of the 1844 crop the planters again attempted c ombined action to force down wages by about 25 per cent, after a six-week strike halted work in some areas. But at the start of the 1845 crop wages had climbed back to 50 cents again. It was the financial crisis of 1846-8 that made it really urgent for the planters to reduce wages, and after 1846 wages settled down to about 30 cents per task or per day for field labour, rising occasionally if there was a labour shortage in a particular locality.

The high wages offered between 1838 and 1846 were paid by the planters, however reluctantly, as an inducement to get the ex-slaves to work for them. For the same reason, they continued to pay some of the traditional 'allowances' of slavery days. Resident workers still occupied rent-free huts and provision grounds; and all the workers were given saltfish and rum. But the planters decided that these allowances were too expensive to continue, and most planters stopped giving them after January 1842, with no compensation in money. Bushe told the 1842 Select Committee that the withdrawal of allowances did not increase the planters' problems in obtaining labour, but it must have made plantation labour even less attractive to the ex-slaves.

Despite the high wages, the planters felt that their labourers were not performing steadily and continuously, above all during crop. Instead of regular and docile labourers, they had to employ mobile workers who refused to be bound by any contract, whose work patterns could not be predicted from week to week or day to day, and who would quit an estate for no clear reason. This is why some planters tried to use the ex-slaves' huts and grounds as a means to pressure them into regular work. Planters in Trinidad did not try to charge rents for the huts and grounds, but they did try to enforce a system known as tenancy at will: the labourer resident on an estate was obliged to work for that estate and no other, on pain of immediate eviction from the cottage and grounds. The worker paid no rent, but he was tied to work for the estate, and he had no security of tenure. This linking of tenancy with labour was implicit - there were no written contracts; there was merely an understanding that rent-free residence in an estate hut was dependent on at least a few days' labour per week. Bushe stated that four tasks per week during the slack season, and four nine-hour days during crop, would be expected on average from a resident labourer. He said that he would evict a worker who did less than two days a week, though he stated that in practice he had never had to evict such a person. The point was not that evictions were frequent - after all, frequent evictions would have defeated the whole point of the strategy - but that the worker had absolutely no security or independence. As the American journalist William Sewell noted, the resident worker was in a position of virtual serfdom, and the system gave every incentive for him to leave the estate and seek independence as a smallholder and a part-time wage labourer.

The ex-slaves' objective was to make freedom meaningful, to achieve a measure of economic and social independence of the planter. There was no mass disappearance into the bush, as many planters had feared. The ex-slaves were reluctant to settle far in the interior at a distance from existing centres of population with their schools, churches and rudimentary social amenities. In Trinidad the bush was left to the Amerindians, now fast dwindling away, and the 'peons', of Spanish-African-Amerindian descent originally from Venezuela. But if the ex-slaves did not disappear into the forest, many of them saw no reason why they should continue to live on the estates. And this feeling was accentuated by the tenancy system, the withdrawal of allowances in 1842, the reduction in wages after 1846, and countless other irritants. Hence very many ex-slaves left the estates to live elsewhere. Sewell estimated that of the 11,000 field slaves in 1834, 4,000 remained on the estates by 1859, while 7,000 had left. The majority of the ex-slaves who left the estates remained in agriculture. They bought, leased, or squatted on parcels of land, becoming small cultivators, giving part-time labour to estates, and living in new villages close to existing plantations which sprang up in the years after 1838. During crop, wrote Sewell in 1859, between 4-5,000 of these smallholders would give labour to the neighbouring estates. Ex-slave villages developed near Port of Spain (East Dry River, Laventille, Belmont) and San Fernando (Rambert and Victoria Villages), and a ribbon development of settlements along the Eastern Main Road between Port of Spain and Arima. By 1846 an estimated 5,400 were living in these new villages, and by 1847 the resident estate labour force had shrunk by 40 per cent. Sewell estimated that five-sixths of those who had left the estates had become land-owners by 1859, holding one to ten acres, and he thought that their condition was far better, materially and socially, than that of the resident estate workers. The smallholders cultivated vegetables and provisions, to feed themselves and to sell locally, but they also grew crops like cocoa and coffee, and a little sugar for local use.

Some ex-slaves left agriculture altogether. Many became petty traders or hucksters, and a large internal trade grew up with ex-slave hucksters selling cloth, clothes, flour, tobacco, saltfish and so on. A few became more prosperous shopkeepers in towns and villages. Quite a large number entered the skilled trades; of course many slaves had been skilled artisans who could begin to work on their own account after 1838, and it became a matter of pride to apprentice a son into a trade rather than see him labour in the field. Burnley said in 1842 that 'there is a very great tendency to collect in towns ... the general opinion is, that the towns have increased one third, or more, since emancipation'. Sewell said that in Port of Spain, four-fifths of the black inhabitants were in trade, and were independent and prosperous by 1859. This was certainly an exaggeration, and many of the ex-slaves who congregated in Port of

Spain and the other towns after 1838 were probably unemployed, or at best irregularly and casually employed. Lord Harris claimed in 1851 that there were as many as 8,000 persons in Port of Spain alone over the age of ten who did not work, or over one-half of the total population of the capital. Perhaps this claim was as exaggerated as Sewell's. In any case, the fact that many of the more ambitious and potentially mobile ex-slaves practised skilled trades and settled in Port of Spain, San Fernando and the larger villages is important. This pronounced urban orientation would be significant for the development of Trinidad society in the post-emancipation generations.

Another important development was the withdrawal of most of the ex-slaves' children from field labour. During slavery children over the age of six had been an integral part of the plantation labour force. Now parents made great efforts to keep their children from the fields. The manager of two large estates said in 1842 that there was no single case, on the two estates he managed, of a child emancipated under the age of ten subsequently working in the fields. Parents tried to send the children to school in San Fernando: 'they exult very much in the idea of sending them to school; and it gratifies them very much when one of the children can read'. Parents felt that field labour would degrade their children, and often they sent their offspring away from the estate to live with godparents or relatives.

For the ex-slaves who left the estate, land was abundant, and squatting on Crown lands or on abandoned estate lands was universally resorted to, There was some sale of estate lands to the former slaves; a few planters sold small lots at very high prices in order to settle labourers close to their estates. But on the whole planters were very reluctant to sell estate land, and when they were forced to do so they charged exorbitant prices. The Crown lands were made inaccessible by rules that set a high price per acre and forbade the sale of small or medium-sized lots. Squatting was the obvious solution. It had been resorted to long before 1838, and now it greatly increased. Since there were over a million acres of Crown lands in 1838, and since the government made it impossible for the ex-slaves to buy small parcels, there was nothing surprising in this development. A Proclamation of March 1839 authorized magistrates to evict squatters of less than one year's standing - in other words, ex-slaves who had squatted after August 1838 - and imprison them if they refused to move. But this law was a dead letter because planters refused to lay information against neighbouring squatters who were a source of labour; if they were removed they would only work for someone else. As Burnley said in 1842, 'for any useful purpose, we have no law in Trinidad to prevent squatting'. It was not until the 1860s that the related issues of squatting and the Crown lands would be effectively dealt with.

Sugar: Fluctuating Fortunes

For the planters, the decade after 1838 was fraught with difficulties. Yet sugar suffered no disastrous decline in Trinidad, as it did in Jamaica and some of the other colonies. At first production did decline. In 1838 the planters made 14,312 tons of sugar; in 1840 only 12,228 tons, although production costs had risen. But there was a recovery in 1840-6, and in these years the planters sustained their sugar exports, on the strength of the island's fertility, though at the expense of the quality of their sugar and the physical condition of their fields and buildings. One well-informed observer, writing in 1854, said that although Trinidad was fairly well equipped with steam-engines in the factories, the quality of sugar was inferior to that of Barbados. He wrote that the cane plants were planted too closely, the use of fertilization was almost unknown, and the hand hoe was used rather than the plough. This reluctance to use the plough in Trinidad may be explained by the wet heavy soils, the extensive ratooning*, and the presence of tree stumps in the fields, all of which made ploughing difficult in many parts of the island. In any case, it was generally agreed that cultivation was much sloppier than in Barbados, and that the sugar made in Trinidad in these years was not of a high quality. But up to 1846 things were not disastrous. Prices on the British market remained fairly high. Burnley made a profit of £3,433 in 1840 on his Orange Grove estate; which compared reasonably well with his profits during the Apprenticeship. Orange Grove was a well-run estate whose owner had plenty of capital; for small estates the outlook was less good.

But the real crisis came in 1846. In that year the Sugar Duties Act was passed by the British Parliament, providing for the gradual equalization of duties on foreign and British colonial sugar. This meant that the British West Indian producers had lost their preferential position on the British sugar market, and that they now had to compete on equal terms with cheaper foreign producers. The Act caused a drastic fall in sugar prices, and a loss of confidence on the part of British merchant firms and mortgage-holders in West Indian sugar estates. This situation was compounded by a disastrous financial crisis in Britain in 1847-8 which led to the failure of a number of firms that were heavily involved in the West Indian trade. In 1847 the failure of the West Indian Bank brought commercial transactions of every kind virtually to a halt. The Colonial Bank, in Trinidad, had to suspend payments temporarily and only just survived without total collapse. Trinidad was hard hit by this double-edged crisis, and it was in these years that the sugar industry faced its severest difficulties.

Thirteen estates were abandoned in 1838-48, which compared well with other colonies in the period. But Governor Lord Harris reported in 1848 that during the first decade of freedom, 159 estates (the great majority) had been operating at a loss: after running expenses had been met, insufficient money was left to cover the cost of property maintenance. The resulting deterioration in the condition of the estates caused a decline in the market value of Trinidad plantations. Writing in 1848, the Attorney-General noted '64 petitions of insolvency have been filed; estate after estate thrown upon the market, and no purchaser found . . . Many estates have been abandoned from the inability to raise money on the faith of the coming crop.' He instanced the Jordan Hill estate in South Naparima, making an average annual profit of £3,000 in the 1830s, which had just been sold for a mere £4,000; also, he said, 'men here wonder, not at the sacrifice of the vendors as much as at the rashness of the purchasers'. Needless to say, the labourers were hard hit. On most estates there were long delays in the payment of wages, or even a total stoppage, and in 1846-7 the planters combined to force down wages. Revenues fell off as production declined. By May 1848 Harris reported that the Colonial Treasury was virtually empty. To many planters and officials, the very survival of the Trinidad sugar industry seemed threatened.

Yet the abandonment of sugar production on a plantation basis was never a real possibility in Trinidad. Too much capital had already been invested, and the island represented a fresh frontier of sugar lands for the planters of the 'old' colonies, as well as for British capitalists. The island soon recovered from the crisis of 1847-8. As a measure of relief, the British government agreed in 1848 to advance the money needed to finance Indian immigration, and to relieve the island from the cost of introducing African immigrants. Lord Harris showed considerable ability in managing the crisis. He reduced expenditure as far as possible, and he repealed differential duties in favour of British imports and generally reduced import duties, a measure designed to revive trade and production. The arrival of immigrant labourers from India, Africa and the eastern Caribbean began to alleviate the planters' labour difficulties.

Signs of recovery were clear as early as 1849. In that year, exports exceeded in volume the average for the preceding eight years. Revenues for 1849 had increased by £25,000 over 1848, while imports had increased by £170,000. This recovery continued into the early 1850s. In 1852 exports of cocoa were the largest ever, and the export of sugar had increased since 1850. As the revenues recovered, Harris was able to abolish the export duty as an incentive to production, although it was later reimposed to pay for Indian immigration. He was able to embark on a modest programme of public works, particularly the improvement of roads, and limited social services, including government primary schools; he financed these projects by levying a special land tax on all land-owners in the Wards, the administrative districts that he established in 1848. By 1854, when Harris left the island, Trinidad had clearly recovered.

Plate 2 Orange Grove Estate, Tacarigua

In the 1850s planters began at last to expand their cultivation, replanting abandoned land and even clearing and cultivating virgin soil. Sugar estates reached the foothills of the Montserrat range and the Oropouche lagoon by the late 1860s. Production rose steadily. In the 1850s it never fell below 20,000 tons per annum; in 1866 it reached 40,000 tons; only in one year subsequently (1875) would it fall below 40,000 tons; and by 1880 production was 53,436 tons. Sugar was expanding both in exports and in acreage. The prosperity of the Trinidad sugar industry between 1850-84 was the result of Indian immigration, the abundance of fertile land, and a revival of confidence by British capitalists.

After the 1840s large sums of money were invested in the Trinidad sugar industry, mostly to modernize the manufacturing side in order to reduce costs and produce a better grade of sugar. By 1897 at least £2.5 million had been invested. The large British firms or individual capitalists who came to control much of the Trinidad sugar industry had access to metropolitan capital, and they carried out the modernization of the industry in 1860-97. One of the most important developments was the extension of vacuum pan technology in the manufacture of sugar; the process resulted in a higher grade of sugar than the 'muscovado' traditionally made in the British islands. Muscovado sugar became less and less profitable as the century went on, while the semi-refined sugars made by the vacuum pan and centrifugal technologies were much more widely consumed in Britain. So the trend was for the old muscovado factories to be scrapped and the new technology introduced.

Modernizing the factories was expensive, but the new factories could handle much more cane than the old ones. So those owners who had the capital would amalgamate several small estates, scrap their old factories, and build a single modern factory to serve the new, larger plantation. For instance Norman Lamont, the Scottish capitalist, concentrated on the Naparima district, buying up small estates that were too weak to survive as separate units, scrapping their old factories, and tagging them on to his existing holdings. By 1897 most muscovado factories had been phased out, and in 1895 over three-quarters of Trinidad's sugar was produced by the vacuum pan method. The Royal Commission that investigated the West Indian sugar industry in 1897 found that the manufacturing side of the Trinidad industry was modern and efficient.

In the last forty years of the nineteenth century, therefore, British capital came to dominate the Trinidad sugar industry at the expense of local planters, particularly the French Creoles who had been involved in sugar since the 1780s. By 1895 thirty-four out of fifty-nine estates were owned by British corporations or individual capitalists, while twenty were owned by resident British planters and only three by French Creoles. But this does not tell the whole story; the British owners tended to control the biggest and most productive estates. By 1897 most of Trinidad's sugar was produced by eleven units, owned by British corporations or individual capitalists. The situation was, therefore, that sugar estates were being increasingly amalgamated, British concerns were consolidating their hold on the most productive estates, French Creoles were no longer by the end of the century important owners of sugar estates, while even resident English planters had lost ground to the metropolitan concerns.

The giant combine was the Colonial Company, incorporated in 1866 to take over two private firms operating in Trinidad, British Guiana and Puerto Rico; the company has been called the first example of conglomerate capital in Trinidad. It led the field in the amalgamation of small estates and the modernization of production. In 1872 the company completed the Usine St Madeleine, the first central factory to be built in Trinidad. The largest of the British empire at the time, it cost over £180,000 to build - a very large sum at that time - and was equipped with the most modern machinery. It reduced production costs by nearly 50 per cent in 1884-94. By 1896 the Usine represented a total investment of £339,342, comprising the factory, railways and rolling stock. It took in the canes of fourteen company-owned plantations totalling 10,340 acres in 1896, plus 19,341 tons of farmers' canes; its throughput was then 12,000 tons per annum. Other large British concerns were Tennant & Co., which owned Malgretout and La Fortune, a total of 12,925 acres with an investment of £400,000 in 1896; Gregor Turnbull & Co. with Brechin Castle, Caroni and Lothian estates; and the Lamont family owning

Palmiste, with 2,190 acres and an investment of £124,600 in 1896. These large concerns, and others like them, built central factories, acquired large land-holdings and had light railways to transport the canes to the factory.

The existence of central factories made possible the development of cane-farming. It began in Trinidad in 1882, when farmers were allowed to occupy land belonging to the Colonial Company to plant cane to be ground at the Usine St Madeleine. The depressed sugar market in the 1880s and 1890s accelerated the pace at which cane-farming was adopted. More land became available for farmers when smaller estates were abandoned or when large estates decided it was more economic, at a time of low prices, to let the farmers share in the costs and risks of sugar production. Many workers were retrenched in the sugar industry in these decades, and these unemployed persons, both Creoles and 'free' Indians, turned to cane-farming to make a living. It suited the large companies, which bought the farmers' canes more cheaply than they could have been grown on the plantations, and the system ensured that the new central factories were fully utilized. For the farmers it provided the chance of a better livelihood and somewhat more independence than was possible for the wage labourer. By 1890 cane-farming was firmly established in the Naparimas and it soon spread all over the sugar belt. Creoles, British West Indian immigrants and ex-indentured Indians all became farmers; not until 1906 did Indian farmers outnumber the rest. By the turn of the century a substantial proportion of the sugar crop was grown by farmers.

One of the major factors in the prosperity of the Trinidad sugar industry after about 1850 was Indian immigration. The Indians 'solved' the labour problem that had been so acute in the 1840s. As early as 1852 Lord Harris had expressed the view that Indian immigration had saved the sugar industry by providing reliable labour: reliable because, as we shall see, the indentured Indians were tied to the plantation by the indentureship laws, and cheap because they were paid low wages and because the taxpayers subsidized the cost of immigration up to one-third of the total. By the 1850s Indian labour was the backbone of the sugar industry, and gradually Creoles withdrew until by the end of the century even the skilled factory jobs, hitherto monopolized by Creoles, were increasingly held by Indians. By 1870 any situation of labour shortage was over; by 1897 the position was one of an overstocked labour market and depressed agricultural wages as a result. Yet the planters never gave up their cry of labour shortage, not even in the 1880s and 1890s, when all the evidence pointed to an abundance of agricultural labour and much rural unemployment.

The planters found it necessary to claim a continuing labour shortage in order to back their insistence on continued Indian immigration, which they wanted because it suited them to have a core group of indentured workers, and because they hoped to depress the wages of the non-indentured labourers, both Creole and Indian. Some of the evidence given to the 1897 Royal Commission is revealing of the planters' attitudes to labour. Indentured labour, they thought, was absolutely essential for sugar production, for without it, it would be impossible 'to begin work early and end it late'. The manager of the Usine St Madeleine said 'I should prefer to be able always to call on them [i.e. as he could in the case of indentured workers]. I should prefer to have twice or three times as many people as we have now - with much lower wages.' Wages should be reduced and immigration stepped up, he said; thousands of workers lived comfortably on five cents a day, so wages could be reduced from 25 cents to 18 cents without any hardship; there were never enough hands for the work. This evidence was given at a time when rural unemployment was mounting and when even the indentured workers were failing to earn the minimum average wage stipulated in the indentureship laws.

The last two decades of the nineteenth century were years of crisis for the sugar industry. Cane sugar producers faced severe competition on the British market from beet sugar produced in Europe; the European governments artificially boosted beet exports by paying subsidies on every ton exported. Cheap beet sugar flooded the British market. In 1884 Germany doubled the bounty, or subsidy, on exports, and France stepped up her exports. Prices on the London market dropped drastically; the price for muscovado in 1884 was only 13 shillings per hundredweight, which was usually below the cost of production, and the severity of the crisis depended largely on how far the industry had broken away from the old muscovado process. Although the Trinidad planters were far better situated to survive the crisis than their counterparts elsewhere, because the vacuum pan process had been extensively introduced by 1884, they reacted with the traditional prophecies of utter ruin and anguished cries for help. In 1884 the legislative council stated that the existence of the colony was threatened by the depression in sugar, and asked to be allowed to make reciprocal tariff arrangements with the USA to facilitate the sale of sugar to that market. Similar pleas came from the Agricultural Society, while a petition from sugar planters, also in 1884, complained of imminent ruin and called on Britain to impose countervailing duties on bountied beet imports (i.e. duties to the value of the bounty paid on exports by the European governments). The Colonial Office rejected this request, but it agreed to try to negotiate arrangements with the USA for more advantageous terms for British West Indian sugar entering that country.

The second round of the crisis came in 1895-7. Both France and Germany doubled their bounties and prices fell even lower; and the USA, despite efforts by the British government, imposed heavy duties on British West Indian sugar. A petition from the Agricultural

Society in 1895 stated that sugar was the most important industry in Trinidad and that the welfare of the whole population depended on it. Prices on the British market were ruinous, far below the cost of production even on the best estates. Bounties on European exports prevented the investment of British capital in the Trinidad sugar industry. The petitioners asked for countervailing duties and a reciprocal agreement with the USA. The governor, F.N. Broome, supported their case. In his view, if sugar collapsed, 'it will bring down with it both the government and the community'. He thought investment would soon stop if sugar prices continued so low, and inevitably the finances of the colony would suffer. In 1897 even the best Trinidad estates could make a profit of only 6s per cwt, and others were producing at a loss.

Some relief came in 1898 when the USA imposed countervailing duties on bountied beet imports to the full value of the bounty. This virtually shut out beet sugar from the US market, and by 1900 nearly three-quarters of British West Indian sugar was sold on that market. But US tariff policies were notoriously changeable, and the Trinidad planters continued to agitate for the imposition of countervailing duties in Britain as a form of pressure on the European governments to abolish bounties. The British Cabinet, however, decided against this strategy, and instead applied diplomatic pressure. In 1902 the Brussels Convention finally ended the paying of bounties on beet sugar exports, and in 1900 Canada offered a general preference to British West Indian sugar. These developments enabled the sugar industry to recover and enjoy a modest prosperity in the early years of the twentieth century.

The Emergence of Smallholders and the Cocoa Industry

Until the turn of the nineteenth century, sugar remained the principal export of Trinidad, and it was always more heavily capitalized than any other industry. But the economy was not completely dominated by sugar, nor could the plantocracy prevent the emergence of a smallholding class and the development of other crops. For at the time of emancipation Trinidad was still an undeveloped country, with over a million acres of Crown lands, and much of the land in private ownership still uncultivated or under-cultivated. The disposal of the Crown lands was to be a central issue in the nineteenth century, reflecting the interests and concerns of the local government and the local ruling class.

The official policy for the disposal of the Crown lands was laid down in a dispatch from the Secretary of State for the Colonies in 1836: they should be kept out of the reach of the masses in order to preserve the estate labour force after complete freedom, and to concentrate the population near the 'civilizing influences' of church, police and schools rather than allowing them to scatter into remote districts in the interior. At the end of the Apprenticeship, the smallest parcel of Crown lands that could be bought was fixed at 340 acres, and later the Colonial Office actually agreed to a minimum acreage of 680 acres, or one square mile. By this policy, the Crown lands were for all practical purposes closed to any legal enterprise. No sensible capitalist would buy a square mile of virgin forest for sugar cultivation in the depressed 1840s, while the ex-slaves could not possibly raise the purchase price. Instead, of course, they squatted illegally wherever they could.

The point of the policy was to prevent the ex-slaves becoming land-owners and to preserve the estate labour force. Although Lord Harris was essentially in agreement with that policy, he was prepared to make minor concessions. He sold one-acre lots of Crown land at Arima and Arouca for housing plots; both townships grew rapidly as a result. Then he tackled the 'problem' of squatting. A Proclamation in 1847 stated that squatters in occupation before December 1838 had six months to have their holdings legalized at 6s per acre and legal and surveying costs; those who had settled later were to pay £1 per acre plus costs. Squatters who failed to regularize their position in this way could be evicted by the magistrates and sentenced to up to six months in jail. But the problem, as always, was enforcement; many of the squatters lived deep in the interior, and bad roads and the absence of a rural police force made Lord Harris's laws a dead letter. Only 295 squatters took advantage of the new law to buy their lands; most were content to let things slide, and it soon became clear that as little was being done to evict them after Harris's laws as before. Sales of Crown lands were virtually at a standstill. Labourers found it easier to squat, planters preferred to buy land on the private market. In 1847-65 only 3,425 acres were sold. At the same time squatting had increased in the 1850s and 1860s. By the mid-1860s squatters included cocoa farmers, some of whom owned thousands of trees, especially in the Northern Range, in the districts east of Arima and in the Montserrat area.

It was Governor A. H. Gordon (1866-70) who decisively tackled the related issues of squatting and the Crown lands. An 1869 law radically changed the conditions under which Crown lands were sold. The price was reduced to £1 per acre and the minimum lot to five acres. Legal fees were also cut, and surveys were to be done by government officers at a moderate and uniform fee and within a reasonable time. The entire transaction could be carried out locally at the Warden's offices so that the applicant need never come to Port of Spain, an important consideration when travel was so difficult. The result of the new law was to makes sales far easier and quicker; in some cases grants could be made within days of the sale. The applicant would pay £13 18s 10d inclusive for ten acres and the whole process might take about three months.

Gordon then moved to deal with the squatters. He chose the district of Montserrat to try out his policy; it was an area notoriously settled by Crown land squatters. He created it a Ward Union and in 1867 he appointed Robert Mitchell Warden and Commissioner of Crown Lands. It was a brilliantly successful appointment; Mitchell, a Creole, spoke Spanish and patois as well as English, and he was an energetic official who thought nothing of difficult trips into the remote interior where the squatters lived. After only a few months at work, Mitchell reported that 408 squatters had applied for 5,533 acres, and new settlers had applied for 3,000 acres of unoccupied land. These Montserrat squatters included peons, Creoles, British West Indian immigrants, Yorubas, Ashantis, Congos and Mandingos. Mitchell's report for 1868 indicated that the African squatters had co-operated in buying their holdings, and some had voluntarily removed to new settlements. Mitchell noted that nearly all the squatters were ready and anxious to pay for a legal title to their land in return for the protection of the law, and access to schools, markets and churches when roads were built in the new districts. By the end of 1870, Mitchell thought, most of the squatters would either have paid for their holdings or abandoned them, and by the end of 1872 he reported that new cases of squatting were rare. The Montserrat experiment had shown that squatters could be persuaded to become legitimate land-owners if reasonable terms were offered to them, and the new rules for the sale of Crown lands were designed to facilitate the orderly sale and settlement of these lands in the future. In 1869 Gordon was able to offer twenty-five 'free' Indians grants of Crown lands in commutation of their right to return passages to India. He felt that this was a development of great significance to the country, and this land commutation scheme was continued until 1880.

Gordon had opened up the Crown lands to the small man. Some of his successors changed the rules for the sale of these lands and made the process more difficult, but they could not reverse his achievement. After 1869 the Crown lands were steadily sold, mostly to small buyers who purchased between five and twenty acres. In 1875-85 3,350 grants were made with a total acreage of 54,193; the average grant was 16 acres. In 1890-1900 the average annual sales totalled 6,800 acres and in 1899 alone 14,600 acres were sold. As the Crown lands were sold, cultivation spread. By 1890 the natural vegetation on the central plains had disappeared, leaving only the three hill ranges still covered with forest. The work of clearing the land and advancing cultivation was done almost entirely by smallholders - Creoles, peons, Africans, British West Indian immigrants and, from the 1870s, Indians.

Most of the Crown lands alienated in this way - and much private land too - were cultivated in cocoa. Cocoa was only moderately prosperous in 1840-66, but it enjoyed a tremendous boom period in

1866-1920. By the turn of the century cocoa exports had overtaken sugar in value to become Trinidad's leading export staple. If sugar was becoming heavily capitalized and largely foreign owned, cocoa was the reverse: it was owned almost exclusively by locals, and although there were large cocoa planters, peasant producers were always an important element in the Trinidad cocoa industry. The small cocoa farmers in the foothills of the Northern Range, who were mainly patois- or Spanish-speaking, experienced difficulties in the 1840s. Their labourers often deserted for the higher wages on the sugar estates, so cocoa faced for the first time a labour problem. But their most serious difficulty had to do with the market for their cocoa. Spain was by far the largest importer, and Spanish prices determined the market situation of Trinidad cocoa. They had dropped drastically in 1820-42. Furthermore, Spain imposed high duties on foreign cocoa imports, and these were even higher if they were carried in foreign ships; securing Spanish ships to take the cocoa to Puerto Rico or Cuba for trans-shipment to Spain involved long delays and heavy costs for the Trinidad producers. In Britain the demand for cocoa was very small in the 1840s and 1850s; neither the beverage nor chocolate were items of mass consumption.

But important technological advances in the processing of cocoa resulted in the drink becoming a staple item of the masses in Britain, Europe and the USA. In 1866 Cadbury Brothers introduced their 'cocoa essence' and eating chocolate of the modern kind began to be manufactured in Britain by the 1840s. All this was to create a tremendous expansion in the British market, and this was the principal reason for the boom in cocoa production in Trinidad after the 1860s. Within the island, the elimination of squatting and the opening of the Crown lands gave a great boost to cocoa; so did the extension of roads and the building of railways. The depression in sugar after 1884 released land, labour and capital for cocoa. Montserrat, Gordon's experimental district, became the finest cocoa district in the island. In 1871-81 two-thirds of the new land opened up to cultivation was planted in cocoa.

The great boom came in the 1870s. Sewell, writing in 1859, said that people thought that cocoa would ultimately go out of production because it was so unprofitable; only 7,000 acres in the whole island were in cocoa. Another writer said that in the 1860s cocoa was 'negligible'. The industry was 'in its infancy' in 1874; in 1869 exports exceeded 6 million tons but this accounted for only about ten per cent of the island's exports. But the last thirty years of the century would see cocoa overtake sugar as the island's leading export.

The Trinidad cocoa industry was pioneered and built up by peasants, and there were two ways in which cocoa estates were established. A peasant might buy a portion of Crown land, clear it, and plant cocoa. After the trees began to bear he would sell his plot to a cocoa planter, getting up to ten shillings per bearing tree, plus the value of his land. Often he would use the proceeds to buy areas of fine virgin soil in new districts and repeat the whole process. The peasant was the real pioneer and the planter simply followed, buying up the plots when they were already in production, and thus forming large estates. The second method was the contract system: the capitalist would buy a large block of Crown land and fell the forest; he entered into an agreement with contractors who agreed to plant cocoa on a 'quarrée' of land (just over three acres). When the trees were bearing the owner took over the land, paying agreed sums for each tree according to the stage it had reached. The contractor was free to plant and use food crops and he often also gave wage labour to nearby cocoa estates. The contract usually lasted for five years, and the contractor could normally expect to make a reasonable sum. It suited the planter, who incurred very light expenses - buying the land and clearing the bush - while the growing trees were security on which he could raise loans when the five years were up. He could build up an estate cheaply, while the contractor would never be more than a transient in the cocoa industry. Probably most of the estates were built up by contractors.

Many of these freeholders and contractors were peons, the true pioneers of the cocoa industry. But they also included Creoles and natives of Africa, and from the 1870s 'free' Indians entered cocoa as contractors or smallholders. On the larger estates the wage labourers were mainly Creoles or peons. Most cocoa estates, scattered and isolated, could not comply with the hospital requirements of the immigration laws and so did not qualify for indentured immigrants. But from the 1880s the larger cocoa planters began to apply for and receive indentureds; a number of neighbouring estates would combine to build a common hospital. Barracks were built and indentureds employed on the same terms as in sugar. Still, the number of indentureds employed on cocoa estates was always low. The Indians made their contribution to cocoa mainly as small proprietors or contractors, rather than as indentured labourers.

The larger cocoa planters were overwhelmingly French Creoles, and so were the cocoa dealers in Port of Spain who exported the produce and advanced supplies and credit to the planters; often the dealers themselves owned estates. By the turn of the century, cocoa was predominantly controlled by French Creoles, and only twelve estates were owned by British companies. Many French Creoles were owners of small sugar estates, which had probably been in their families since the early years of the nineteenth century, or even since the late eighteenth century, and these estates, producing muscovado sugar for the most part, became less and less profitable in the second half of the century. With the depression in the 1880s and 1890s, many of these weak estates were sold to the heavily capitalized, mainly British concerns which were consolidating their hold on the Trinidad sugar industry. The French Creoles, forced to sell out of sugar, used the proceeds of the sale of their estates to buy Crown lands and build up large cocoa estates. By the 1880s cocoa was clearly profitable, and the capital required to buy Crown lands and pay off contractors was willingly extended by merchants and cocoa dealers, who were usually French Creoles themselves. It was easy and profitable to go into cocoa. Cocoa was the backbone of French Creole prosperity: the 1860s and 1870s witnessed their economic recovery; the 1880s and 1890s were decades of relative affluence for the 'third generation' of French Creoles.

Cocoa prices were consistently high between 1890 and 1920, and this commodity was the favourite investment of Trinidadians in these years. Sales of small sugar estates, profits from other industries or crops, individuals' savings and proceeds from cocoa itself, were all invested in cocoa mortgages at interest rates of six to twelve per cent. Any planter could get a loan on the security of his trees, and estates yielded between 15 and 20 per cent profits. Planters extended cultivation to areas that could only be profitable if prices remained high, and mortgagors were willing to postpone the period of repayment indefinitely because of the high rates of interest and the general buoyancy of the industry. Many planters owned several estates, all heavily mortgaged and liable to immediate foreclosure. While prices remained high, therefore, conditions were favourable for an extremely rapid expansion of cocoa cultivation. Exports averaged eight million lb per annum in 1871-80; by the decade 1911-20 they averaged 56.3 million lb. The crash came, but not until after the First World War. In the last decades of the nineteenth century and the first two of the twentieth, cocoa provided a relatively comfortable livelihood for many peons, Creoles and Indians, and made fortunes for the larger French Creole planters.

Adrian de Verteuil, for instance, owned the Tortuga estate in Montserrat, and cocoa production was so profitable in the later years of the nineteenth century that he could 'live the life of the French aristocrat to the full, with frequent visits to France and Paris, and all the pretensions of a Count'. Gaston de Gannes was another typical French Creole planter of the same period, one of the pioneers in the rebirth of the industry. From about 1860 (long before cocoa became really profitable) he was engaged in building up large estates in Central Trinidad, Guaico, Manzanilla and Mayaro; then he moved to Arima in the 1880s and built La Chance, a splendid estate house. For the rebirth of cocoa in the last thirty years of the century was the economic base for the French Creoles' social and political renaissance and La Chance, with its lavish life-style, symbolized their recovery.

For the Trinidad peasantry, cocoa provided a profitable export crop that required neither considerable outlays of capital nor a large labour force. Because of cocoa some peasants were relatively well-off between 1870 and 1920, but the attitude of the government towards them tended to remain indifferent or even hostile. The local government's policy on economic matters, during the nineteenth century, usually reflected the bias towards the plantation and sugar. Both the Colonial Office and the local officials tended to accept the idea that the plantation was a 'civilizing agency' necessary for the control of the black and Indian labourers. This made them hostile to measures that might facilitate the growth of a peasantry and thus perhaps deplete the estates' labour force. Up to 1884 sugar remained prosperous, even on fairly small estates, and so there seemed no real need to question the plantation system. Taxation, immigration and land policies all reflected the plantation bias. We can see this in the issue of the disposal of the Crown lands. Essentially the question was whether the interests of the planters or of the peasants would determine economic policy. The small cultivator wanted easy and cheap access to the Crown lands, and a good system of roads serving the newly opened areas. But free access to the Crown lands would tend to draw away from the plantations resident and non-resident labour, both Creole and Indian. So between 1838 and 1869, the Crown lands were placed beyond the reach of the small purchaser. Governor Gordon was able to reverse this policy, and his great achievement was to resist the sugar planters and open the Crown land to the peasants. But after he left changes in the regulations were designed to obstruct the rapid alienation of the Crown lands to peasant purchasers. The government could not prevent this - smallholders did buy extensively after 1869 - but the restrictions certainly made the progress slower. Furthermore, this policy was persisted in even when the plantation system showed signs of severe distress. In the crisis years after 1884, there was ample evidence that the plantations could no longer absorb the rural labour force. Yet there was no new policy to give easier access to the Crown lands.

In the same way, until 1885 no serious efforts were made by the government to diversify the economy. Cocoa was developed without much aid or encouragement by the local government. It was not until the sugar crisis of 1884-5 that a real programme of diversification was launched by Governor Sir William Robinson. He offered grants of land on easy terms to anyone who tried to introduce new commercial crops. He started the experimental cultivation of new crops at the government farm at Chaguanas and set up a tobacco plantation at Siparia. Robinson was anxious to encourage an export trade in bananas and citrus to the USA, and to this end he established in 1889 a subsidized steamship service around the Trinidad coast, to Tobago, and thence to New York. He hoped to awaken a spirit of enterprise among the small fruit growers along the coasts. Robinson established District Agricultural Boards to stimulate the introduction of new crops and encourage and instruct small farmers, and a Central Agricultural Board to co-ordinate the work of the eleven

District Boards. A journal was produced with articles about new crops and better farming methods. All this represented a serious effort to diversify; but Robinson had little success. The export trade in fruit did not materialize and after a few years the subsidy to the steamship service was withdrawn. Tobacco failed. Other new crops failed to be widely cultivated; cocoa and coconuts developed without government help. So did rice, the only really successful new crop developed in this period. The cultivation of paddy rice and irrigated fields began in the 1860s on the Caroni and Oropouche lagoon lands, by 'free' Indians living in the new villages formed at this time. By 1896, 6,000 acres were in wet rice, providing about one sixth of local consumption.

One reason for the failure of government efforts to diversify after 1885 was a shortage of capital and inadequate credit facilities for the small farmers. Government lending to farmers was considered impossible, and the Colonial Bank, Trinidad's major financial institution at this time, did not lend money to small cultivators. Small farmers had to rely on private money-lenders and dealers who charged very high rates of interest, and they preferred to grow a crop like cocoa which was sure to yield a high profit margin, rather than untested and possibly unprofitable crops like fruit or tobacco. The very profitability of cocoa reduced a farmer's incentive to try other crops. Because of the expansion of cocoa, the development of cane-farming and the introduction of rice, the last years of the nineteenth century and the early years of the twentieth did see some increase in employment opportunities for the rural labourers and the peasants. But the point was that government participation in rice and cocoa had been virtually non-existent.

By the beginning of the twentieth century, Trinidad's economy was still overwhelmingly agricultural, with sugar and cocoa dominating the plantation sector. After all the difficulties of the 1880s and 1890s, the sugar industry was fairly prosperous in 1900-20; cocoa production continued to boom until after the end of the First World War. The 'minor industries' like coconuts and rice made some progress, and smallholders of all races, but particularly the Indians, grew food crops for local consumption. But it was not agriculture that would dominate the modern Trinidadian economy; and in the early years of the new century, hardy pioneers in the forest were beginning the commerical exploitation of oil. The story of the twentieth-century Trinidad economy would be, in large measure, the story of oil.

---

1. After harvest, the cane shoot is allowed to grow again for reaping at the following harvest; this process can continue for several years.

SIX

The Newcomers, 1838-1917

New Arrivals after Emancipation

Despite the alternate policies of conciliation and coercion followed by the planters in their efforts to retain the ex-slaves' labour in the years after 1838, and more particularly after 1846, labour became less and less available to the Trinidad planters; at least, the kind of steady, manageable labour that they wanted. Most of the planters were sure that there was only one viable remedy, immigration: the importation of fresh labourers, and some system of regulations that would keep the immigrants on the estates. Immigrants would provide labour directly; and by creating competition they would force down wages and perhaps drive some of the ex-slaves back to the estates. Immigration was seen as the remedy for all the planters' troubles; but where would the immigrants come from, and under what terms?

The first source of immigration was the most obvious one, the islands of the eastern Caribbean. This was a free emigration of blacks attracted by the high wages, job opportunities and availability of land in Trinidad. In November 1838 the legislative council passed a resolution calling for recruiting agents to be appointed who would receive a bounty on every immigrant they introduced. Though the authorities in the other islands objected, the inter-island traffic was impossible to check; Trinidad was the Mecca for the small-islanders. When the British government forbade the payment of bounties on inter-island immigration, the movement was hardly affected. Between 1839 and 1849, an estimated 10,278 West Indians came to Trinidad in a small armada of inter-island sloops and schooners, though not all of them settled permanently. But there was one great drawback for the planters in this emigration: most of the immigrants joined the Creole blacks in leaving the estates to settle in the towns or become independent cultivators. Their background and aspirations were similar to those of the Creoles, and, in time, they began to merge into the general black population. The Barbadian immigrants in particular were disliked by the planters for being too independent and 'insolent'; by 1847 less than 3,000 of the West Indians were said to be still working full time on the sugar estates.

Nevertheless, the movement of blacks from the eastern Caribbean continued all through the nineteenth century. Between 1871 and 1911 about 65,000 immigrants entered Trinidad, the majority of whom settled permanently; in 1897 there were about 14,000 Barbadians living on the island. Though many gave seasonal labour to the sugar estates during crop, they tended not to work as full-time wage labourers for long; after 1847, when wages were reduced, plantation labour was not attractive to them. Many found jobs on public works projects, especially in the 1870s and 1880s when there was an active programme of road and railway construction. Some became policemen, teachers and nurses, particularly the Barbadians who tended to be better educated and more literate than the Creole blacks. Others were skilled craftsmen who settled in Port of Spain, San Fernando and the larger villages, especially the villages between the capital and Arima. The immigrants were a valuable and important addition to the island's population, but from the planters' perspective, they were unsatisfactory: they did not remain on the estates, they would not sign contracts, they were capable of defending their independence and they were not the manageable labourers that the planters always wanted.

One possible source of labour was the USA; free blacks whose situation was very difficult in the 1840s might be induced to settle in Trinidad. The influential planter spokesman W. H. Burnley was the main advocate of US immigration, and as agent for Trinidad he went to New York to persuade free blacks to emigrate. His success was very limited. Between 1839 and 1847 only 1,301 had arrived; and most of them, from the cities of the northern states, were not agricultural labourers but artisans and mechanics whose skills were hardly needed on the Trinidad estates. In 1848 only 148 Americans were still working on the estates, and most of the others had returned to the USA; there was no further immigration from this source.

The experience of Caribbean slavery made everyone assume that Africans were the best fitted for agricultural labour in the tropics. If blacks from the eastern Caribbean and the USA were unsatisfactory, what of Africa? A few Africans liberated by British naval ships on anti-slave trade duty had already been landed occasionally in the West Indies, so that a precedent existed for a systematic immigration of Africans freed from foreign slave ships by the British navy.

There were two British colonies where Africans could be procured for the West Indies: Sierra Leone in West Africa and St Helena in the Atlantic. Since 1815, British warships had been bringing liberated slaves to these colonies. St Helena, a small barren island, could only be a temporary station, and even Sierra Leone was too crowded to support the liberated Africans indefinitely. So they seemed ideally suited for an organized emigration of liberated

Africans. At first the emigration to Trinidad was in merchant ships chartered by private individuals, but in 1843 for the first time the imperial government took a direct and controlling interest in the West African emigration. The prospects of better wages and employment opportunies in Trinidad induced numbers of Africans to emigrate from Sierra Leone in 1841. The first immigrants were English-speaking Christians, and accustomed to European ways; they had lived in Sierra Leone for some time. But after 1841 most of the immigrants were people just rescued from the slave ships, or liberated for a short time; they were not Christians and their indigenous customs and culture were still strong. Since they spoke no English and knew little of European life, they tended to settle with their own countrymen in African settlements in Trinidad, and these Africans remained separate and distinct from the Creole population all through the nineteenth century.

By the 1850s the emigration of liberated Africans slackened. The slave trade had by then fallen into the hands of illegal US operators for the most part, and the US government objected to British warships searching these slave ships and seizing the slaves. The numbers of liberated Africans dwindled; by 1861 African immigration to Trinidad was at an end. Trinidad had received a total of 3,383 from Sierra Leone and 3,198 from St Helena between 1841 and 1861. These were hardly the kind of numbers that the planters had hoped for. Nor did the Africans live up to expectations: many left estate labour, chiefly to squat and cultivate as smallholders. When Governor Gordon came to deal with the squatting problem in the late 1860s, many of the squatters in the Central Range were Africans. Others settled in or near towns. The Radas from Dahomey settled in Belmont, while other Africans lived in the East Dry River district of the capital. Louis de Verteuil, writing in 1858, thought that the Yoruba were outstanding among the liberated Africans for their industry, intelligence, honesty and pride, and for their tradition of self-help: 'the whole Yoruba race of the colony may be said to form a sort of social league for mutual support and protection'. By contrast, he thought the 'Congos', from Angola, were idle and worthless. Until the twentieth century, the Africans and their descendants formed a self-contained section, quite distinct from the Creole and West Indian blacks, often speaking their own languages, and tending to settle together with their fellow countrymen in villages and suburbs.

Africa and the Americas had failed the planters; Europe was frequently put forward as a source of immigrants for Trinidad. It was often argued that the immigration of Europeans would create a white middle class of farmers which would be a stabilizing influence and would increase the number of whites in relation to blacks and coloureds. But the immigration on a large scale of European peasants or labourers was never really feasible in nineteenth-century Trinidad. For such a movement would conflict with the basic strategy for developing a tropical colony, that Europeans owned and managed, while the coloured races did the manual labour. Any large influx of white labourers would have upset the racial structure of society and undermined the dominance of the whites in the colony. Only a few Europeans came to Trinidad in the decades after 1838, and most of these were people from Britain going to posts in the public service or in business firms, or to professional practices as doctors and lawyers; above all, they were going to take up jobs on the sugar estates as overseers and managers, particularly the Scottish immigrants.

But two groups of Europeans came to Trinidad in these years who did not fit into the category of British managers, or professionals, or colonial civil servants. In 1839-40 two groups of 866 French and German immigrants arrived. These people had been brought by ship captains who were paid a bounty of $40-50 for each passenger by estate owners in Trinidad; they had been lured by promises of high wages on the sugar estates. However, mortality among the first group was extremely high, since they arrived during the rainy season and had no immunity to tropical diseases, as well as being unused to manual labour in a hot climate. The immigration was stopped, and the survivors mostly found their way to the USA. Compared to the opportunities offered in the undeveloped temperate lands like North America and Australia, Trinidad had few real prospects for European immigrants without capital or posts in the existing firms or estates.

It was believed, however, that Europeans could safely work on cocoa estates where the workers were shaded and the work was less exhausting than on the sugar plantations. The British government allowed an immigration of Portuguese labourers from Madeira to work on the cocoa estates. The first group arrived in 1846, but they were employed on sugar estates, contrary to the government's instructions, and nearly half had died from tropical diseases within a few months of their arrival. Later other Madeirans arrived, including a group of Presbyterians converted by Scottish missionaries and driven from Madeira by persecution. In all 1,298 Madeirans came to Trinidad in these years. Some stayed on the plantations, but most of them became market gardeners or small shopkeepers. They contributed to the economy of the island, but they hardly met the planters' requirements.

The population of Trinidad was, therefore, augmented in the years after 1838 by immigrants from the USA, the Caribbean, Africa and Europe, adding new elements to an already diverse people. But none of these immigrants had satisfied the planters' requirements of a massive influx of cheap, easily managed labourers. There remained Asia. Although it was, of course, India that eventually provided the 'solution' to the planters' difficulties, there was also a much smaller immigration from China. The drawbacks of Chinese immigration were the high cost of their passage, and the problem of persuading them to sail across the world merely to do agricultural work which they could find much nearer home.

Despite the difficulties, about 2,500 Chinese immigrants were brought to Trinidad between 1853, when the first three shiploads arrived, and 1866, when Chinese immigration to the West Indies was ended because the Chinese government insisted on a free return passage. The immigrants came under much the same indenture rules as the Indians, but they were not entitled to a free return passage: this would have made Chinese immigration prohibitively costly.

Mortality was high among these early Chinese immigrants, but some of them prospered. Many bought out their indenture and became shopkeepers; other took up market gardening and butchering. They soon took Creole wives, and were far more receptive to Christianity and western ways than the Indians. But for the planters, these immigrants were quite unsatisfactory. Often artisans and tradesmen by profession, they did not make docile agricultural labourers. For the wider society the Chinese were a valuable addition to the population; but Chinese immigration was always too small-scale and too costly to be a viable solution to the planters' labour needs. There remained India.

Indentured Indian Labour

India seemed to offer an inexhaustible reservoir of labour: its population was huge; most of its people were accustomed to agricultural labour in tropical or similar conditions; many lived close to destitution and might be persuaded to emigrate; much of the subcontinent was under British control so that difficult negotiations with foreign authorities would not be necessary; and the cost of immigration, though high, was not prohibitive as in the case of the Chinese. From the start, the imperial government closely supervised and regulated the whole traffic in Indian immigrants. The advantages of India as a source for labourers seemed overwhelming, and in 1844 the British government sanctioned Indian immigration to Jamaica, Trinidad and British Guiana. By this decision a large movement of people began that was not to end until 1917, and which radically altered the racial composition of the Trinidad population. But in the early stage of Indian immigration, and in fact until the late 1860s, few persons in Trinidad or in London envisaged a permanent, settled Indian population. The government of British India insisted on a free return passage for all immigrants, and this made the scheme seem impermanent: the immigrants were seen as temporary labourers who would return after a short spell in the West Indies. As a result, few people thought about the long-term consequences of importing large numbers of immigrants of a different race, religion and culture. In the first quarter-century of Indian immigration to Trinidad, people were concerned with securing labour for the sugar estates and devising ways to keep that labour tied to the plantations; the long-term implications could wait.

In May 1845 the first immigrant ship, the 'Fatel Rozack', arrived from Calcutta with 225 immigrants, and a total of 5,392 Indians came in the first three years of Indian immigration, 1845-8. There were immediate problems. Some deserted the estates, for they were not legally tied to their employers, others fell ill or became destitute vagrants, and many died. Lord Harris, the able governor who served between 1846 and 1854, believed that a system of contract or indenture, and strict regulations to prevent desertion or unauthorized absence from the estates, were essential for the Indians' own safety as well as being in the planters' interests. In 1846 he issued a set of rules which provided that contracted (indentured) Indians could not leave their estates for any reason without a ticket of leave from their employer, nor could they give up work at the end of their one-year contract without a certificate of discharge which had to be shown to the new employer. But these strict regulations were seized on by the Anti-Slavery Society in Britain and its allies as proof that Indian immigration was only slavery in a disguised form, and so the Colonial Office disallowed them.

Yet the planters and the local authorities were convinced that something had to be done to check the tendency to desert the estates and to ensure that the planters were guaranteed some steady labour. Gradually the Colonial Office was coming round to the view that some form of indenture system was essential in the interests of both employers and Indians. The new thinking was reflected in an 1847 Ordinance. This featured the concept of an 'industrial residence': five years' actual work in Trinidad before the immigrant was entitled to a free return passage. For five years the immigrant either had to work under contract (five one-year contracts) or had to pay a monthly tax to help towards his return passage, with prison terms the penalty if he failed to do one or the other. Here was the element of coercion and discipline that Harris and the planters wanted: the Indian was forced to work under contract for five years or pay a special tax, subject to criminal sanctions. But this 1847 Ordinance never had a fair trial. Immigration problems were overshadowed by the acute financial crisis of 1847-8. The Treasury was empty, and immigration to Trinidad came to a temporary halt in 1848.

But the crisis soon eased, and by 1849-50 Trinidad planters were asking for the reopening of immigration; the first arrivals had almost worked out their time and most were due for repatriation in 1851 or 1852. Harris, although still doubtful about the long-term implications of Indian immigration, supported their call, and the British and Indian authorities agreed to resume immigration. In 1851, 173

Indians arrived in Trinidad and from then on they arrived steadily each year until 1917. Things were better organized now; a Superintendent (later called Protector) of Immigrants was appointed to supervise the system and to guard the welfare of the Indians, and in 1850 Harris appointed Henry Mitchell, a Creole doctor who soon became the leading authority in Trinidad on all aspects of immigration - and a real friend to the Indians.

The financing of the system had presented problems at first, but in 1860 the Colonial Office decided that the planters should pay twothirds of the total cost of immigration. This was to be paid partly through the indenture fees (paid on each indenture signed) and partly through export duties on sugar, rum and cocoa. The remaining one-third was to be paid from the general revenues, that is, by the ordinary taxpayers. This remained the arrangement throughout the indentureship period, with the export duties being altered from time to time. The cost of immigration remained a burden on the revenues. During the 1860s Trinidad spent 25 to 35 per cent of the revenues each year on immigration expenses. In general the planters usually paid less than their fair share, and by the 1870s there was an increasing demand that planters actually employing indentured labourers should bear the whole cost.

In 1854 an important Ordinance consolidated the body of law relating to the Indian immigrants, and the principles embodied in this law remained operative all through the indentureship period. The planters had won a major concession from the Colonial Office in that the time which the immigrant had to spend in the colony before qualifying for his free return passage had been extended from five to ten years, while the period of 'industrial residence' was to be five years. An immigrant on arrival had to serve an initial indenture for three years with a single employer; this was another concession, for now the Colonial Office had allowed three-year contracts. After the three-year contract, the immigrant could reindenture himself for two further one-year contracts with an employer of his choice to complete the industrial residence of five years, or he could buy out the remaining two years by a lump sum of £6 or a monthly tax of 5 shillings. On completion of the industrial residence, in order to qualify for the 'free' return passage, the Indian either had to engage in yearly contracts or pay a special annual tax of £2 10s 6d. Thus even after the industrial residence was over, the Indian was subjected for a further five years to a restraint on his freedom (an indenture) or to a tax that did not apply to the rest of the population.

An important provision of the 1854 Ordinance was that indentureds had to carry tickets of leave when off the estate during working hours, on pain of criminal punishment (jail sentences). This was the same rule that had been disallowed in 1846. Even unindentured Indians had to carry their 'certificates of industrial residence' with them at all times, and these had to be shown on demand to policemen and employers. There were jail terms for unauthorized absence, desertion and helping or sheltering deserters. Thus this Ordinance incorporated one of the most obnoxious features of the immigration system: the use of criminal sanctions (jail) for what was really a civil offence, breach of contract. Needless to say, the employer who broke his side of the contract was never jailed; the worst that could happen to him was that he might be refused more immigrants in cases of gross maltreatment. And the provision about tickets of leave and certificates of industrial residence set the immigrants apart from the rest of the population, emphasizing their unfree status. But the planters were satisfied with the 1854 law. It meant they had secured the system of contractual labour they had always wanted - a system that lasted without significant changes until 1917 - and in 1862 they won a further victory when an initial five-year contract was allowed.

Large numbers were involved in Indian immigration to Trinidad: over the whole period, 1845-1917, a total of 143,939 people came to the island. The vast majority came through the great port of northern India, Calcutta, but a small number came through Madras in the south. These 'Madrasi' were said to be less efficient and more troublesome workers; the reason seems to have been that many of them came from the city itself rather than the surrounding country, and thus did not adapt easily to agricultural labour. After 1870 only a few Indians came to the island through Madras.

The people who came through Calcutta came overwhelmingly from the densely populated Gangetic plain, the vast majority from the United Provinces (today Uttar Pradesh), Bihar and Oudh. Much smaller numbers came from Bengal and the Punjab. Between 1876 and 1879, for example, 45.5 per cent of the immigrants were from the United Provinces, 27.9 per cent from Oudh, and 16.2 per cent from Bihar: a total of 90.6 per cent. For these peasant people from the Gangetic plain, the motive for leaving India - despite strong caste and religious sanctions against 'crossing salt water', and despite the deep-rooted Indian attachment to the ancestral village and land - was to escape harsh economic conditions: low wages, small landholdings, drought, hopeless debts to money-lenders, economic dislocation caused by British imperialism, a living standard often close to destitution for the agricultural classes. Famines were frequent and devastating. The Indian Mutiny or Uprising (1857) and its savage repression further worsened conditions, and it was followed by poor harvests and a rise in prices. People might be induced to emigrate for personal reasons - a quarrel, a crime, a caste dispute, the hardships of widowhood - but for the main part, economic necessity forced Indians to leave their homes.

The great majority of the immigrants were Hindus, and they continued to practise their religion in Trinidad. From the beginning of Indian immigration Hindu household worship was carried on, and by the 1850s Hindu temples had been built on estates; Brahmins

Plate 3 Breaking cacao

resumed their priestly functions and enjoyed much the same reverence as in India. The smaller Muslim community was also able to carry on its religious observances, and the Muslims provided the great annual festival that was to become in Trinidad the major 'Indian festival': Hose or Muharran, observed by Shi'ite Muslims to commemorate the murder of the Prophet's grandson, Hosein. First celebrated in Trinidad in the 1850s, in time it lost much of its special religious meaning, and Sunni Muslims (the majority group) and Hindus participated enthusiastically. It became largely a chance for festivity for an overworked and oppressed labouring class; almost from the start Creoles joined in, often as drummers.

By the late 1860s, what had begun as a temporary measure to meet an acute labour crisis had become an apparently perpetual and regular importation of labour on a large scale. It seems clear that in the first phase of Indian immigration, 1845-70, the scheme did fulfil the purpose for which it was begun: to ensure the survival and expansion of the sugar industry by providing steady, manageable labour anchored to the estate by stringent regulations.

But Indian immigration, in its first phase, also benefited to some extent other sectors of the economy and the population as a whole. Although the cocoa industry did not employ many indentured workers, it did use many free Indians as labourers and contractors, and they thus contributed to the great expansion of cocoa in the later years of the nineteenth century. A rising population offered more opportunities for hucksters and petty shopkeepers, and widened the market for provisions and other local food crops. Most estates continued in this period to employ Creoles for heavy field work and for factory labour, and these jobs increased as cultivation expanded. The general economic development that the island experienced in the years after 1850 opened up wider fields of employment for Creoles as traders, artisans and small farmers. Public facilities improved: by 1872 Trinidad possessed a rudimentary medical service as a result of the need to look after the immigrants' health.

But it was the sugar industry that gained most from Indian immigration, and its prosperity between 1854 and 1884 was largely due to Indian labourers; by 1870 they were the backbone of the sugar industry. In 1871 Indians comprised 25.1 per cent of the total population; in that year there were 27,425 Indians in Trinidad, 4,545 of whom were locally born. The vast majority were still working on the estates, and nearly 40 per cent were still indentured. Although a few Indians had prospered as money-lenders or shopkeepers, the great majority remained low wage-earners, tied to the estates and relegated to the bottom of the social and economic ladder. They had hardly improved their material condition since 1845, nor had they made much progress in establishing their own social organization and institutions.

The last thirty years of the nineteenth century witnessed fundamental changes in the social and economic situation of Indians in Trinidad. In 1871 the great majority of Indians were resident on the estates (67.6 per cent), and nearly 40 per cent were still indentured. By 1901 only 21.6 per cent of the Indian population still lived on the estates, and a mere 8.5 per cent were indentured. Further, while Trinidad-born Indians made up only 16.5 per cent of the total Indian population in 1871, by 1901 they constituted 44.8 per cent, nearly as many as the India-born immigrants. By the early years of the twentieth century, most of the Indians were off the estates, living in villages and scattered settlements as small cultivators. The centre of gravity of the Indian population had shifted from indentured labour in sugar to peasant proprietorship, and a settled Indian community emerged that was recognized as such by the rest of the society.

This transformation was caused, in part, by worsening conditions on the plantations in the last two decades of the nineteenth century, the years when the sugar industry suffered from depression as a result of competition from beet exports to the British market. The planters continued to insist that there was a shortage of plantation labour, and that continued - even increased - immigration was therefore necessary. But all the evidence suggests the exact opposite: that by the 1880s there was a surplus of agricultural labour available in the colony. Wages tend to fall when the labour supply is abundant, and there were at least three occasions after 1870 when the planters successfully reduced wages of unindentured workers, while there was a downward pressure on the actual earnings of the indentureds as well. The plantation labour force was increasing at a time when the expansion of cultivation in sugar had virtually halted: the increase in the area in sugar between 1879 and 1900 was only 1,057 acres, an insignificant expansion. Yet the number of indentured and free Indians resident on the estates continued to rise in this period. The fact that planters had an adequate labour supply in these years was also revealed by their cancelling orders for immigrants and refusing to accept labourers who had to be transferred from their original estates. These features were especially marked in the late 1880s and 1890s; by contrast, the transfer of immigrants had been no problem in the 1860s, a period of expansion for the industry. The combination of a halt to the spread of cultivation, depression in the industry, and an ever-increasing labour supply, meant a reduction in the work-load and earnings of the resident labourers, and a decline in the amount of work offered to non-resident workers. On Couva estates during the 1897 crop, for example, residents labourers could only get three days a week, while outside workers were offered nothing. We have to conclude that despite the continued cries of labour shortage, there was in fact an abundant supply of indentured and unindentured plantation workers in the years after 1880.

In theory, a legally fixed wage rate should have benefited the indentured Indians during the depression; but in actuality there was a downward pressure on indentureds' wages at such times. The 1870 Immigration Ordinance had stated that indentureds should be paid not less than the prevailing wage rate for unindentured workers, and in 1872 a minimum wage of 25 cents per day or per task was fixed for the male indentured Indian. Despite the 1870 law, indentureds continued to be paid less than non-indentureds; in 1884-5 indentureds were given heavier tasks and were paid 25 cents per task while non-indentureds were paid 30 cents. Even when the planters deliberately reduced the wages of non-indentured workers, in 1884-5 and in 1895, the differential in favour of these workers still remained. Because the statutory minimum wage of 25 cents had been fixed for indentureds, the planters usually reacted by lengthening their tasks instead of reducing their wage rate; but increasing the task at the same money wage had precisely the same effect as reducing wages.

In 1884-5, and again in 1895-6, the planters made a major effort to increase tasks and reduce wages, and to economize on labour costs by offering less work to labourers, both indentured and free. As a result, the actual earnings of resident Indian labourers, both indentured and free, declined markedly in these years. In the 1880s and 1890s many strikes took place as a result. The indentureds became so disillusioned by the increasing size of their tasks that during the strikes of the mid-1890s the Protector of Immigrants reported that they wanted to replace tasks by day work. In fact, although the legal guarantee of a minimum wage rate should have protected the indentured immigrants against economic crises, the guarantee proved ineffective, and the immigrants' real earnings were pushed down.

The effect of the reduction of wages and the low actual earnings of resident Indian labourers, both indentured and free, was to accelerate the departure of free Indians from the sugar estates, particularly after 1884. Plantation labour became unattractive for free Indians when wages were reduced and less work was offered. The majority moved away from the estates to reside in new villages or more isolated settlements in the newly opened districts of the island. A substantial number succeeded in becoming peasant proprietors, and the economic interests of the majority of Indians shifted from plantation labour in sugar to small-scale cultivation on their own account.

This shift was possible because land could be obtained once their indentures had expired. In 1869 a scheme started whereby male Indians who had lived in Trinidad for ten years could be granted ten acres of Crown lands in commutation of all claims to a free return passage to India, and this scheme lasted until 1880. Its purpose was to reduce the colony's financial liability for return passages, and to retain the services of experienced and seasoned labourers. The lands granted under this scheme were usually close to existing estates, in order to provide them with a potential supply of 'outside' labour. In just over a decade (1869-80) 2,643 male immigrants (and their families) had been settled on 19,055 acres. In terms of the acreage involved the land commutation scheme was substantial, and it marked the beginning of a settled Indian peasantry. Most Indians, however, obtained their land not through the commutation scheme, but by purchasing lots of Crown land in the normal way. In the 1880s and 1890s, free Indians responded to the deteriorating conditions on the estates by moving away and acquiring lands. It was the policy of Governor Robinson (1885-91) to make the Crown lands easily available to the labouring classes and to enoourage the 'minor' industries, in order to offset the harmful effects of the sugar depression on the labourers. There was, in fact, a steady rise in the sales of Crown lands to free Indians in the last twenty years of the nineteenth century. In addition, many Indian peasants rented their land, either from Indian land-owners or from estates; for instance, the Ne Plus Ultra and Palmyra estates were rented or sold in small plots and Indian villages were established on them.

Once established, the Indian smallholders grew food crops for their own consumption and for the local market: they pioneered the cultivation of paddy or wet rice; they went into cocoa as contractors and as freeholders, especially after 1885; and they began to grow sugar as canefarmers from 1882. In general, the Indian peasantry contributed a great deal to the modest progress towards diversification in this period, and to the increase in local food production.

The Establishment of the Indian Community

For the Indians themselves, the transformation from indentured estate workers to smallholders living in their own settlements provided the basis for the emergence of a settled Indian community with its own social organization. When most Indians lived on the estates, it was difficult for a real community to develop because social life and its institutions were subordinate to the needs and the discipline of the plantation. But as increasing numbers settled in the new Indian villages, traditional Indian institutions could re-emerge, sometimes hardly changed, often drastically modified. With the breakdown of traditional sanctions, the rigid division of Indians in the caste system weakened and there was a tendency for all the Indians in Trinidad to be compressed into a single group, except for the important Hindu-Muslim division. Free from the constraints of the estates, and no longer dependent on the continual importation of immigrants to maintain the population group, the Indians were able to become a permanent and settled community in the last years of the nineteenth century. One indication of this change is that, increasingly, Indians began to regard Trinidad as their homeland. The majority, after all, chose to remain rather than to return to India, despite their strong attachment to the land of their birth. And the growth of the locally born Indian community reinforced the commitment to Trinidad; Creole Indian children often persuaded their India-born relatives to remain. The locally born Indians tended to identify strongly with Trinidad. By the 1890s Indians had come to resent the use of the word 'immigrant' when applied to Indians who had been in the island for ten years, and especially when applied to Trinidad-born Indians. In the same way they began to object to their designation, in all the official documents and in the Press, as 'coolies'. At a meeting in 1889 Lal Behari, the first Indian to be ordained a Presbyterian minister in Trinidad, was asked when the word would cease to be used as a description for all Indians, even respectable and wealthy people. The Canadian Presbyterian missionaries were among the first to realize that the word was offensive to the Indians, and so they used the term 'East Indian'. From the 1890s onwards, 'coolie' was used less and less in the official documents and the newspapers, reflecting changing perceptions of the status of the Indian community both on the part of the Indians themselves and the wider society.

At about the same time, educated Indians began to make their views known in the island press, and what may be called an 'Indian opinion' emerged, a body of views held by articulate Indians about issues important to the community. The *San Fernando Gazette* was especially interested in Indian views and an anonymous letter writer, Son of India, wrote numerous letters to this paper in the 1890s. These articulate Indians projected the image of a group justly deserving good treatment for having saved the colonial economy, but being unfairly deprived of their deserts. Such an image, however justifiable, contributed to the increasing sense of group solidarity among the Indians.

In 1897 this sense of group identity was crystallized by a formal Indian organization, the East Indian National Association (EINA). The organization was formed in response to an Ordinance in that year which infringed the rights of 'free' Indians. One clause authorized the arrest of free Indians if found on a public highway without their certificates of exemption from labour; another required an employer to demand to see this certificate before employing a free Indian. In other words, unindentured Indians were subjected to legal restrictions that did not apply to the rest of the population. The Indian leadership organized a protest against the Ordinance, which led directly to the formation of the EINA at a meeting in Princes Town; the *Port of Spain Gazette* called it 'an influential association which will have to be reckoned with in all matters of legislation affecting the Indian population'. While the protest did not lead to any important amendments to the Ordinance, it was significant because it forced on the government and the society an awareness that an Indian community did exist and was capable of organizing itself in defence of its group interests. Also in 1897 the Indian leadership had submitted a memorandum to the West India Royal Commission and had, for the first time, asked for a special representative in the legislative council. Though unsuccessful at the time, the request indicated a growing political awareness. And the EINA, originally formed to oppose a particular law, outlived the protest to become a permanent organization which played an important role in the next century.

Yet the Trinidad society took a long time to recognise the changes taking place within the Indian population, and to accept that the Indians had come to stay. The Indians entered what was an essentially hostile environment, and the host society became even less sympathetic as time went on and it became clear that they would be a permanent element in the population. Planters, officials, upper-class whites, educated coloured and black Creoles and the black working class all, to different degrees and for different reasons, reacted unsympathetically to the arrival of the Indians. Interaction between the races was at a low level, and the Indians were quickly consigned to the lowest rung of the socio-economic-cultural ladder. The reasons for this crucially important development need to be carefully examined.

In the first place, the degrading and coercive conditions under which indentured Indians were forced to live made them appear, in the judgement of the society as a whole, as inferior beings. They were unfree, hedged in by a multiplicity of laws restricting their freedom of movement and action. A large section of the Indian population occupied a peculiar legal status, sanctioned by the criminal law, restricted to compulsory work and residence on the estates under coercive conditions of service. Even the 'free' Indians had to show their certificates to policemen and immigration agents. Thousands were sentenced to jail terms for desertion or unauthorized absence from the estates. Further, occupation is always an important index of status, and the Indians performed the low-status jobs on the estates which the Creoles preferred to avoid, like weeding or transporting canes. In general, right up to the end of the indentureship period most Indians remained low-paid manual labourers in agriculture or poor smallholders; in 1917, 70 per cent of the Indians were agricultural labourers of some kind. In the towns, where they flocked from 1884 on in response to worsening conditions on the estates, they filled miserably paid, generally despised jobs as scavengers and porters, 'coolies' in the true sense of that term. Very few Indians, up to 1917, occupied any of the positions that society defined as prestigious; in 1921 only 187 Indians were classified as 'officials and professionals'.

Furthermore, the economic conditions under which the majority of Indians were forced to live were so wretched that the notion of them as inferior beings willing and content to live in squalid surroundings gained credence. On the estates, the barrack ranges provided miserably insanitary and overcrowded housing. Diseases were rife, especially debilitating ones like malaria and hookworm infestation; and low wages meant that the Indians' diet was nearly always inadequate. In Port of Spain destitute and decrepit Indians were only too visible, broken-down refugees from the plantations. Even in the new Indian villages and peasant settlements, where conditions were better, poverty was still pervasive; their houses were simple huts, their household goods at a minimum. In the city, quite a high proportion of the Indian population at any given time was to be found in the hospital, the House of Refuge and the jail, because sick and destitute Indians gravitated towards the town for succour, and because breaches of the indentureship laws were punished by jail sentences. In short, the coercive indentureship, the legal separation of the Indian population, the harsh economic conditions of their existence, the low-status jobs that they filled, all operated powerfully to make all sections of the Trinidad society despise them - even the planters for whose benefit they came.

Under these circumstances, Trinidadians of all ethnic groups evolved a set of stereotyped judgements about Indians, almost invariably unfavourable. Indians were regarded as deceitful and prone to litigation; there was no understanding that the Indian might not understand the moral force of an oath in a western court, or that he was often forced into litigation - for instance, to inherit his father's property if he died without a will, since the vast majority of Indians in this period were illegitimate in the eyes of the law. Violence and crimes of passion were an important element in this stereotyping, especially the murders of wives by Indian men. Again, there was little effort to understand the root cause of this tragic development: the scarcity of women on the plantations, the breakdown of traditional Indian restraints against adultery, the abnormal living conditions in the barracks. More generally, there was a fear of the Indians' potential for violence and rebellion, a fear that never was realized, although it was reinforced by the Indian Mutiny or Uprising of 1857. The planters wanted increased immigration, yet they feared the growing Indian population as a menace, an attitude similar to that of the slave-owners towards their African slaves.

Attitudes towards money were yet another aspect of the stereotype: the Indians were accused of being misers. Like most first-generation immigrants, the Indians would save their miserable wages and put off present comforts for future goals. Again, the Indians did not share the Creoles' interest in western clothes, and they could easily be derided for their 'uncivilized' way of dressing; similarly, the women were sneered at for the Hindu habit of decorating themselves with bangles and rings.

The religions and culture of the newcomers contributed to their low status in the host society. Trinidad was a society in which Christianity and western culture were accepted by virtually all groups as the norm to be aspired to, even though many blacks did persist in their African-derived religious and cultural forms. It was a time when the superiority of Christianity to all other creeds was hardly questioned in the West. The official attitude to Islam and Hinduism in Trinidad was one of contempt; Indians were officially referred to as 'our heathen population'; government grants were made exclusively to Christian denominations; Muslim and Hindu marriages were not recognized as legal until 1936 and 1945 respectively, with the result that the vast majority of Indians were technically illegitimate. John Morton, the pioneer Canadian missionary to the Indians, wrote that Hinduism was a sinister, 'unclean' faith that fostered 'a low sense of sin'. He claimed that the Hindus themselves had no respect for their gods, and that their creed had led to a degraded morality. The Trinidad press articulated a similarly harsh judgement on Indian religions. Its editors and contributors criticized Hindu and Muslim rites as degrading and uncivilized.

However, in the face of the contempt freely expressed by Trinidadians for Islam and even more for Hinduism, Indians resisted Christian conversion. Despite efforts by the Canadian Presbyterians, the Anglicans and the Catholics, by 1921 only 11.8 per cent of the Indian population had accepted the Christian faith. This clearly shows that the Indians never shared the host society's evaluation of their faiths. For the Indians, religion provided psychological protection, a sense of self-worth with which to arm themselves against the contempt of the society. The pundits and the imams became influential leaders of the Indian community because they could offer this kind of psychological aid.

In the same way as religion, the Indians' cultural forms evoked contempt or indifference. People showed little interest in Indian history, culture, music, dress, or traditional art forms. The normative cultural system was western, and literacy in English, and command of 'good English', were essential to gain respect. Very few Indians were literate in English before 1917; in 1911, 97 per cent of the Indian-born population was illiterate. The enrolment of Indian children in the schools was far below that of Creoles. Indian parents would not send their children to the government primary schools or to the denominational assisted schools, where all the teachers and most of the pupils were Creoles, for fear of ill-treatment, ridicule and pressures to convert. The Canadian Mission schools, established from 1868, did provide elementary education for a large number of Indian children, and these schools were an extremely important westernizing agency for the Trinidad population. Yet even with the mission schools, many parents kept their children away for fear of conversion; others took advantage of the education while rejecting Christianity. Indians were far behind in the education stakes by the end of the indenture system, and this explains their late entry into the high-prestige occupations.

Just as religion was a psychological comfort to the Indians, so was the Hindu caste system and the traditional family and village structure. Caste was seriously weakened, but in the new Indian peasant villages it was partly recreated, along with its traditional sanctions and its 'panchayat' or council of elders. It served to protect the Indians in their own traditional communities. In the Indian villages and the large family, the Indians were partially sheltered from contact with non-Indians and from conflict with western ways.

In fact, interaction with other races during the indentureship period was at a low level. On the estates there was regular contact with white or coloured overseers and managers, in a formal management-labour relationship. But relations between Creole and Indian labourers on the estates were low-level. One planter said in 1897: 'Somehow they do not come into contact with one another. There are certain works that the Negro will not do which are appropriated to the Coolies. You do not generally find them working together in gangs.' Yet up to the 1880s there seems to have been little actual hostility. There was no serious competition for jobs; estates continued to employ Creoles for factory work and for better-paid field tasks, and jobs here became more available when cultivation expanded between the 1850s and 1870s. Indians and Creoles were not generally competing for scarce resources between 1845 and 1880.

In the later period of Indian immigration, with the depression in sugar and improved technology lessening the number of factory jobs, immigration helped to cause rural unemployment and depress wages. Indians took work on the estates that had previously been done mainly by Creoles; by 1917 some estates employed virtually no Creoles. So by the turn of the century competition for jobs was noticeable, and blacks were well aware that the Indians depressed wages and increased unemployment. The Trinidad Workingmen's Association, the spokesman for skilled black workers, argued in 1909 that while Indian immigration was not objectionable up to the late 1870s, its continuation after that time had injured the interests of Creole labourers. Yet although tension between the races increased after 1884 because of worsening economic conditions and heightened resource competition, there is little evidence of serious inter-racial conflict. Cases of violent clashes between Indians and Creoles on the estates did occur, but in view of the numbers involved and the long time span, they were not frequent or serious, and there was no large-scale violence. On the estates, although conditions were deteriorating, the interaction between the races during the indentureship was at a low level, and was usually non-violent.

The Indians were concentrated in particular areas of Trinidad;

the great majority lived on the estates, or in villages and rural settlements that were predominantly Indian. Indeed, many of the new Indian villages established after 1869 were virtually exclusively Indian communities, as their names suggest: Calcutta, Madras, Barrackpore, Fyzabad. So geographical and residential segregation reinforced occupational separation. Port of Spain and San Fernando were places where Indians interacted with other races, but relatively few Indians lived in these cities before 1917: Indians were rural people at a time when Creoles were increasingly moving to the two chief towns and their environs. In general, most Indians could limit their contacts with others to a minimum: occasional trips to the town or brushes with officialdom; if they lived on the estates their contacts with management personnel and Creole workers could be kept purely formal; if they lived in the rural settlements, the village community and the extended family cushioned them from wider contacts.

This is strikingly illustrated by the reluctance of Indian men to cohabit with Creole women (and vice versa), despite the shortage of Indian women. As late as 1871 the Protector of Immigrants believed that no single case of cohabitation of male or female Indians with Creoles existed; and up to 1917 such cases were rare. Of course language, customs, religion and caste were powerful obstacles to such unions, but individuals have always broken through such sanctions, and in the Caribbean miscegenation was the general rule. Perhaps the Indians, who were mostly Hindus from northern India, brought with them the caste-linked Indian contempt for the darker-skinned, which reinforced the existing race and colour prejudices in the host society. Whatever the reason, miscegenation was not to be an integrating factor in this period.

The attitudes of the host society to the Indians were influenced by the opposition to indentured immigration which became important in about 1870. Immigration was seen as a symbol of the power and privileges of the sugar planters, and so it was opposed by groups hostile to the sugar interest, especially black and coloured middle-class professionals. Hostility to the immigration system was quite likely to develop into hostility to the Indians themselves, and the opposition to the system got mixed up with generally unfavourable notions about the people involved. *New Era* and the *San Fernando Gazette* were two newspapers representing the coloured and black middle class that consistently opposed immigration in the last thirty years of the century. Another spokesman for this group was Henry Alcazar, who used his membership of the legislative council after 1894 to oppose Indian immigration. In 1895 he argued that the labour market was glutted and further immigrants would only depress wages and cause unemployment. He elaborated his views in two memoranda submitted to the Royal Commission in 1897, arguing that immigration had become by then merely a weapon to allow planters to control the labour market by depressing wages to starvation levels. C.P. David, the first black Unofficial member of the legislative council (1904), was the chief opponent of immigration in the system's last years. Every year, in a minority of one, he would oppose the annual vote for immigration. We have already noted that the Trinidad Workingmen's Association, representing skilled black urban workers, attacked the continuation of Indian immigration after the 1870s because of its effect on the wages of Creole labour. The transition from attacking the system to attacking the people was easy enough, and many of these coloured and black politicians began to express fears that Indians might come to outnumber Creoles, and thus eventually threaten the nature of society and civilization in the island.

Against this background we can understand why Indians took so long to enter Trinidad politics, and why their first forays into the political field were hesitant and defensive. When a number of Indians qualified to vote for the San Fernando borough council from about 1870, fears were expressed that Indians would be elected to the council by a 'block' Indian vote, and the first Indian borough councillors were greeted with hostility. The EINA, and the East Indian National Congress, formed in 1909, were both communal organizations, reacting only to issues that affected the community. In 1909 they called for an Indian representative in the legislative council to speak for the community, and this was granted in 1912 when George Fitzpatrick, the President of the EINA, was nominated a member of the council. The leadership of both organizations was mainly Christian and westernized; a small elite was no doubt felt to be better equipped to deal with the authorities. At least until 1917, Indian participation in politics was hesitant and limited, yet even this brought out hostile or nervous reactions from the other ethnic communities.

The essential reality was that the Indians came to a society that was hostile to them, a society whose attitudes ranged from fear to contempt to indifference. They reacted defensively. Geographical, residential and occupational separation was reinforced by the Indians' protective use of caste, religion, village community and traditional family organization to cushion them from contacts with a hostile society. This would be the pattern of race relations long after the system of indentured immigration was ended in 1917.

SEVEN

The Development of Creole Society, 1838-1938

Trinidad in the century after emancipation was a divided or 'segmented' society, consisting of sectors that perceived themselves, and were perceived by others, as separate and distinct. The segments were hierarchically arranged, and, generally speaking, most people accepted the place of each sector in the hierarchy. At the risk of over-simplification, we can say that Trinidad in this period was divided into four major sectors. There was the white upper class; few questioned its ranking as the political, social and economic elite. There was the black and coloured middle class, distinguished by education and by white-collar jobs. There was the Creole working class, mainly of African descent. Finally, the Indians, although strong numerically, were separated from the rest of the population by culture and religion, by race and by legal restrictions, and by their relatively late arrival. They were not generally considered to be a part of 'Creole society' in this period.

The White Creoles

The powerful white elite was the ruling class of Trinidad for the whole of this period, and its position was not seriously challenged until the late 1930s. It consisted of two main groups: there were the British officials and the English and Scottish merchants, planters and professionals resident in the island, and there were the white Creoles, born in the island, descended from French, Spanish, English, Italian or German immigrants who had settled in Trinidad since the eighteenth century. Trinidad was home for these people, and they felt that they had a 'natural' right to form the local aristocracy.

The French Creoles were the most numerous group among the white Creole sector. They were mostly descended from French settlers, but the term was understood to include people of English, Irish, Spanish, Italian or German descent, born in the island and traditionally Roman Catholic. People born in Europe, but resident in Trinidad for many years and linked by marriage to this group, were also considered to be French Creoles. They formed a closely united elite, racially exclusive, imbued with aristocratic traditions, de-

Plate 4 St James Barracks, St James

scended (for the most part) from the royalist French immigrants who had come to Trinidad after 1783. They greatly valued family traditions and kinship; to be a true French Creole, one had to belong to one of the 'good' families, one had to bear one of the 'respected' names. Before a person could be accepted into the group by marriage, he had to satisfy this requirement. Even more crucial, a member of the French Creole elite had to be 'pure white' and a Roman Catholic. Formal education was not especially important to the French Creoles, but ownership of land was a significant measure of status, for this group was essentially a land-owning aristocracy.

The critical points, for the French Creoles, were racial purity and aristocratic tradition; marriage outside these two boundaries meant loss of one's membership in the elite group. Some of the leading French Creoles were descended from minor French noblemen, like the de Verteuils or the de Gannes; others were not, but still adopted aristocratic pretensions. There was an exaggerated deference to birth and breeding. A member of the de Verteuil family wrote as late as 1932 'I am a respecter of the old blood...I still have that which they cannot buy'. Naturally, the French Creoles hardly ever married outside the group, and intermarriage was extensive. So few families were acceptable: free from any taint of 'Negro blood', impeccably Catholic, aristocratic enough to meet the requirements. So everyone who mattered was related to everyone else. Frederick de Verteuil wrote of the time he was born (1887) 'about a dozen families were intimate, the others just did not exist'. So the well-known French Creole families were all interrelated; there were perhaps about fifty families who felt they could risk marrying each other. In one of his novels the English writer Evelyn Waugh describes a fictional French Creole girl going home from her school in Paris to get married. She explains to the hero that she is not yet engaged, 'but you see there are so few young men I can marry. They must be Catholic and of an island family ... There are two or three other rich families and I shall marry into one of them.' Poor Therese de Vitre was limited to seven possible candidates, and one of them was eliminated because although he was very rich 'he isn't really a Trinidadian. His grandfather came from Dominica and they say he has coloured blood'.

More than the resident Europeans or the English Creoles, the French Creoles were open to the suspicion of having 'coloured blood.' Legal marriage to anyone known or reputed to have coloured ancestors would have been impossible for a French Creole in this period. Non-legal unions with coloured or black women were a well-established convention, but in these relationships the element of superiority/inferiority was carefully preserved, and the children of such unions could not of course move in French Creole circles, even though they often bore the 'respected' names. Legal marriage was limited to members of the group; French Creoles might marry a Catholic European long resident in the colony, but that was generally as far outside the fold as they would venture.

French Creoles did not mix with non-white Trinidadians except in contexts where the element of inequality was present. Coloured persons would not be invited to private gatherings at French Creole homes; indeed even white English Creoles would rarely be invited to such affairs. In public life, French Creoles would sometimes mix with educated coloured people at official functions, in certain church and charitable activities, and on some occasions in politics, business and in the professions. Apart from these limited contacts, French Creoles dealt with non-whites only in class relationships: employer-servant, planter-labourer, magistrate-offender. Especially significant was the intimate relationship that so often existed between black women domestics and the children of the white elite. Such contacts gave white Creoles confidence in dealing with blacks and Indians, whose status was defined as inferior. Many of the French Creole planters preserved the traditional patriarchal attitudes towards their labourers - their 'people'- much as in the days of slavery. It seems clear that the French Creole planters had far more influence over the black rural population than the British planters. Most of them were Justices of the Peace and some were Wardens (civil servants in charge of the administrative districts called Wards), and they exercised a considerable control over the labourers, black and Indian.

Although the French Creoles were more numerous, the English Creoles were also influential. They were people of English descent born in the island, invariably Protestant. Perhaps religion, rather than national descent, was the real dividing line between the French Creoles (who included Catholic families of English or Irish descent) and the English Creoles. The Warners were the 'first family' of the English Creoles, corresponding to the de Verteuils for the French Creoles. Charles Warner, Attorney-General in 1844-70, was the powerful spokesman of the group for much of the nineteenth century after emancipation. So far as private life was concerned, English and French Creoles formed two quite distinct entities well into the twentieth century.

Scots were prominent and influential as merchants and retailers in Port of Spain and San Fernando, dominating the dry goods business. They would be sent out as young men to work as shop assistants or clerks, often in stores owned by relatives in Trinidad. If they were ambitious they would in time set up their own businesses, or be admitted as partners in established firms. A prominent Scottish businessman was William Gordon Gordon, who came to Trinidad about 1867 and founded the firm Gordon Grant & Co. Other influential Scottish merchant families were the Alstons and the Todds. If these Scottish businessmen and their families settled permanently in the island, they might be assimilated into the English Creoles; as Protestants, intermarriage with the French Creoles was unlikely.

The white Creoles resented the presence of the British officials; the old Creole families felt that the 'upstart' Englishmen were trying to displace the locally born aristocracy. The Trinidad newspapers in this period are full of expressions of this sense of grievance. One editorial in 1879 rebuked:

> 'the impertinent affectation of a section of those who arrive here, whether as simple residents, as Government officials, or as employees of some of the large sugar estates or of the private establishments of the Colony, and the members of which never lose an opportunity of parading their contempt for everything colonial. . . What Creoles do not like is to see men no better than many who could be found here to fill the same posts, sneering at the land from which they draw their salaries, which gives them a position they would never have been able to attain in their own country, running down and snubbing those whom they have supplanted, and above all claiming for themselves a mental, moral, and social superiority over all who have not, like themselves, been born on the other side of the Atlantic'.

No doubt this expressed a deeply felt Creole resentment. Yet the truth was that the British officials during their residence in Trinidad identified with the land-owning class and moved in white social circles. Many officials were land-owners themselves and had an identity of interest with the Creole planters. Their education, background and values were similar to those of the white Creoles.

The important division within the white upper class in the decades after emancipation was that between the French-Catholic and the English-Protestant sectors. Fundamentally, the issue at stake was whether Trinidad was to become essentially English in institutions and values, or whether the 'foreign' whites were to continue to dominate the society. One powerful group wanted to anglicize the island - to make Trinidad essentially an English society - while the Creoles of foreign descent resisted the anglicization policy. Many aspects of the issue agitated the public mind: the law, language, church-state relations, the position of the Catholic and Anglican churches, and education.

Tension was heightened by the mutual suspicions between France and Britain in Europe. The old British mistrust of radical and Republican France was not dead, particularly with the revolutions in France in 1830, 1848 and 1870, and from time to time doubts were raised about French Creole loyalty to Britain and the British Crown. In fact, the attachment of the French Creoles to France was cultural and sentimental, not political; their allegiance was to the old royalist France, not to revolutionary or republican regimes, and when they did take part in movements of opposition to Crown Colony government, it was always within the conventions of the British empire. Certainly the French Creoles resented the arrogance of the English residents, for Victorian Englishmen were tremendously complacent about the superiority of Britain over all other nations, and this was very irritating to the French Creoles who prized their good birth and aristocratic traditions. Relations between the two groups deteriorated markedly after 1838 when the British government allowed the local authorities to mount a systematic policy of anglicization. Charles Warner was the leading figure in this campaign. His politics were animated by a simple principle: to make Trinidad English in feeling and institutions. He doubted the loyalty of the foreign Creoles and was suspicious of the Catholic church as a supranational body. Whether the new policy was directed from London or from Port of Spain, it was carried out without enough consideration for the feelings of the foreign whites and the Catholics, and Warner, as the epitome of the campaign, became easily the most unpopular public figure in nineteenth-century Trinidad.

Religious policy was the major arena for conflict between the French and English 'parties'. The majority of the people were Catholics, but the Anglican Church, if numerically weak, was very influential. In 1841 only one member of the legislative council was a Catholic, and the Bishop of Barbados was an ex officio member (for Trinidad was then a part of the Anglican diocese of Barbados). The Catholics had a strong case when they claimed that they were under-represented in favour of a minority church, while the anglicizers accused the Catholic Church of being a foreign organization, since most of its priests then were Frenchmen who often spoke no English. In the 1840s the government showed a quite new hostility to the Catholic Church, culminating in the Ecclesiastical Ordinance in 1844, which established the organization of the Anglican Church in Trinidad on English lines. It clearly favoured a minority church at the expense of the far more numerous Catholics, and it added a deep religious resentment to the existing suspicion between French and English.

In the 1850s there was further conflict, this time focusing on the right of the Catholics to appoint a foreign bishop to a British colony. For three years (1854-7) this question, involving the Italian Bishop Spaccapietra, outweighed all other matters in the public mind. The last great religious crisis was in 1863, when the government enacted a Marriage Ordinance which Catholics thought interfered with the sacred functions of their priests. Afer a sustained campaign of protest organized by a Catholic committee of prominent laymen, this law was amended in 1865 in the Catholics' favour - the first significant setback to the anglicizers and Warner's first major defeat. Also about this time, two French Creoles were appointed to the legislative council, giving them more adequate representation there.

In the last three decades of the nineteenth century the national and religious divisions between French and English whites lost some of their importance, and tensions between them were eased. Much of the credit for this change belongs to Governor A. H. Gordon (1866-70). His approach to religious problems was sympathetic and tolerant, and he took care to show due respect towards the elite French Creole families. His education policy, as we will see, had a calming effect on religious tensions because it allowed state aid to denominational schools. His government effected the repeal of the Ecclesiastical Ordinance in 1870; the two churches were put on an equal footing, with state aid being granted to each in proportion to the number of their communicants. Furthermore, Warner - for so long regarded by the French Creoles and the Catholics as the evil genius of anglicization - was forced to resign as Attorney-General in 1870 and retire into private life. After 1870 the conflicts between French and English within the white elite, although not entirely ended, were far milder than in the thirty years after emancipation.

It is interesting to note that often these tensions between the French and English sections became so absorbing to the white elite that they seemed to ignore altogether the non-white majority. The white society was curiously isolated from the wider island milieu. It seemed possible to ignore the existence of non-whites except as domestics and labourers. When upper-class Trinidadians spoke of 'our heterogeneous society', as they often did, they were thinking of the national divisions in white society: English, French, Spanish, German, Italian. As the historian Donald Wood puts it, 'as with Boer and Briton in South Africa, so also in Trinidad did the relations between two sets of Europeans sometimes take precedence in their own minds over their relations with those of other races'.

But as the century drew to its close, the differences between the English and French Creole whites became blurred. Before the 1870s the children of the French Creole elite received an essentially French education; at St Mary's College and at St Joseph's Convent the nuns and the Fathers were French, as was the language of instruction. But this changed about 1870. Both schools anglicized their teaching methods and used English as the language of instruction. More French Creoles (if they could afford it) sent their children to Catholic public schools and girls' convent schools in Britain rather than in France. While the older generation, like Sir Louis de Verteuil, were educated in France, and French was their chief language, the younger French Creoles at the end of the century had received their education in Britain or at St Mary's and English came as naturally as French to them. P. E. T. O'Connor, a member of a prominent French Creole family of Irish descent, writes that during his boyhood in the early 1900s, his older relatives spoke French fluently but did not pass it on to their children; in fact his parents and their friends would chat in French so that the children would not understand the gossip. His generation of French Creoles, born at the turn of the century, did not speak French, and he correctly sees this as a major landmark in the assimilation of the French Creole elite.

The French Creoles continued to have a sentimental feeling for France, but it became more and more sentiment, less and less actual contact. They hung on to their cherished aristocratic notions and their 'old blood'. But in fact the French and English white Creoles formed a single power block, with British businessmen, planters and officials, exercising economic, political and social control over society - subject, of course, to the imperial power and its agents.

Education and Mobility

But the position of the white elite as the colony's effective ruling class was slowly undermined by the rise of an educated black and coloured middle class that would eventually assert a claim to political leadership. To a very large extent it was education that made this possible. The system of education established in Trinidad after 1838 exercised a powerful influence on social development. It offered a chance, however limited, for mobility, for an escape from the harshly restricted world of the manual labourer, and this was an opportunity that was grasped by coloured and black families.

Two things were probably most responsible for the establishment of a system of public education in Trinidad: the imperial government's recognition that it had some responsibility for the education of the ex-slaves and their children, reinforced by the energy and interest of a few exceptional officials in the island; and the rivalry between the Christian denominations, especially the Catholic and the Anglican, which saw schools as the best means of increasing their flocks and thus improving their position at the expense of their religious rivals. When Lord Harris became governor in 1846, he found fifty-four primary schools, most of them run by the different denominations. The quality of instruction they offered was extremely low, and they were totally unsupervised; most children of the labouring classes were not attending any school at all. Harris was an unusual governor in that he had a genuine interest in education, and he believed that education was essential for the lower class in order to fit them for freedom. He disapproved of handing over education to competing religious bodies, for he felt that their competition served to deepen the divisions in the society, and he advocated a system of state schools which would be secular and totally controlled by the government.

The result was the Education Ordinance of 1851, which set up a system of Ward schools in each Ward, free and secular, to be run by a Board of Education and a salaried inspector. Instruction was to be entirely secular, but each week at stated times the clergyman of the majority faith in the Ward would undertake to teach religion, with parents free to withdraw their children if they wished. No church school was to receive government aid. In Port of Spain, a Normal (teaching-training) School was to be set up to train teachers for the Ward schools, with practising schools called Model Schools attached to it. The whole structure was to be under government control. For the first time in Trinidad, a system of government-run secular schools had been set up.

But the Ward school system ran into problems. Too few were established to serve the needs of the population; only thirty had been set up by 1870. There were difficulties about attendance; acute language problems since English was the only language of instruction in the Ward schools while the majority of the pupils were patois-speakers; inadequate buildings; poorly trained and motivated teachers. By the time Gordon came to the island in 1866 there was plenty of evidence that the Ward schools were not working well, and by then too the Catholic Church had taken the position that only state-aided denominational schools would be acceptable to them, for they had concluded that the secular schools - godless in their view - were a danger to Catholic youth. These two difficulties, the inefficiency of the Ward schools and the Catholic objections, motivated Gordon to take up the education issue as one of the major concerns of his government.

On his request, the Colonial Office sent out an Irish education expert, Patrick Keenan, to investigate the situation and make recommendations. His 1869 report, a major document in the history of education in Trinidad, was a serious indictment of the Ward school system. His recommendation was that church schools should be allowed state aid under certain conditions, which would have met the Catholic demands. Gordon agreed, and the Education Ordinance of 1870 set up a dual system of state-aided church schools existing side by side with government schools in the Wards. Church schools, if approved and licensed by the Board of Education, could receive state aid on condition that they were open to children of all faiths and that they were subject to government control and supervision. When a state-aided school was working satisfactorily, the Ward school could close down. But under the 1870 Ordinance the church schools had to meet high standards in order to qualify for state aid, and the result was that very few schools were able to qualify. In 1875 the law was changed to make it far easier to obtain aid, and the result was a considerable increase in the number of assisted schools. By 1885 there were sixty-one assisted and fifty-five government schools. The increase in the number of schools meant that children were able to attend a primary school in greater numbers, and figures for attendance and enrolment rose steadily in the last years of the century.

Yet large numbers of children remained outside the school system; Governor Robinson thought that nearly one-half of the island's school-age children were not enrolled in any school. A large proportion of these were Indian children. Few attended the Ward schools. Some planters did set up small private schools on their estates for the children of their immigrant labourers, and in 1857 an orphanage was set up at Tacarigua for orphan Indian children. Then the Canadian Presbyterian Mission started to open primary schools for Indian children, and after 1870 these qualified for state aid. These schools offered an elementary education for a growing number of Indian children after 1868; the drawbacks were that there was, inevitably, a proselytizing element in them, and that, because they were for the most part racially exclusive, the Mission schools were not an integrating agency.

By the beginning of the twentieth century, then, many children, especially Indians, remained outside the schools; but the state-aided and government schools provided an elementary education for most of the island's Creole children.

Secondary education remained the preserve of the upper and middle classes. Like elementary education, the provision of secondary schools became embroiled in the secular versus sectarian issue. Indeed, the question of a college in Port of Spain for upper-class boys caused so much controversy in the 1850s and 1860s that it seemed at times to push the education of the great mass of the colony's children into the background. In 1857 the government established the Queen's Collegiate School (QCS), a government run and financed college offering a secular and classical education on the lines of the British public (meaning elite private) schools to those boys whose parents could afford the high fees. Keenan found in 1869 that most of the pupils were the sons of Protestant officials, merchants and professional men in Port of Spain; only 19 per cent were coloured and there were no black or Indian pupils. Catholics objected to QCS because it was secular, and in 1863 they set up their own college, St Mary's, staffed and run by French Fathers of the Congregation of the Holy Ghost. In 1869 its pupils were all Catholics and mostly boys from the foreign Creole families, though there were some from English Catholic families and a few coloured boys. The language of instruction at St Mary's was French, and this was objectionable to those dedicated to anglicization.

Governor Gordon was concerned, not so much that the two secondary schools were closed to all but the wealthy, but that the upper-class youth of Trinidad were being educated in separate schools according to their religion or nationality, instead of meeting together on common ground in their formative years. He felt that the divisions in the white upper class were being perpetuated by this segregation. In 1870 he set up machinery for granting state aid to St Mary's, as Keenan had recommended. There was to be a Royal College, financed by the government, to which private secondary schools could be affiliated once they had reached a defined standard. St. Mary's was affiliated in 1870, and from then on it received government funds calculated on the basis of a fixed grant for each boy who passed an annual examination. Pupils of St Mary's now competed with those of the Queen's Royal College (QRC), as the government college was renamed, for the annual Island Scholarships. Gordon had intended that the pupils of the two colleges should combine for all secular classes, but this never happened. St Mary's continued to be run on strictly denominational lines, and the Royal College remained merely a device for granting state aid to private secondary schools; Naparima College was the second school to qualify. It remained the case well into the next century that only upper-class boys could gain access to the colleges, with the important exception of the small number of boys who won free places to the colleges from the government and assisted primary schools.

Yet despite all the difficulties and limitations, it remains true that the system of public primary education that existed after 1851 provided a schooling for black children that might allow them to rise above wage labour and to achieve a kind of lower-middle-class status as artisans, small shopkeepers, minor civil servants, clerks and store assistants. The Normal School took in Ward school pupils and trained them to be teachers, and this represented a means of mobility that did not require a secondary education in the colleges. School teaching was badly paid, but it was one of the surest avenues for social mobility for black and coloured men and women. The primary school teachers were clearly members of the middle class, because of their command of culture and their 'good' English, and their white-collar occupation, however miserably paid; so that teachers formed the nucleus of the emerging black and coloured middle class in nineteenth-century Trinidad.

A black boy from a poor family might, if he was lucky or very able or both, gain access to one of the colleges by winning one of the exhibitions or free places offered each year to boys from the government and assisted primary schools. The difficulties were great: the quality of the rural primary schools was so low that few of their pupils had a real chance in the examination; rural working-class parents often could not keep a son in the city even if he did win a place; boys from the city schools, especially the Boys' Model School in Port of Spain, were always at an advantage. Yet the free places opened up a secondary education to a small number of black or coloured boys from poor families, and these boys often succeeded in climbing up into the middle class as a result. To take just one example, in 1890 Arthur McShine won a free place to QRC from the Eastern Government School, Port of Spain, later proceeding on an Island Scholarship to study medicine in Britain: the start, one might say, of a prominent Trinidadian dynasty of black professional men.

A secondary education opened up various possibilities for white-collar jobs: teaching, the civil service, journalism, minor positions in business, a practice as a solicitor. Then, to complete the meritocracy, pupils of the two colleges competed for two Island Scholarships awarded each year, which financed three years' study at a British university. They were nearly always won by fee-paying, upper-class boys. But occasionally - frequently enough to make officials boast that the island's education system was entirely open to talent regardless of birth or means - exhibition boys would win these scholarships, like McShine, enabling them to qualify at a British university for the professions of law and medicine, which offered relative wealth and secure social status to the tiny handful who gained access to them.

For the great majority of the working-class children, especially in the rural areas, the schools offered little real chance for social mobility, and this is one reason for the general apathy about education showed by many rural parents. Why support education if it did not clearly lead to material or social advantages for their children? The schools offered a chance of upward mobility to a small minority of the working-class population. This minority tended to be urban, for the primary schools in San Fernando, Arima and Port of Spain were always of a higher quality than the rural schools, and there were always more opportunities for urban boys to win the exhibitions. The boys who were able to advance socially tended to be the children of an upper-working-class group: skilled workers rather than rural labourers, often literate themselves, church-goers and 'respectable' people. For them, the schools did represent a real chance that their children would be better off than themselves, and so they were correspondingly more anxious than rural parents to take advantage of them. Despite all its deficiencies, the system of public education established after 1851 was the crucial factor in the emergence of a black and coloured middle class.

The Emergence of the Black and Coloured Middle Class

It was not, however, the only factor. The nucleus of the coloured and black middle class comprised the free coloureds of pre-emancipation society, and the descendants of the French free coloured planters continued, after 1838, to form a distinct and separate group within the non-white middle class. Like the white French Creoles, they cherished aristocratic traditions and respected birth and breeding, often intermarrying among themselves. Catholic, French-speaking until the turn of the century, highly conscious of their descent from wealthy coloured planters and slave-owners who had settled in the island since the 1780s, these people formed a kind of aristocracy within the coloured and black middle class. Although most of them had lost their family estates by the later years of the century, many were well-educated businessmen and professionals. Among the leading families of this group were the Philips, the Romains, the Saturnins, the Espinets and the Maresses. This group belonged to the middle class by right of birth rather than through education.

But they were few in number, and the expansion of the middle class after emancipation was due to black and coloured persons rising in the social scale through their own efforts and through the schools. For these people it was important that so many ex-slaves and British West Indian immigrants settled in the towns, especially Port of Spain. By 1871 at least a quarter of the total population was urban, a high proportion for a nineteenth-century tropical colony. It was naturally in Port of Spain and the other towns that schools and other social and religious amenities were most available. The pronounced urban orientation of many of the more ambitious ex-slaves and British West Indian immigrants, and their children, was an important factor in the emergence of a non-white middle class.

Most of the 'self-made' black or coloured men who rose to middle-class status were teachers, professionals, clerks or civil servants. Few owned plantations, unless they had inherited estates from their families, because of the difficulty of acquiring capital to buy land. Nor did the large sugar or cocoa estates offer employment to educated coloured or black men. Only a few owned businesses; the island's commercial establishments were almost exclusively owned by whites in this period, and even the clerks and shop assistants employed by these firms tended to be young white Creoles or Britons though coloured clerks were also employed. Large-scale commerce was effectively closed to non-whites, though a few owned and operated small businesses or shops. But on the whole the established plantation and commercial sector, dominated by metropolitan capital and a group of white families, offered few opportunities to educated and socially mobile non-whites.

Teaching was, probably, the most important occupation open to the men and women of this group. A significant number of the emerging black middle class were teachers themselves, or the sons and daughters of teachers. But law and medicine were far more lucrative and prestigious professions, although they could only be entered after a university education. Lawyers formed an important and articulate element in the black and coloured middle class, and they provided political leadership to the group: Michael Maxwell Philip was Solicitor-General between 1869 and 1888; L.P.Pierre was the first black Stipendiary Magistrate; Edgar Maresse-Smith and Emmanuel Lazare were two radical lawyers who were active in the agitation that led up to the Water Riots in 1903; Henry Alcazar, appointed a member of the council in 1894, had an active political career; so did C. P. David, the first black appointed to the council (1904). Medicine was a favoured profession for those who could get to a British university. Stephen Laurence won a free place to QRC and then proceeded to Edinburgh University on an Island Scholarship, qualifying in 1888. Early in the 1900s he was to be a prominent member of the council and spokesman for the coloured middle class.

Most middle-class blacks and coloureds were employed in white-collar occupations, as teachers, minor civil servants, journalists and printers, druggists, doctors, lawyers and clerks. And education was the key to all these occupations, the crucial factor in the upward mobility of non-whites after emancipation. As the Trinidadian economist Lloyd Best has written, 'black people's investment was in education, our business was the school. The tycoons of industry in this country have been the Primary Headteachers, the men who held the precious ladder which let our fathers out the hatch - first the College Exhibition and finally the Island Scholarship supreme.' It was the development of a meritocracy, a coloured and black elite (later, from the early years of this century, joined by a few Indians), narrowly based at first, but gradually becoming more numerous.

These men had a 'natural' claim to leadership of the non-white population. They became prominent in campaigns against Crown Colony government from the later nineteenth century. They bitterly resented the discrimination against them in the civil service, especially the appointment of expatriates or local whites to the medical and legal posts. They also resented what they identified as social and racial snobbery on the part of the expatriate and local whites. These men believed that their education qualified them to participate in political life, and they kept closely in touch with political movements in Britain and in the empire. Indeed, British colonialism, by providing a public education system, however limited, made possible the emergence of an educated middle class that would become increasingly politicized and would eventually turn against Crown Colony government.

Educated blacks and coloureds participated in the movement to reform the constitution in the 1880s and 1890s. During the campaign of the 1890s, leadership was in the hands of coloured lawyers (Alcazar, David, Vincent Brown), and no doubt this was a factor in the eventual refusal to grant elected members in the council; for the Colonial Office had a long-standing mistrust of coloured 'agitators', would-be politicians. Politically minded blacks and coloureds also sat on the three elected borough councils (Port of Spain, San Fernando, Arima), one of the few political forums open to them. M.M.Philip became the first coloured mayor of Port of Spain in 1867; Alcazar was mayor for several terms in the 1890s. Both men were coloured, but there were two black lawyers who became prominent in political life around the turn of the century. Emmanuel M'Zumbo Lazare, a solicitor of 'pure African descent', was one of the three radicals who were prosecuted and acquitted for instigating the Water Riots. He served as a member of council in 1920-4. C. P. David won an Island Scholarship in 1885, the first black to do so, and was called to the Bar in 1889. A prominent supporter of the campaign to reform the constitution, he served as Secretary of the Reform Committee in 1892-5 and joined the council in 1904. The careers of Lazare and David mark the emergence of black men in Trinidad's political life.

Educated blacks and coloureds also expressed their political views through the press. There were always one or two papers owned or edited by members of this group and representing their outlook and aspirations. William Herbert was one of the prominent coloured newspaper editors and proprietors, owning or editing several papers. Born in Barbados, he lived in Trinidad between 1857 and 1873. His views were liberal, even radical, and his anti-government editorials incurred the anger of several governors. *New Era* (1869-90), owned and edited by Joseph Lewis, was the self-acknowledged spokesman for the coloured middle class, and it was noted for candid editorials and articles on questions of colour and race. *San Fernando Gazette* was owned and edited by Samuel Carter, a mixed-race Tobagonian, and it was perhaps the most consistently liberal paper in the later years of the nineteenth century. Carter wrote 'a Crown Colony is a despotism tempered by the Press'; his lively columns attacked all those groups or institutions that seemed to oppress the African race in Trinidad.

Historians have often assumed that middle-class blacks and coloureds in this period aspired to adopt white values and to reject or repudiate their African heritage, their slave past and their race. Yet this idea needs to be modified. While many members of this group no doubt did try to reject their racial heritage, a significant number in Trinidad expressed pride in their race and advocated race consciousness. They did not, as a group, downgrade their black identity. The local papers owned by members of the group in this period contain many articles, editorials and letters that express race awareness and pride, and these papers often defended blacks against racist attacks. Racial pride was also expressed in celebrations of the anniversary of emancipation. The jubilee in 1888 was observed by a group of young radicals led by Edgar Maresse-Smith, and their celebrations revolved around an appeal to race pride. There were many appeals for unity among people of African descent of whatever shade. One of the most prominent champions of the race in nineteenth-century Trinidad was J. J. Thomas, the self-educated black scholar and writer, author of *Creole Grammar* and *Froudacity*. He was a consistent advocate of race consciousness. In 1901 branches of the Pan-African Association (founded in London by the black Trinidadian H. S. Williams) were established in the island, supported mainly by members of the educated middle class. The evidence suggests that many blacks and coloureds in nineteenth- and early twentieth-century Trinidad expressed pride in their race and called for black solidarity. In fact, they were beginning to construct an ideology of race consciousness with which they could confront the racism that pervaded West Indian societies at this time.

The Creole Masses

The black and coloured middle class emerged in the century after 1838 from the Creole masses, the working class of mainly African descent. This was by no means a homogeneous group. In fact the Creole working class consisted of a number of distinct elements. The nuclear group comprised the Creole ex-slaves and their descendants, mainly Roman Catholic and patois-speaking. Then there were the British West Indian immigrants, mainly Protestant and English-speaking; the 'Americans' who were the descendants of the US ex-slave soldiers settled in the Company villages; the descendants of the demobilized soldiers of the West India Regiment; natives of Africa who had come to Trinidad between 1841 and 1861; and the 'peons' of Spanish-Amerindian-African descent who came from Venezuela all through the nineteenth century, with their Trinidad-born children, Catholic and Spanish-speaking. There were marked linguistic and cultural differences among them, although there was some tendency for the other groups to adopt the patois of the Creole blacks as a kind of lingua franca. Yet the British West Indians were distinct from the Creoles, and the natives of Africa remained separate from both. Perhaps the only things they had in common (aside from their African ancestry) were their exclusion from political life, their general poverty and their low level of exposure to formal education.

Although most working-class blacks lived in the rural.areas in the century after 1838, a significant and growing number of them were urban; by the turn of the century over a quarter of the whole population lived in 'Greater Port of Spain'. The rapid growth of the city's population after 1838 was due partly to internal migration, and partly to British West Indian immigration, for these people tended to gravitate to the city and its environs. Few Indians lived in Port of Spain; the 1881 census recorded only 970 in the city proper, although they were certainly a more significant element in the population of San Fernando by that time. Working-class blacks lived in the old heart of the city, around Nelson and Duncan Streets, and in the newer, lower-class districts of Laventille, East Dry River, Corbeaux Town and Belmont. They held a variety of jobs: they were domestics, washerwomen, seamstresses, petty traders, porters, carters, cab-drivers, dockworkers, messengers, workers in the small light industries of the city. Perhaps a majority of the men were skilled artisans, carpenters, masons, mechanics, tailors, printers, furniture-makers and the like. A large number of urban blacks were probably habitually unemployed, part of the floating population of petty criminals, prostitutes and so-called vagrants.

The great majority of the working-class blacks lived in the notorious barrack ranges, situated behind the front of each city

Plate 5 Corbeaux Town, Port of Spain

street, with its respectable stores and houses, hidden from the passer-by. These ranges offered the most primitive standards of accommodation, ventilation and sanitation. Often six or more adults were crowded together into unventilated rooms of eight or ten square feet. It is not surprising that the barrack dwellers were the victims of endemic diseases, especially dysentery and malaria, as well as periodic epidemics of cholera and smallpox. One editor, writing of Port of Spain in 1885, described 'hordes of destitute and suffering creatures, more or less ill-fed, their diseases unattended to and their abodes the scene of squalor and every unwholesomeness'. The wretched housing conditions worsened after about 1860, as continued immigration into the city put increasing pressure on totally inadequate lower-income housing in the slum sections of the capital.

These harsh physical conditions of life gave rise to characteristic urban social problems. Juvenile crime and vagrancy were widespread; if the newspapers can be believed, there were hundreds of children on the streets who lived on errands, casual jobs and petty crime. Prostitution was much in evidence in Port of Spain. Nothing alarmed respectable people as much as the extent of 'vagrancy', as it was called, among the lower classes of the city. The traditional belief in the virtues of honest labour for the masses was outraged by the spectacle of able-bodied men and women on the streets with no legitimate means of support. The point was, of course, that at least after 1880 there was a serious unemployment problem in the city. Some of the vagrants were between jobs; others had simply given up trying to find work and lived by occasional jobs, gambling, prostitution and petty crime. In the 1870s and 1880s the situation became especially obvious as overcrowding and unemployment worsened, and the press was full of complaints about the lawless behaviour of the urban vagrants.

This class of unemployed men and women was organized into loose associations, bands or gangs, and it was these bands that took over Carnival in the 1860s and 1870s. Their semi-criminal activities brought them into almost daily collisions with the police, and made them the subject of outraged letters and editorials in the press. It was from this Port of Spain underworld, the world of the jamets*, that cultural forms like calypso emerged, and Carnival became a festival of the urban black underworld until it was purged and made respectable around the turn of the century.

The urban blacks were highly visible, but the majority of working-class blacks in this period probably lived in the rural areas, as small cultivators, field labourers in cocoa and sugar, and artisans working in the villages or on the estates. The black peasantry had been formed in the years after 1838 when many of the ex-slaves left the sugar estates to become independent cultivators, and the opening of the Crown lands to small purchasers had given this development a considerable impetus. The peons were a very important element in the peasantry; they were pioneers of cultivation and of the cocoa industry in Trinidad. They moved to the northern foothills, the district east of Arima, and the Montserrat area to grow cocoa, either as peasant growers or as contractors. At first they were mostly squatters on Crown lands, but after 1868 many acquired legal titles to the land they cultivated, along with Creole and African squatters. Cocoa was the chief peasant crop in this period, and it was cultivated by black, 'peon' and Indian peasants.

Most peasants lived in small huts of tapia or wood, thatched with palm leaves. Usually they had only one room that contained little furniture. Cooking, living and sleeping were conducted in this one room and on the surrounding land. Often the peasants in the interior were very isolated, separated by miles of difficult tracks from the nearest village, school, church and police station, facing tremendous obstacles in getting their produce out to the market. Communications in nineteenth-century Trinidad were unbelievably primitive. People wrote of journeys to Mayaro or to Blanchisseuse as if they were exploring the source of the Nile. The peasants' produce would perish because it could not be conveyed to a market. The situation improved in the last thirty years of the century; Gordon gave an impetus to the building and maintenance of roads and bridges, and railways began to reach the new cocoa districts by the 1890s. Yet many of the peasantry remained isolated in their remote and scattered clearings until well into the twentieth century.

Significant numbers of blacks were still employed on the sugar estates in the second half of the nineteenth century, whether as field labour or as skilled artisans and mechanics. By 1870 the majority of field labourers were Indians, but an official estimate made in 1878 indicated that Creoles accounted for about 25 per cent of the field labour force on the sugar estates, and black peasants also gave seasonal labour during crop. Further, most of the artisans on the sugar estates - coopers, boilers, carpenters, mechanics, factory hands - were Creoles, although Indians were increasingly entering these jobs by the 1890s. Resident Creole labourers were housed either in the old slave huts, or in the newer barrack ranges built to accommodate the Indians but also used for resident Creole workers.

The harsh conditions of lower-class life inevitably bred crimes, and the courts usually proceeded on the assumption that a black or Indian labourer was guilty unless he could prove himself innocent; the whole machinery of law enforcement was directed against the lower classes. Corporal punishment was inflicted for praedial larceny (theft of growing crops) and the practice of obeah, and the victims were invariably working-class blacks, or, less often, Indians. All through this period there was a strong feeling of resentment against the police. One reason was that the ranks were predominantly Barbadian; in 1892, of 506 men, 292 were Barbadian, 137 from other islands, and only 47 were Trinidad Creoles. The government deliberately employed 'small-islanders' as part of the classic imperialist policy of divide and rule. The popular view was that Barbadians were often admitted to the Force even though they had a known criminal record, and they repaid the Creole population for their contemptuous attitude by systematic police brutality and persecution. Lower-class Creoles used their knowledge of patois, which most Barbadians did not understand, as a kind of weapon against the policemen. The deep resentment against the Force came to a head in 1880-4, when Captain Baker, the Chief of Police, broke up the Port of Spain bands and brought Carnival under tight control. It is not surprising that the official report on the Carnival riots of 1881 mentioned a 'very strong prejudice' against the police on the part of Trinidadians of all classes, but especially the black working class.

The black masses were able to retain and practise some of their own cultural forms, often African in derivation. The ex-slaves and their descendants had no first-hand memories of Africa, but between 1841 and 1861 some 8,000 liberated Africans came to Trinidad. As time passed, of course, the numbers of the natives of Africa dwindled. Nevertheless, many elements of West African life and religion persisted in this period. One group succeeded in keeping their religion almost intact well into the present century; these were the Radas in Belmont, a group of Africans from Dahomey who settled on Belmont Valley Road in the 1860s under their leader. These Radas practised their ancestral religion, but to the authorities there was no distinction between their ceremonies and the practice of obeah for monetary gain. Any 'African' worship tended to be classified as obeah which had been made an offence in 1868, punishable by jail and flogging. This is why several members of the Rada community in Belmont were prosecuted and often convicted of obeah. In 1886 the leader, then a very old man, was convicted and sentenced to thirty-six lashes; but the Appeal Court reversed the conviction, much to the alarm of respectable people, who felt that it would strengthen the people's belief in obeah.

The term 'obeah' was used in this period to include any religious or magical practices, including healing and conjuring of all types, which were believed to be African-derived. Most working-class blacks believed in the efficacy of such practices and consulted obeahmen and women; probably many upper- and middle-class Creoles did too. People saw no contradiction in attending Christian churches and consulting the obeahmen; it was only prudent to be on good terms with both sets of gods. In the same way, the less orthodox Christian groups often combined African religious practices and tendencies with Christian theology and ritual, like the Shouter or Spiritual Baptists who held noisy, emotional services that featured loud preaching, singing and movements by the congregation. The more orthodox Baptists regarded this kind of behaviour with concern and contempt. Yet it was a genuine fusion of fundamentalist Baptist worship with African religious practices, and it evolved into an indigenous church, which was especially strong among the 'Americans' of the Company villages who had been converted as Baptists in the southern USA and had kept up their religion in Trinidad.

Other mainly African-derived cultural forms kept up by the black masses were drumming and drum dances, and the playing of other African musical instruments; calypso emerged in its modern form at about the turn of the century. African musical forms were subject to legal restrictions all through this period, and evoked great hostility from the upper and middle classes. Urban blacks evolved a kind of sub-culture in the slums of Port of Spain, based on the barrack yards, dominated by the jamets, the singers, drummers, dancers, stickmen+, prostitutes and badjohns[#] in general. This group was organized loosely into bands, each with its clearly defined 'territory'. Carnival was the focus of this sub-culture, and in the 1860s and 1870s the jamets took over the festival, using it as their chance to let off steam and pay off old grievances in ritualized band conflict. Carnival was an important means of expression for the blacks who took part in it, and twice, in 1881 and 1884, they rioted against police efforts to control it.

Despite official and upper-class hostility, the black masses succeeded in preserving some of their values, traditions and patterns of life. These would be a source of strength and comfort to people whose material living conditions were usually wretched, just as religion and traditional cultural forms performed the same function for the Indian population.

---

1. Lower-class persons whose life centred on fighting, singing, dancing and Carnival, derived from the French 'diamêtre', or underworld type.

2. Experts in the martial art of stick-fighting, a tradition among the Creoles of African descent.

3. Trinidadian slang for a rough type, always in trouble with the law, and proud of it.

EIGHT

Politics in a Crown Colony, 1838-1914

The Legislative Council and the Unofficials

From the time that Trinidad became British, the authorities in London had resisted the call for an elected assembly, such as the older British colonies had long possessed, to be granted to the new colony. Their determination was strengthened by Trinidad's role as the model slave colony during the period of amelioration, for it was far easier to implement new slave policies in a Crown Colony where the British government could legislate directly by Order in Council, than in the colonies with their own assemblies. But as the end of slavery approached, the Colonial Office decided that the time had come to grant Trinidad a law-making body; not, indeed, an elected assembly, but a legislative council whose members would all be nominated by the governor. At the end of 1831 a purely nominated legislative council was established, which was not to be substantially changed until 1924.

The new council consisted of official members - the leading officers of the local government - and private citizens nominated by the governor 'from the principal proprietors of the Colony', who were called Unofficial members; the governor presided. The legislative council was authorized to enact Ordinances, to which both the governor and the Colonial Office in London had to assent, and after 1831 this became the usual method of making laws in Trinidad, although the British government kept its right to legislate directly by Order in Council. Trinidad's constitution was that of a 'pure' Crown Colony: all the members of the council were nominated by the governor, and in theory at least, the governor could enact any measure he wished by commanding the official members (who were in the majority in 1832-62) to vote for him.

As a concession to intermittent demands for elected members in the 1840s and 1850s, the Colonial Office agreed to allow a majority of Unofficials in 1862, on the understanding that if they frequently voted together to defeat the official vote, the official majority would be restored. Between 1862 and 1898 the Trinidad legislative council had an Unofficial majority, but this did not prove effective in providing opposition to the government. There were few issues on which the Unofficials disagreed strongly enough with

Plate 6 Detail from: Labour meeting at Grandstand, Queen's Park Savanna, Port of Spain, *c.* 1935; Captain A. A. Cipriani in centre

government policy to act together against it, and in any case the governor nominated the Unofficials; he was most unlikely to choose a person unless he had good reason to expect that the nominee would generally support his policies.

When the British government decided to grant Trinidad a legislative council, it expected that the new council would deal with the complex problem of the laws, by gradually assimilating the laws of Trinidad, still mainly Spanish, to those of England. The Colonial Office was anxious for the process of emancipation and apprenticeship to be completed before permission was given for the local government to proceed with a full-scale legal revolution, and it was not until 1842 that this permission was given. Then a great flood of Ordinances, largely drafted and piloted through the council by Charles Warner, finally introduced English laws into the colony which had become British nearly half a century before.

The criminal law was tackled first; it seemed simpler to deal with than civil law, for we have seen that virtually all the property-owners in Trinidad wanted the introduction of English criminal law. The Spanish criminal code was seen as too lenient, too biased in favour of the accused. Once full emancipation had taken place, the upper class felt that harsher laws were necessary to protect their lives and property from the newly freed blacks. Between 1842 and 1843 the legislative council enacted Ordinances that introduced English criminal laws, and trial by jury was allowed in 1844.

The civil law presented greater difficulties, for the upper class was divided on the introduction of English civil laws. But Warner had the upper hand, and between 1843 and 1846 he pushed ahead. Ordinances in 1843 amended the laws that prevented free disposal of property by will, and took away the special 'ganancial' rights of a married woman to property she brought to her husband on marriage. These laws were objectionable to the Spanish and French Creoles, who felt they were a part of the anglicizing process, and believed that Spanish law, with its special provisions for the rights of illegitimate children and married women, was more applicable to Trinidad society than British law. But London endorsed the changes, and by 1846 English civil law had been substantially introduced. The 'legal revolution' was complete: after fifty years of uncertainty and delays, Trinidad's legal system had been largely assimilated to that of Britain and the British empire, although a few relics of Spanish law survived until late in the century. The new legislative council had been successfully used to carry through the transformation of the island's laws.

By the middle years of the nineteenth century, Crown Colony government had come to be viewed as the only form of government suited to Trinidad. The men in the Colonial Office were convinced that the illiteracy of the mass of the population made any real public opinion impossible, and representative government therefore unworkable. The mixture of races and nationalities, the doubts about the 'loyalty' of the French and Spanish Creoles, the influx of Indian immigrants, all reinforced the idea that Trinidad could never be trusted with representative institutions. Indeed, the Colonial Office felt that Crown Colony government had worked well in Trinidad, and that the governor and officials had protected the ignorant and the weak against the planters. For this was the official justification for the Crown Colony government: the Crown was the best guardian of the interests of the masses as against the propertied few.

It was the great myth of Crown Colony government that governors and officials were impartial administrators, and, at the same time, the special protectors of the poor. But the written constitution was one thing, reality another. It was too much to expect that British officials would have operated as impartial arbiters between the social groups. The poor had no access to the policy-makers, while the propertied interests could lobby effectively. The practice of appointing Unofficials to represent the large property interests of the community made it inevitable that they would influence the decisions of the local government. When British officials by and large shared the planters' general ideas about the society and the economy, the process became even easier. There was no need for the governor to assert the autocratic powers that the constitution allowed him, save in very exceptional cases. For the local oligarchs, the governors and the British officials were agreed, on the whole, on what should be the general lines of policy. The central fact about Crown Colony politics in Trinidad was that the planter-merchant community was able to exercise very considerable influence over policy-making. Through the Unofficial members of the council, this group was able to influence and even to make government policies, especially on domestic issues like taxation, finances, immigration and economic policy in general.

Until the end of the nineteenth century, property and wealth (and gender) were the only qualifications for appointment as an Unofficial. The theory was that only men with a large economic stake in the island would have its true interests at heart. So Unofficials were usually planters or planter-merchants. And the interests of the British firms that owned much of the sugar industry were always an important consideration; there was a tacit understanding that the Colonial Company should always have a 'representative' in the council. Sugar planters predominated in the council, but cocoa and commerce, both closely linked with the sugar interest, were also represented among the Unofficials. In 1870, out of eight Unofficials, five were sugar planters, one was a doctor with sugar and cocoa properties, and two were barristers, one of them legal counsel to the Colonial Company. By the turn of the century, members were appointed to represent cocoa, but often they also had investments in sugar. In 1897, out of nine members, six were planters, two were merchants closely connected to the planting interest and one was an independent coloured barrister.

We saw that between 1862 and 1898 there was an Unofficial majority in the council. But this did not, in practice, make much difference to the Unofficials' ability to influence the local government. What mattered more was the informal relationship between Unofficials and the governor, and between them and the Colonial Office. Social and economic power lay behind the planters' political position, and only the strongest governors would be likely to oppose their wishes. The relationship between the governor and the plantocracy decided the local influence of the latter. Between 1838 and 1866 this relationship was usually close. Arthur Gordon (1866-70) was less co-operative, and he encountered considerable opposition from them, especially on his Crown lands policies. Between his departure and Sir William Robinson's arrival in 1885, the relationship was again close. Robinson's policies were certainly less favourable to the planters, but his successors in the last years of the century went very far to co-operate with them.

For its part, the Colonial Office tended to show great deference to the wishes of the Unofficials, especially on all matters involving taxation and expenditure. They were thought to represent the taxpayers, the wealth of the colony, so the Colonial Office was always reluctant to override their views on financial matters. Even on immigration, and on economic policy in general, London was very responsive to their wishes. So with governors usually cooperative, and the Colonial Office deferential to the Unofficials' views, the two possible checks on their ability to influence policy had been neutralized.

The Unofficials were able to exercise some control over the senior officials in the island. For instance, the episode of the Judicial Enquiry Commission illustrates the ability of the Unofficials to make life uncomfortable for officials who did not show proper deference to the local oligarchs, in this case Chief Justice Sir John Gorrie. From 1886, when Gorrie arrived, to 1891, when the Commission was appointed to investigate the administration of justice, the Unofficials conducted a persistent campaign against Gorrie. It was a group of Unofficials whose complaints led the Secretary of State to appoint the Commission, and they formed an 'Unofficial Committee' which acted like a prosecuting counsel during the inquiry, retaining legal help to cross-examine Gorrie and his witnesses. Gorrie's unforgivable sin was to administer justice impartially, and to reform judicial procedure so as to make the courts more accessible to lower-class suitors. Gorrie was correct when he said of the Unofficial Committee 'they are subject to every local bias and prejudice, men who have no sympathy with an impartial administration of justice, men who would not and do not hesitate to use their public position to make charges and demand enquiries with a view to getting control of the judiciary'.

Moreover, the Colonial Office felt that the Unofficials, as representatives of the community's wealth, should have considerable weight in all decisions affecting taxation and expenditure. For instance, in 1883 a petition signed by the representatives of all the leading absentee sugar firms, and by over 800 resident planters and merchants, requested the withdrawal of three recently introduced taxation bills. The governor announced to the council that 'in view of the strong adverse opinions therein expressed, by so many whose opinions are of great weight and which it is the Governor's duty to respect, without entering into the arguments adduced, His Excellency had decided to withdraw the bills in question'. In fact, the system of taxation that existed for much of this period is partly explained by the respect shown by the governors and the Colonial Office for the interests of the plantocracy: few property taxes, heavy import duties on articles of mass consumption, exemption of buildings used for sugar manufacturing from the building tax, no income tax.

The Unofficials exercised even greater control over finances with the establishment of the finance committee of the legislative council in 1886. Consisting of all the Unofficials and three official members, it was to consider the annual estimates before they were presented to the council. In announcing the innovation, the governor stated that the Secretary of State had 'practically handed over control of finances' to the Unofficials. In time the Committee usurped some of the functions of the Executive, and made a habit of attacking officials by voting cuts in their salaries. The convention was established that any item rejected in the committee would not be included in the estimates when they went to the full council. In effect the Unofficials could reverse the policy of the government by a simple majority in the committee, and thus they exercised a powerful, if negative, control over expenditure. And there were other standing committees of the council through which the Unofficials could influence policy, notably the immigration committee, consisting of the Protector of Immigrants and all the Unofficials, which decided the annual intake of Indians and other matters related to immigration. Officials showed great deference to the opinions of this committee, and considerable reluctance to override its requests. In normal circumstances, this committee got its way on immigration matters, even when the government disapproved of its recommendations.

As Crown Colony government actually operated in nineteenth-century Trinidad, the large property interests were able to exercise considerable, even decisive influence over policy-making, and the Unofficials, representing those interests, were treated with deference by both the local authorities and the Colonial Office. It was against this background that movements for constitutional reform developed in Trinidad. In the 1840s and the 1850s, groups of planters and merchants requested elected members in the council, but the Colonial Office rejected these demands, arguing that the population was too heterogeneous and uneducated to be trusted with representative institutions. But the idea of reform continued to be agitated. In the later nineteenth century the reform movement, as it was called, revived and there were two well-organized campaigns, in 1885-8 and again in 1892-5.

The Reform Movements

The first campaign was led by Philip Rostant, a white French Creole journalist, who used his newspaper, *Public Opinion*, as his main weapon to mobilize support. After public meetings and a petition for reform signed by over 5,000 persons, a Royal Franchise Commission was set up in 1887 to consider whether Trinidad was ready for elected members in the council, and if so, to recommend a suitable franchise. This Commission produced a majority report in favour of elected members, with a moderately high property qualification for voting and a literacy test in English for anyone aged over 40. But in 1889 the Colonial Office decided to reject the majority report and to refuse elected members; the only concession made was that the Unofficials were to sit for five years instead of for life. This was a blow to the reformers, but the movement revived in 1892, with public meetings, petitions and delegations to London. In 1894-5 a motion calling for elected members was debated in the legislative council and was defeated, and towards the end of 1895 Secretary of State Joseph Chamberlain decisively rejected the reformers' case, marking the failure of the reform movement of the late nineteenth century.

A number of grievances was linked together in the attack on Crown Colony government and the movement for elected members. There was an attack on the system of nominating Unofficials and on their tendency to legislate in the narrow interests of the class they represented. This was consistently attacked in the local press. *New Era*, organ of the educated black and coloured middle class, wrote of the Unofficials in 1885:

'Men who are selected for the business of Government from a particular class will naturally be prone to give undue prominence to their exclusive interests... It is only in the natural order of things that our Legislature would be used as a machinery for the furtherance of the particular interests of the class whose supporters so largely predominate in its composition.'

The tendency of the Unofficials to use their power in the narrow interests of the planter-merchant community was one of the strongest arguments for elected members. The reformers were sure that enfranchising at least some of the people would decrease the power of the planter-Unofficials. C. P. David, Secretary of the Reform Committee in 1892-5, wrote that the introduction of elected members would mean a revolution in Trinidad politics, a decrease in the power of the large land-owners. In general, the reformers were opposed to the political power of the sugar barons.

They tended to support the encouragement of minor industries, the opening up of the Crown lands, and the settlement of the people on the land as smallholders, all policies objectionable to the sugar interest. Reformers were especially hostile to the metropolitan firms that controlled much of the sugar industry and whose spokesman was the West India Committee in London. Some, though not all, of the reformers opposed Indian immigration, regarding state-aided immigration as an unjustified subsidy to the sugar industry, and they argued that indentured labour depressed the wages of free workers. The continuation of Indian immigration at a time of depression was proof, they thought, of the excessive power of the Unofficials.

An important aspect of the reform movement was dissatisfaction with the administration and an attack on incompetent or highhanded officials and extravagant spending, especially on public works. The reformers felt that public money would never be safeguarded until taxpayers had their own elected representatives in the council. They deeply resented expatriate appointments in the civil service, especially to medical and legal posts. J. J. Thomas wrote of 'pure-blooded Englishmen who have rushed from the destitution of home to batten on the cheaply obtained flesh pots of the Colonies'. Expatriate officials were often accused of incompetence and social arrogance. Hence the slogan that the reformers adopted: Trinidad for the Trinidadians. Certainly one goal of the reformers was to open the higher ranks of the civil service to Creoles, and especially to black and coloured Creoles. This helps to explain why coloured and black men led the movement in the 1890s. These men also felt that they were qualified by education and training to take part in government and political life; clearly, if reform had been granted, the leaders of the movement would have been obvious candidates for elected seats. Governor F. N. Broome was at least partly correct when he summed up the movement as 'a middle class upheaval, promoted by some lawyers and businessmen who desire a form of government more open to themselves'.

Leadership was provided, in the 1880s, by Philip Rostant, a French Creole who had taken part in radical Irish politics as a young man. He believed in mass meetings and petitions signed by thousands - radical tactics in nineteenth-century Trinidad. But as a member of an elite land-owning family, he had a deep respect for property rights, and he opposed universal male suffrage. He told a meeting 'we wish to give the franchise to those who represent something, to men who are able to understand thoroughly the responsibilities of citizenship'. Yet as a French Creole, he was bitterly hostile to British officials and British sugar interests; he was a genuine anti-colonialist in a limited way, and his methods were populist in the sense that he tried to mobilize the support of rural peasants and urban labourers. These tactics scared the more conservative planters and merchants who were suspicious of any attempt to involve the working class in political movements, and their defection from the movement was an important reason for the decision in 1889 not to grant elected members.

In the 1890s leadership passed to coloured and black lawyers. Most of them were moderates, and they did not try to mobilize the working class. Perhaps this is because they belonged to an aspiring elite, while Rostant was a member of the traditional land-owning ruling class; they were less secure and so less able to afford the 'luxury' of radicalism. Or perhaps it was their legal training that imbued them with respect for proper procedure, orderly meetings, petitions, delegations. Their meetings were smaller and their petition was signed by fewer people than Rostant's 'monster' petition of 1887.

The reformers all wanted to gain elected members in the council, but they did not envisage a fully elected council. They advocated a mixed council with officials, nominated Unofficials and elected members, on the lines of the reformed Jamaican constitution of 1884. And they were all agreed in opposing universal male suffrage. Henry Alcazar, the main leader in the 1890s, stated in 1897 that 'it had not been proposed to place power in the hands of the working classes, but only in those of the wealthier middle class'. The general consensus was for fairly high property qualifications for voting and for membership. The Majority Report of the Royal Franchise Commission suggested a fairly high qualification plus a literacy test for voters over 40, a franchise that would have resulted in an electorate of less than 6 per cent of the total population. (Women, of course, were to be excluded; this was long before female suffrage was granted in Britain.) Similar proposals were adopted by the Reform Committee in 1893, except that non-British subjects were to be excluded and the literacy test was to be dropped. C. P. David thought that the Committee's proposals would give an electorate of 12,000-15,000, out of a population of just over 200,000.

The people whom the reformers wanted to enfranchise were, in fact, the respectable classes, the men of property and education who were qualified to vote for the town councils and who sat as jurors. No one wanted to enfranchise the working classes, whether black or Indian, for that would have been to give the vote to 'the uneducated and the irresponsible', as one reformer put it. The reform movement was moderate, even conservative, and this was felt to be a positive virtue that would recommend it to the Colonial Office. For when the

Colonial Office considered requests for constitutional change from the colonies, the nature and extent of support for the movement were critical. Numbers were not as significant as influence. Whenever a petition for reform was sent to London, the governor would analyse the signatures in terms of their class and economic position. If a good proportion of the propertied class supported reform, it was said to be 'influentially' supported by those 'with a stake in the colony'. If most members of this class opposed change, the Colonial Office would feel that it was justified in refusing to grant reforms.

As a generalization, the officials and planters were hostile to reform; the working classes were mainly uninvolved; the only section to give consistent support was the urban middle class.

Most of the higher officials opposed reform. The three British officials who were on the Royal Franchise Commission all opposed any change and did much to ensure that the decision was unfavourable in 1889. The evidence of nearly all the official witnesses to the Commission was damaging to the case for reform. In the council debate on reform, six out of eight official members voted against it; the two officials who supported reform were both Creoles and both coloured.

The support of the planter-merchants was crucial to the fate of the movement; if the bulk of the propertied class had supported reform it would have been difficult for the Colonial Office to have refused concessions. At first, a number of important planters and merchants supported the campaign in 1885-7, but they became alienated by Rostant's efforts to mobilize the working classes, and by his close association with the radical Chief Justice, Sir John Gorrie, whom they detested. In the 1890s campaign, very few planters supported reform. Their defection is understandable; the whole thrust of the movement was against the sugar interest. On the other hand, the Port of Spain merchants generally supported the movement in the 1890s. They were not alienated by attacks on immigration or on sugar, and they felt with the reformers that other interests were not fairly represented in the existing council.

It was the coloured and black middle class which consistenly supported reform. Lawyers provided leadership and black men like C. P. David and the Grenadian-born radical J. S. de Bourg took an active part in political movements. Teachers, journalists and artisans provided active support in the towns and villages and no fewer than eighty-seven lawyers and law clerks signed the petition of 1893. Barbadians in Trinidad were especially active supporters in the towns and villages, particularly San Fernando, a stronghold of reformers. Unlike most rural Creoles at this time, the Barbadians spoke English well and were often literate, and this gave them the entry to strategic jobs in teaching, the police service and the skilled crafts. They seemed to have advanced faster within the system than the patois-speaking Creoles. It may have been that their command of English, and their familiarity with electoral politics in Barbados, equipped them better than working-class Creoles to participate in political movements. For all the evidence suggests that most working-class Creoles and Indians were uninvolved in the reform movement.

Although it failed in all its objectives, the reform movement of these decades was important in the development of political life in Trinidad. It stimulated a debate on the issues crucial to the island: labour and capital, the influence of sugar, the disposal of the land, immigration and free labour. This debate sharpened the political awareness of educated Trinidadians, and helped also to arouse political interest among the lower middle class of teachers, artisans, clerks and so on. The movement served as a political training for the black and coloured middle class. Men who would lead the more radical movements of the turn of the century, like David, Edgar Maresse-Smith and Emmanuel Lazare, received their political education in the campaigns for reform of the 1880s and 1890s. They accustomed the non-white middle class to participation in political life. And so the reform movement, itself moderate if not conservative, prepared the ground for the more radical attacks on Crown Colony government in the years after 1895.

The Growing Opposition to Crown Colony Government

In these years opposition became more populist in its methods and more radical in its aims, and groups emerged that clearly aimed at lower-class support. This development culminated in the Water Riots of 1903 and their aftermath. The decade after 1895 was an important period in the development of more radical political dissent in Trinidad.

A number of factors helped to make the opposition to Crown Colony government more intense in the mid-1890s. One was the failure of the reform movement at a time when most other Crown Colonies were being granted semi-elective councils. Another was the position of Joseph Chamberlain, Secretary of State for the Colonies between 1895 and 1903. He was openly hostile to the grant of representative institutions to colonies where the majority of the people were not Europeans, and his general opinion of West Indians was low. In deciding in 1895 to refuse elected members for Trinidad, he was rejecting the advice of the officials in the Colonial Office, something only a very determined minister would do. He wrote in 1896:

'Local government (falsely so-called) is the curse of the West Indies. In many islands it means only the rule of a local oligarchy of whites and half-breeds-always incapable and frequently corrupt. In other cases it is the rule of the negroes, totally unfit for representative institutions and the dupes of unscrupulous adventurers.'

It is hardly surprising that a Secretary of State with these views came into headlong collision with the opposition in Trinidad. Chamberlain served notice, as it were, in 1898 by ending the Unofficial majority that had existed in the legislative council since 1862. When an acting governor reported that the Unofficials were meeting together before council meetings to concert their votes and were acting as an opposition to the government, Chamberlain added two new officials to give a permanent official majority, even though the substantive governor, Jerningham, denied the report. This was certainly a high-handed action that seemed to take away the modest concession of an Unofficial majority.

Far more serious an issue was Chamberlain's abolition of the Port of Spain borough council. An elected body, set up in 1853, it had always been an important forum for local politicians, especially black and coloured radicals. With the defeat of the reform movement in 1895, it was more than ever the only area in which educated Trinidadians not belonging to the capitalist class could participate in political affairs, however limited in scope. Though the property franchise for voting for borough councillors was fairly high, and though only a small proportion of the electors actually voted, the borough council was crucially important to the small group of active opponents of Crown Colony government. This explains the significance of the dispute between the borough council and the local government in 1897-8. It centred on money: the council was always in financial straits, and it claimed that the central government ought to relieve it by exempting it from certain charges and by granting it certain new revenues.

More generally, the borough council thought that its powers should be enlarged, and the citizens (the voting ratepayers) should be given greater powers to manage municipal affairs. Complex negotiations between the council, the local government and the Colonial Office took place in 1897 and 1898. Chamberlain formed the view that the council had displayed great irresponsibility over the years, by borrowing instead of supplementing its revenues, and by failing to collect the rates with proper efficiency. He rejected all the council's requests and suggestions, and finally announced his decision in August 1898. He offered limited financial relief to the council, but only on condition that the council's budget should be submitted yearly for government approval, and that its accounts should be audited annually by a government officer. This would, of course, have destroyed the council's independence of the central government. If the council refused to accept these conditions, the governor was to abolish the elected council and vest the administration of the city in a nominated Board of Commissioners; an outcome, said Chamberlain, he would 'much regret as distinctly a retrograde step; but it must be understood that if Municipal Institutions are to continue they must be self-supporting, and that the grant of privileges implies the acceptance of responsibilities'.

By a majority of two, the borough council refused to accept Chamberlain's conditions, claiming with some justice that if it had done so, it would have ceased to exist as an independent body. An Ordinance was rushed through the legislative council at the end of 1898, abolishing the borough council. At its last meeting in January 1899, the 'no surrender' group in the council voiced their indignation at Chamberlain's high-handed ultimatum. Maresse-Smith called the abolition 'one of the greatest crimes in the annals of Trinidad'. Randolph Rust* lamented the 'killing' of a 'school to teach the people to manage their own affairs'. They recorded a formal protest: 'This Council, at its last meeting and on the eve of its abolition, wishes to place on record its strongest protest against the injustices and unfair treatment they have received from the Government of this Island.' A petition signed by thirty-six citizens was sent to Chamberlain protesting his action as repugnant to British principles of local self-government. But Chamberlain was not arguing, and the issue was closed as far as he was concerned. A Board of Commissioners consisting of officials and ratepayers nominated by the governor was established to run the city's affairs.

The whole episode was regarded by the Trinidad liberals as a classic example of high-handed, authoritarian interference by the Crown Colony regime with the rights of local citizens. It took away the small measure of self-government that they had enjoyed, on the specious plea of financial responsibility. It showed the powerlessness of the colonial faced with the Crown Colony system of government. After 1898 political agitation centred around two points: the ending of the Unofficial majority in the legislative council and the abolition of the borough council.

But neither of these issues was well suited to win mass support. After all, only a handful of people were actually ratepayers qualified to vote for the borough councils. Some more popularly based organizations were needed to widen the area of dissent. The first organization in Trinidad that explicitly appealed to working-class support was the Trinidad Workingmen's Association (TWA), founded probably in 1897 by Walter Mills, a Port of Spain druggist. He claimed about fifty members in that year, mainly Port of Spain skilled workers, though it was open to all categories of workers. In his evidence to the 1897 Royal Commission, Mills said that the TWA stood for reduction of taxes on food, the extension of roads, the encouragement of minor industries, the opening up of the Crown lands and (significantly) elected members in the legislative council. The TWA sent a number of petitions and letters to the government, but the local authorities refused to take it seriously, and it seems to have been inactive in 1900-6.

There was, however, one other organization that appealed to a wider section of the community, and this was the Pan-African Association. H. S. Williams, a Trinidadian lawyer based in London, had founded this organization in 1897 as a pressure group to lobby in the interests of the coloured races in the British empire. He came to Trinidad in 1901, and as a result of his visit several branches of the Pan-African Association were formed in Trinidad. The black middle class responded enthusiastically to what was then a novel appeal to race pride. The *Mirror* felt that Williams was 'moving the masses and the middle class to a sense of responsibility to themselves and to the greater body of the African race'. Although black race consciousness continued to be important, the Pan-African Association in Trinidad soon split up and then faded away; it was really a burst of enthusiasm caused by Williams's visit. By 1902 many of its members, including the leader of the Port of Spain branch, Emmanuel Lazare, had moved to a new organization, the Ratepayers Association (RPA).

The RPA was founded in 1901 by prominent city businessmen. Its stated object was to safeguard the interests of Port of Spain ratepayers, in the absence of an elected municipal body. Its membership was chiefly middle class, including a number of merchants and professionals, white, coloured and black. Governor Sir Alfred Moloney thought it was formed 'for the express purpose of supervising the expenditure of public moneys, because there was no representation'. Certainly its leaders were partly motivated by their desire to have elected members in the legislative council, and by their indignation at the abolition of the borough council, of which many had been members. Only 185 city ratepayers were members, but it soon acquired a wide influence and capitalized on the government's failure to win public confidence.

The specific issue that the RPA took up was water, long a vexed question for Port of Spain residents. The unpopular Director of Public Works, Walsh Wrightson, was trying to control wastage by paying unannounced visits to city homes and cutting off their supply if their taps leaked; the government was also preparing legislation to control wastage by meters in private homes. This was not exactly an issue calculated to win working-class support, since the great majority of the city's residents lived in tenements where, at best, there was a single communal stand-pipe. But Wrightson's policy aroused a great deal of upper- and middle-class indignation, and the RPA seized on the issue as yet another example of government interference in the rights of citizens, another proof of the authoritarian nature of Crown Colony rule. In this way the RPA leadership succeeded in mobilizing the city's working class on an issue that, in fact, affected them not at all.

Their agitation forced the government to postpone its meter

legislation at the end of 1902, but in February 1903 it tried again. The RPA got busy with meetings and press articles, and the meeting of the legislative council on 16 March had to be stopped because of disorder in the public gallery and outside the Red House, the principal government building in Port of Spain where the council sat. It was adjourned to 23 March. To prevent further disorder, the government announced that only persons with special tickets would be admitted to this meeting. The RPA claimed that this was illegal, and urged the public to attend. A public meeting on 21 March denounced the government and told the people to assemble before the Red House on the day of the council meeting to prevent the reading of the Water Bill. Moloney, the governor, prepared for trouble. On the morning of 23 March, the RPA radicals made strenuous efforts to excite the assembled crowd against the government, yet at the same time they advised the people, according to the *Mirror*, 'to be calm, insistent on their rights but on no account to put themselves in the wrong by beginning a disturbance'. At best, the radicals of the RPA left their followers uncertain of what they were expected to do.

The outcome was a major riot in the course of which police fired on the crowd, killing sixteen and wounding forty-three, and the Red House was destroyed by fire. Although the RPA consisted mainly of upper- and middle-class ratepayers, the victims of the police action were nearly all lower class, and none of the leaders of the RPA were involved in the actual rioting. They had whipped up the crowd's indignation against the government on an issue that had nothing much to do with the people, and then left them to face the police bullets.

The riot was followed by a spread of anti-government feeling and the formation of new pressure groups, to the alarm of Moloney, who requested a warship and 200 white troops. Meanwhile, the Colonial Office had set up a Commission of Enquiry into the riot, which reported in July 1903. It found that the riots were the result of public opposition to the Water Bill incited by the RPA. The police firing was 'amply justifiable', except in some cases where there was irresponsible firing, and in the case of two or three people who 'were brutally bayoneted and killed by the police without any justification whatever'. The government failed, the report stated, 'to take adequate measures to correct the misrepresentations about the draft ordinance with a view to allaying public excitement', and in the Commission's view there was 'without doubt, a regrettable and serious division between a large influential portion of the community in Port of Spain and the Executive Government regarding public affairs'.

In concluding that the cause of the riot was the dispute between the RPA and the government on the Water Bill, the Commission was disagreeing with Moloney's view that the whole agitation really had to do with the demand for representative government. The Commission said that no evidence was given to substantiate this view, and concluded 'the agitation for any change in the system of government formed an insignificant element in creating the riots'. In fact, there was a clear link between the agitation that led to the riots, and the demand for representative government. Alcazar, an Unoffical member of the council, stated before he walked out of the 23 March meeting in protest, 'this public movement...is the inauguration of a more serious movement which I hope will end in the people having their own representatives at this table'. Wrightson was of the same view. He wrote:'It is quite true that no direct evidence was brought forward to show that the real object of the RPA was and is to obtain some form of representative government at least as far as the municipal affairs of Port of Spain are concerned, nor was any asked for by the Commissioners, but no doubt exists locally on the subject...The Water Works question was the spark which caused the explosion.'

One of the commissioners dissented from the majority opinion and called for the restoration of the elected borough council, as this would divert 'malcontents' from radical politics. This probably prompted Chamberlain to go beyond the Majority Report and tell Moloney to consider the restoration of the borough council as a partly elected body. Chamberlain clearly recognized that the riot was more than just a dispute over water, and he told Moloney to consult wherever possible with the Unofficials on legislation and expenditure, and to give them every confidence and consideration. This indicated the direction in which the government proceeded after 1903: debate on the restoration of the borough council and an attempt to involve the radicals in the legislative council. Thus C.P.David, a black and a prominent supporter of the RPA, was appointed an Unofficial in 1904; another coloured professional sympathetic to reform, Stephen Laurence, was appointed in 1911.

After 1903, radical opponents of Crown Colony government devoted themselves to the restoration of the borough council, and to new groupings involving the working class. The borough council issue was extensively aired in 1905-6. A committee was appointed to recommend what kind of municipal authority should be established for Port of Spain, and its members included radicals like David, Rust, Lazare and Alcazar who had been members of the old council or had been active in the agitation of 1902-3. They wanted a fully elected borough council, but the moderate majority favoured a mixed council of electives and nominees. The legislative council was similarly divided. The general view of the official members was expressed by Wrightson: 'the people of Port of Spain and of the Colony generally are not yet fitted by their personal qualities, character and education to exercise such an important privilege as self-government on English lines'. Governor H. M. Jackson (1904-8) was in favour of an elected council, but most of his officials wanted a nominated body. In the event, it was agreed in 1906 that a wholly nominated town board should be established for two years, after which the legislative council should review the whole issue.

But it was not until 1913 that there was a sufficiently numerous body of Unofficials who supported an elected borough council to make it worth their while to reopen the question. By 1913 five Unofficials were in favour of an elected body: Laurence, Alcazar, George Fitzpatrick (the first Trinidadian Indian member), C. de Verteuil and Dr E. Prada. The legislative council agreed to a scheme by which an elected borough council would be restored in stages between 1914 and 1917, and the Secretary of State agreed. This left the critical issue of who would be allowed to vote. A fifteen-man committee was divided (as usual) between radicals and moderates; the former wanted low property qualifications for voting and for membership. But the majority recommended fairly high qualifications for voting and even higher ones for membership; women could vote if they qualified but could not be elected. Despite protests from radical groups, these high qualifications were incorporated into the 1914 Ordinance which reconstituted the Port of Spain city council as an elective body. The fairly narrow electorate was a setback for the radicals; but the restoration of the elected borough council between 1914 and 1917 was regarded as a victory for the opposition to Crown Colony government, and it meant that the major objective of politically minded Trinidadians, after 1914, was elected representation in the central government, the legislative council.

One of the more radical groups that agitated for the restoration of the borough council was the TWA. It revived in 1906 to protest against the decision that year to establish a wholly nominated town board; its new president was Alfred Richards, a city druggist of Afro-Chinese descent. Its aims were stated to be the promotion of the interests of working men, but in joining the campaign for an elected borough council and for elected members in the legislative council, the TWA was primarily concerned with the same goals as the middle-class reformers. In 1906 TWA had about 240 members, mainly white-collar workers and skilled artisans from Port of Spain. In 1907 it petitioned the Secretary of State on behalf of railway workers; in 1908, significantly, it petitioned against the continuation of indentured Indian immigration.

TWA took an important step when it developed close links with the British Labour Party, which assigned one of its MPs to,act as 'Trinidad representative' in the House of Commons, receiving memoranda from the TWA, asking questions and lobbying at the Colonial Office. This was a very sound move; the importance of direct influence in London had always been appreciated by the plantocracy, and the tactic ensured that Trinidad's problems were regularly put before the British Parliament and the Colonial Office. Joseph Pointer, the Trinidad 'representative' from 1910, visited Trinidad in 1912. He toured the island and held meetings organized by TWA. His visit helped to politicize Indian workers; he met with the executive of the East Indian National Association and toured rural Indian settlements. At the end of his visit, TWA organized a mass meeting in Port of Spain, attended by some 3,000 including Indians, which passed resolutions for the restoration of an elected borough council and for elected members in the legislative council.

In 1913-14 TWA supported those radicals who wanted a low property qualification for voting for the restored borough council, and called several meetings to agitate the issue; Pointer put their case to the Secretary of State. When the high property qualifications were incorporated into the 1914 Ordinance, TWA protested to the Secretary of State again. The point was that TWA had consistently, since 1906, supported the campaign for an elected borough council; now the franchise had been put out of the reach of many, perhaps most, of its members. It meant a betrayal of the radical and working-class groups represented by TWA. When TWA re-emerged into political activity in 1918, its politics would be far more radical, and more directly oriented to a working-class constituency.

But between 1914 and 1918 it was hardly active at all. It was seriously damaged by the conviction in 1914 of its main officers for fraud in connection with funds contributed by members. Whether or not these charges were framed, the organization was discredited, and it split up. J. S. de Bourg led an anti-Richards faction (de Bourg was a relatively militant radical) and organized a coup ousting Richards and declaring his faction the legitimate TWA. The organization was damaged; and, in addition, the start of the First World War in August 1914 meant an end to virtually all political activity. At the war's end in 1918, Trinidad would enter a new era of radical political and labour movements.

Tobago becomes a Ward of Trinidad and Tobago

By the beginning of the twentieth century, however, Trinidad was not alone in these movements, for the island was linked to the smaller neighbouring colony of Tobago in two stages in the 1880s and 1890s. This was not the result of agitation for union by the people of either island, or even by powerful interest groups; it was by imperial fiat, the outcome of Britain's anxiety to shuffle off responsibility for an impoverished little colony by tacking it on to a more prosperous one. For by the last decades of the nineteenth century, Tobago's economic situation seemed hopeless.

Sugar, the traditional staple, had fallen into hard times ever since the 1820s, and especially since the 1840s. The adoption of metayage, or share-cropping (by which part of the estate land was cultivated by labourers without wages in return for a share of the proceeds of the crop) had salvaged Tobago's sugar estates for a time. But many were abandoned when the production of muscovado sugar became increasingly unprofitable in the 1870s, and by 1880 Tobago was exporting only about 2,000 tons each year. The final blow came in 1884-5, when sugar prices on the London market fell steeply as a result of the competition of European beet exports. This crisis caused the collapse in 1884 of Gillespie Brothers of London, and over half of Tobago's sugar estates had depended on this firm for advances of credit and supplies. Tobago was still producing muscovado sugar, which was almost worthless for export by the later 1880s. Land values crashed, estates could be bought for a song: the Bacolet estate, of almost 1,000 acres, was sold for a mere $2,880. By 1894, sugar exports were a pathetic 599 tons, and the value of Tobago's exports of sugar, rum and molasses was only £5,029. The total value of all Tobago's exports in that year was £15,872. Revenues fell steeply, public works employees went unpaid for months, the public services - such as they were - were cut back. Tobago's export sugar industry, lacking capital and immigrant labour, faced with drastically falling prices for crude sugar, was going under; the island was virtually bankrupt.

Politically, too, Tobago had suffered reversals. Unlike Trinidad, Tobago had enjoyed the dubious blessings of a 'British constitution'; in other words, after its cession to Britain in 1763 an assembly had been established, elected by the white land-owners, and this assembly had survived into the post-emancipation decades. A small, impoverished island supported nine privy councillors, seven members of the legislative council (the nominated 'Upper House') and 16 elected representatives in the assembly. But the electorate was a minute fraction of the population: in 1857 it only numbered 102 people; after franchise reform in 1860 the grand total of 215 was reached. Exactly ninety-one people voted in the 1860 elections, and two representatives (for St John and Plymouth) were returned by one voter each. Clearly, the old representative system was a farce in a society like Tobago's and after 1865 it was the policy of the British government to bring pressure on the West Indian assemblies to modify their constitutions in the direction of Crown Colony government. In Tobago, the change took place in two stages. In 1874, a single legislative council was established consisting of six nominated and eight elected members; then an 1876 Act, which became effective at the start of 1877, made Tobago a 'pure' Crown Colony like Trinidad by setting up a wholly nominated legislative council. As a further measure of rationalization, in 1880 the offices of lieutenant-governor and colonial secretary were amalgamated to form a new post, the administrator of Tobago. Yet the island remained a separate colony supporting its own legislative council and bureaucracy. By the 1880s London had decided on the unification of Trinidad and Tobago in order to save money and - it was hoped - to improve the quality of administration in the smaller island.

In 1886 the Secretary of State announced his intention to unite the two islands, either by complete annexation, which he thought preferable, or by a loose union that would allow Tobago to retain a separate Treasury and a subordinate legislature. Predictably, the Tobagonian planters and merchants, while agreeing in principle that union would be an advantage, were reluctant to give up their control of local taxes and expenditure through the Tobago legislative council. That body resolved in January 1887 that union would only be advantageous to Tobago if Trinidad's tax laws were not applied to the smaller island, if Tobago's revenues were used only for local purposes, and if a financial board, consisting of the governor's representative, a nominated Unoffical and two elected members, retained control of internal taxation and expenditure. As a parting shot, the Tobago council resolved that if in the future union proved to be disadvantageous to Tobago or unacceptable to its people, 'the colony shall on petition have granted back to it the form of self-government which now exists' - a built-in secession clause that the Secretary of State not surprisingly vetoed. In Trinidad, the Unofficial members of the council were even less enthusiastic about union, on the grounds that Tobago would inevitably be a financial burden and that Trinidad would be inundated by Tobago paupers, criminals and invalids rushing into the larger island's jails and hospitals. A cautiously worded resolution was passed after long debate in March 1887: 'This Council has no objection to the administrative annexation of Tobago with this Government, Tobago retaining, however, a separate Treasury and a separate internal Financial Board, on the understanding that ... no pecuniary charge is now or hereafter to be imposed on the Revenues of Trinidad for any service connected with the Island of Tobago.' Neither partner really wanted marriage; but in January 1889 Tobago was duly united to Trinidad, with a single governor, judiciary and code of laws, and with Tobago retaining its own financial board and its separate Treasury, administered by a resident commissioner who was ex officio a member of the Trinidad legislative council.

This arrangement satisfied no one, and the Tobago merchants began to complain of a loss of trade and customs duties as a result of the union. But these complaints failed to impress the British government, and the West India Royal Commission of 1897 dismissed them decisively, recommending instead 'the complete amalgamation of Tobago and Trinidad and the abolition of the separate account of revenue and expenditure. Tobago would then become a Ward, or district of Trinidad, and the two islands would have a common exchequer. To this measure objections would, no doubt, be raised locally, though we believe that the majority of the inhabitants of Tobago are in favour of it ... The traders seem to fear that amalgamation with Trinidad would reduce their business in connection with the import trade, and possibly with the export trade. This result might follow, but from the point of view of the general interest, no sound argument against the amalgamation can be based upon it.'

The British government accepted this recommendation, and in October 1898 an Order in Council constituted Tobago a 'Ward of the Colony of Trinidad and Tobago; and the revenue, expenditure and debt of Tobago shall be merged in and form part of the revenue, expenditure and debt of the united Colony. . . All future Ordinances enacted by the Legislature of the colony shall extend to Tobago. . .' Tobago was thus made a Ward of the new colony of Trinidad and Tobago, losing its own financial board, treasury and statute book. It remained to be seen whether Tobago - on the verge of bankruptcy after suffering neglect and maladministration under first the old representative system and then Crown Colony government - would fare any better as a Ward of Trinidad and Tobago.

---

1. An English businessman and public figure, and one of the main pioneers of the oil industry.

NINE

Constitutional Reform and Labour Movements, 1917-36

Unrest and Organization after the First World War

The First World War marked something of a watershed in the development of political organization and political protest in Trinidad and Tobago; the immediate postwar years saw an upsurge in labour organization and radical political activity. During the war, worsening economic conditions caused considerable hardships for both Creoles and Indians; the colony's merchants saw the war as a signal for an immediate rise in prices. The Colonial Office calculated that in 1914-19, prices had risen in Trinidad by 145 per cent, a rate of inflation that was far higher than in Britain itself. This inflation, especially marked in basic foods, led to demands for higher wages, and labour protests when these were refused. In 1917 oil and asphalt workers went on strike and damaged property; troops were called in, and five leaders were arrested and imprisoned under wartime defence regulations. Economic hardships also led to the establishment of the East Indian Destitute League by Mohammed Orfy in 1916. The aims of this body were to agitate on behalf of impoverished Indians in Trinidad, and to work for the abolition of indentureship and the repatriation of all those entitled to a free passage to India. Because of inflation, and because ships were not available during the war to repatriate Indians, there was some unrest among the Indian population; the government felt nervous about Orfy's activities and he was summarily deported in 1918. By war's end Creoles and Indians alike were restless and dissatisfied in the face of rising prices imposed - mostly without any real justification - by the merchant elite.

This climate of unrest was heightened by the return of Trinidadians who had served in the armed forces during the war. Black West Indians who volunteered to serve king and country were disgracefully treated by the military authorities, and their experiences helped to politicize them and to orient them towards radical political and labour movements on their return. At first, the British government categorically refused offers by black West Indians to serve; it was only when the Colonial Secretary and the king himself took an interest that the War Office agreed to accept a West Indian contingent, as a separate unit that would not be a part of the British army. It was made clear that the black troops of the British West Indies (BWI) Regiment, as this unit was to be called, would be given lower rates of pay and allowances than British soldiers. Further, the army refused to give officers' commissions to men 'who are not of unmixed European blood', and would not allow the West Indian troops to engage in actual combat against European troops. Most of the battalions of the BWI Regiment spent the war in Egypt, performing labour services, although in 1917-18 some of the men took part in action against Turkish troops in Palestine and the Sinai. Some battalions served in Europe as ammunition carriers and 'pioneers' (performing labour services like digging trenches), but they were never allowed to engage in actual fighting, and the military authorities took every opportunity to humiliate and degrade the black soldiers. A Trinidadian soldier serving in Egypt wrote privately to a friend, 'We are treated neither as Christians nor as British citizens, but as West Indian "niggers" without anybody to be interested in or look after us.'

This was the background to a 'mutiny' by some men of the BWI Regiment who were stationed at Taranto, Italy, at the end of 1918. These men had been forced to perform degrading services - cleaning latrines, washing linens - which were properly the work of labour units, not soldiers. They were given segregated and inferior canteens, cinemas and hospitals. When the commander of the regiment complained to the South African camp commander, he was told that 'niggers' had no right to expect to be treated like British troops, and the army dismissed charges of discrimination raised by officers of the regiment, including Captain A.A.Cipriani of Trinidad. The sequel to the 'mutiny' was the establishment of the secret Caribbean League by some BWI Regiment sergeants at Taranto. They advocated industrial and social reforms for the West Indies, closer union among the colonies, the vote for black men, and strike action after demobilization to press for higher wages. The League was disbanded when its meetings were reported to the authorities, and West Indian governors were told to keep a close watch on the leaders when they came home in 1919; but its aims were taken up in the postwar period, and the League's ideas influenced several leaders and reform groups, especially Cipriani, who had been present at Taranto. It is hardly surprising that the ex-servicemen, embittered by their experiences and exposed to new ideas and socialist influences in Britain and elsewhere, took a leading part in the postwar agitation.

But before the war ended (November 1918), an event occurred of great significance for Trinidad: the final end of indentured Indian immigration. As we saw in Chapter 6, opposition to indentured immigration within the island had begun to develop from the 1870s.

The arguments of local politicians like Henry Alcazar, C.P.David, Stephen Laurence and others, and of newspapers and organizations like the TWA, led to the appointment in 1909 of the Sanderson Commission to investigate indentured immigration. This Commission rejected the suggestion that immigration had caused unemployment, and concluded that state-aided Indian immigration was still desirable for Trinidad and British Guiana, though the numbers should be carefully controlled with reference to the state of the labour market. In fact, Indian immigration was not abolished because of opposition in the West Indies nor because the Colonial Office had changed its mind, but because wider imperial concerns made it necessary. It was the development of a strong opposition in India that ultimately proved decisive. The Indian National Congress, led by G. K.Gokhale, mounted a campaign against indentured emigration, which was seen as degrading to Indian national pride. Led by Congress, public agitation in India mounted after 1910, and by 1915 it had become politically inexpedient for Britain to continue to support indentured emigration; at the same time, the war made the transport of immigrants difficult and dangerous.

By 1915-16 the plantocracy in the West Indies knew that the government in India was reluctant to continue indentured immigration, but they felt confident that the British government would eventually allow continued immigration after the war. In 1916 the Trinidad legislative council debated a new Immigration Ordinance which was supposed to remove the most objectionable features of the indentureship, but which in fact made few significant changes. The planters' optimism was dissipated in 1917. By then the government in India had suspended any further emigration from India, because of the dangers of wartime shipping and because of the need to recruit as many Indians as possible for the armed forces. It had already been decided not to allow indentured emigration to resume after the end of the war; and in July 1917 the imperial government announced that indentured immigration would not be revived after the end of hostilities. The abrupt decision to terminate the indentured immigration system was a victory for Indian popular opinion and the Indian National Congress. For the planters, it was a severe blow.

They turned to the alternative strategy: efforts to retain on the plantations the existing labour force during the transition period while indentureship would gradually disappear (by 1921 no Indians in Trinidad would still be indentured). Their major weapon was the Habitual Idlers Ordinance (No. 7 of 1918). Its objective was to prevent the rural labour force, predominantly Indian, from leaving the sugar districts and drifting to the towns in search of work. It defined a habitual idler as 'a person who has no visible means of subsistence, and who being able to labour, habitually abstains from work', and had not worked for at least four hours during each of three days of the week before his arrest. It was to operate, at first, in

Port of Spain, San Fernando and Arima, but the governor was empowered to extend it all over the colony. The arrested man had to prove that he had lawful means of subsistence, or that he did not habitually abstain from work; in other words, the accused had to prove himself innocent, violating a basic principle of English law. If convicted, he was detained in a 'settlement', which was in fact a penal labour camp. This repressive law was passed by the legislative council without a single dissenting vote. TWA* petitioned against it, and the Colonial Office had its doubts; the Colonial Secretary noted that the Ordinance went 'considerably beyond anything in the UK, in that it makes the mere fact of refusing to work and being without visible means of subsistence a punishable offence'. Questions were asked in the House of Commons, but the Colonial Secretary did not veto the Ordinance, which became law in 1920.

To control rural labour yet further, labour exchanges were set up in 1919, with separate exchanges for Indians and for Creoles. These exchanges were designed to mobilize Indian labour once indentureship had ceased to exist. And to limit the geographical and occupational mobility of the rural poor, the humble urban jobs that Indians had taken up in the towns, like coconut selling and portering, were made difficult to get: in 1916 the fees for licences for selling coconuts in Port of Spain were doubled, and in 1918 porters' licences were raised. All these measures were intended to prevent the rural population from retreating from plantation labour and drifting to the towns, to keep the estate-resident Indian population in the sugar districts after indentureship had ended. They provide a good example of the tenacity of the planters, and their ability, under Crown Colony government, to get their own way.

But it was not the rural Indians who played the leading role in the industrial unrest of 1919-20. The strikes of the immediate postwar period were carried out by urban and industrial workers. General unrest caused by severe inflation and by the return of embittered ex-servicemen opened the way for the revival of TWA as a vibrant body offering leadership to the whole working class. New elections were held in 1918, and a 'rebel' group took over the leadership. James Braithwaite, a Barbadian docker, became secretary, and other prominent new leaders included David Headley, also a docker; J. S. de Bourg, the radical commission agent who had been active in Trinidad politics since the 1880s; and William Howard Bishop, a journalist and teacher from British Guiana. TWA was not highly organized nor did it have a large membership in 1918-19; but it became the main agency through which worker grievances were articulated, and it taught Trinidadians the methods of collective political and indstrial action.

Early in 1919, the TWA leadership decided to take an active part in the agitation for higher wages, and it called on any existing labour organization to join. In the first months of 1919, there were strikes by dockers, railwaymen, city council employees and workers at the Electric and Telephone Companies. At La Brea, labourers of the Trinidad Lake Asphalt Company asked TWA to negotiate for them; the company agreed to meet with TWA, and in May 1919 its team secured a 33 per cent increase and a reduction in working hours for them. This was an important victory that boosted TWA's status among workers, leading to an increase in its membership, and the establishment of two branches at La Brea and San Fernando.

The major cause for this wave of strikes was undoubtedly rampant inflation and worsening economic conditions, but racial feeling played an important role in heightening tensions in 1919. The returning servicemen came home resentful at their disgraceful treatment by the racist military authorities. Throughout 1919 the local press carried reports of race incidents in Britain. There were major anti-black riots in Liverpool and Cardiff; hundreds of blacks were attacked by whites, and in Liverpool a Trinidadian seaman, Charles Wotten, who had served in the navy during the war, was murdered by a white mob. These riots, and the shabby behaviour of the British government, which refused to give blacks adequate police protection from white mobs and tried to pressure black British subjects to be repatriated, heightened racial tensions in the West Indies. A Trinidadian in London, F. E. M. Hercules, who was secretary of the Society of Peoples of African Origin, publicly defended blacks in Britain during and after the riots, and his activities made him a well-known spokesman for blacks. Hercules visited Trinidad in September 1919, giving lectures and recruiting members for his society, and his strongly race-conscious views contributed to the development of black nationalism in Trinidad. Naturally the authorities were alarmed, and the governor refused to allow Hercules to land when he tried to return to Trinidad at the end of 1919, by which time unrest had escalated.

The ideology of race pride was also promoted by a local paper, *Argos*, much to the dismay of local whites who accused the paper of spreading 'all kinds of revolutionary, seditious, and mischievous literature'. Marcus Garvey's publication, *Negro World*, was circulated in Trinidad, often smuggled in by black seamen, and a number of strikers in 1919-20 were probably influenced by Garveyism, while the TWA leaders maintained links with Garvey's organization in the USA. The influence of these two papers, and the *Argos* reports of the anti-black riots in Britain, deepened anti-white feeling in Port of Spain; and this became obvious in July 1919 when some British sailors were assaulted on the streets. Of course the local white community felt threatened, and a committee of six influential white businessmen, headed by G. F. Huggins, wrote to the Colonial Secretary expressing alarm at what they saw as the widespread hostility shown by the black population towards whites. They advocated the suppression of *Argos*, the arming of the white population, and the stationing of a force of regular British troops in Trinidad. Huggins and his cronies warned that the 'Creole Indians' would probably join the blacks against the whites, and rural Indian workers did take part in the general unrest in 1919-20.

The dockworkers of Port of Spain had always been a significant element in the urban working class. Because large numbers were concentrated on the waterfront, the workers could interact among themselves, meet to discuss grievances and begin the task of self-organization. Many were immigrants from the other colonies of the eastern Caribbean, like James Braithwaite. These workers had regular contact with the outside world through the foreign seamen they met, and many had themselves taken jobs on ships and travelled to the USA and Britain. Foreign sailors brought in Garveyite and socialist literature, and a few of them talked to local workers about trade unionism and socialism. Hard hit by inflation, the dockers demanded an increase in wages, overtime pay, and an eight-hour day. TWA took up their case, and when the shipping companies refused to negotiate with them, the dockers went on strike (November 1919). This was a well-planned strike, with a high level of collective organization and action among the workers on the waterfront. Scab labour was used to keep the docks functioning, and on 1 December dockers attacked warehouses, ran the scabs off the waterfront, and marched through the city forcing businesses to close. City employees and coal carriers joined the strike.

What began as a waterfront strike rapidly escalated into colony-wide labour unrest. The governor was advised to negotiate the dockers' demands, and a conciliation board consisting of representatives of the companies, TWA and the government, was established. The company representatives, no doubt impressed by the militancy of the strikers and by their leadership, agreed to a 25 per cent increase. This victory generated a new wave of strikes all over the country. Significantly, Indian rural labourers went on strike on several sugar plantations, and at Woodford Lodge an Indian worker was killed by a white plantation official. In December 1919 the colony faced virtually a general strike. Workers took to the streets in San Fernando, Chaguanas, Couva, Sangre Grande and Toco, downing tools and expressing support for the dockers.

In the sister island, Tobagonians demonstrated their support for the strikers. In the twenty years since Tobago had become a Ward of the united colony, neglect and impoverishment had continued to be the island's experience. Although a vigorous peasantry had been established, growing cocoa, coconuts, coffee and food crops, and raising livestock, estate wages remained very low, and the cost of living was even higher than in Trinidad. In 1898 the British government had directed that Tobago should always be represented in the legislative council by an Unofficial member; but communications between the two islands were so difficult that for twenty-five years no Tobago resident could spare the time to attend council meetings. No wonder, then, that Tobagonians responded to the unrest in the larger island; estate workers struck and marched in the streets of Scarborough. A crowd attacked the Government Wireless Station in Scarborough, the police fired, and a leader, Nathaniel Williams, was killed. Order was only restored when British marines landed in Tobago.

By now the local government and the business community were thoroughly alarmed. The pleas by the businessmen and their friends in Britain for British troops were answered, and early in 1920, 350 British servicemen were dispatched to Trinidad. The white officers of the police, and the governor, doubted whether black policemen could be relied on to suppress riots and strikes, and there was some evidence to suggest that policemen ignored violence against scabs and strike-breakers. A volunteer force, the Colonial Vigilantes, was formed by white businessmen and their friends, while the resident Americans, who were concentrated mostly in the oilfields and at La Brea, formed their own vigilante groups. Local whites blamed 'small-islanders' for 'agitating' the local workers; the Chamber of Commerce called for the deportation of 'these scum of the wharves of the West Indies'. Feeling more secure once British troops had entered, the government cracked down on the leaders of the strikes; ninety-nine persons were arrested, eighty-two convicted and imprisoned, including Braithwaite, and four leading activists who were not natives of Trinidad were deported early in 1920: Brutus Ironman, Bruce McConney, J. S. de Bourg and E. S. Salmon. All four were TWA members, active in the industrial agitation of the time, and the ostensible reason for their deportation was 'seditious activities'.

The strikes of 1919 were critically important for the development of politics and labour organization in Trinidad. They had fused industrial grievances with radical political demands. They had demonstrated the potential strength of organized labour. Yet the strikes had not really been marked by violence: a Colonial Office man noted 'they were the most gentlemanly rioters I have ever heard of', and the official report indicated how few and how mild had been the violent incidents started by the strikers. Race feeling was an element, as we saw, but the threat to the white population had been greatly exaggerated. More significant, the strikes brought new publicity and prestige to TWA. By March 1920 a police report estimated its membership at 6,000. The imprisonment of TWA's top office-holders was tactically an advantage, and TWA got the credit for the 25 per cent increase for the dockers. Further, the strikes had witnessed some co-operation between Indian and black workers, both demanding higher wages. This had been spontaneous, not planned, but it might pave the way to future organized political co-operation, an ominous possibility for the local capitalists. In these ways, the strikes of 1919 ushered in a new era of more radical political-labour movements in the 1920s and 1930s.

But the immediate aftermath of the strikes was repression. The local government and the business community were especially upset by the undercurrent of race feeling, in Port of Spain if not elsewhere, and by the use of socialist ideas and phrases by the TWA leadership. When strikes continued into the early weeks of 1920, the government launched on a policy of full-scale repression. Besides the arrests and deportations, the Strikes and Lockout Ordinance (No. 1 of 1920) was a device for defusing industrial crises by delaying strike action until time-consuming procedures had been carried out. It contained no provision for the legal recognition of trade unions, and this was not to come until 1932. An Industrial Court Ordinance (No. 26 of 1920) provided for an industrial court to arbitrate disputes referred to it by the governor; but it was only an arbitration tribunal without powers to enforce its decisions, and, in fact, this Ordinance remained a dead letter and the court never materialized. A Wages Committee was set up to report on the economic condition of labour with a view to recommending minimum wages. Of its twenty-five members, only two were representatives of TWA. This Committee discovered an enormous gap between the rise in prices and wages between 1914 and 1920, and recommended a minimum wage for unskilled labour of 68 cents for a man and 45 cents for a woman. But the government refused to enact minimum wage legislation, and the report was indefinitely shelved. Finally, the Seditious Publications Ordinance (No.10 of 1920) empowered the government to suppress Garveyite or socialist literature: the governor was authorized to prohibit the importation of any literature deemed to be seditious and the Supreme Court could close any paper it found to contain seditious matter. This was so sweepingly repressive that middle-class liberals protested, but the government was determined to end the influx of Garveyite and left-wing literature. *Argos*, which had consistently supported TWA, was an early victim, and it became increasingly difficult to circulate Garveyite publications.

Despite the repression, TWA emerged by 1921 as the sole representative organization of the Trinidad workers, recognized as such by the British Government and, reluctantly, by the local officials. Under Howard Bishop, the new secretary, the leadership was reformist in the early 1920s and an effort was made to forge an alliance with middle-class liberals. Captain Cipriani, who had become the hero of black soldiers of the BWI Regiment because of his defence of their interests against British army racism, joined TWA in 1919 and was elected president in 1923. Under the joint leadership of Cipriani and Howard Bishop, TWA joined the renewed campaign for constitutional reform, while not neglecting its advocacy of strictly labour demands such as recognition of trade unions, the eight-hour day, overtime pay and workmen's compensation. In 1922 TWA began to publish a party paper, the *Labour Leader*, edited by Howard Bishop. By 1924 at least thirteen branches besides the main one in Port of Spain had been established, and TWA entered a period of steady consolidation.

Constitutional Reform and the TWA

But it was constitutional reform that dominated politics in the early 1920s. The demand for reform revived in several West Indian colonies after the war, and the British government was willing to make concessions. In Trinidad, the leaders of the reform movement were - as in the 1890s - members of the coloured and black middle class, but now with the support of TWA, representing the urban workers. By 1921 the middle-class professionals were preparing to open their campaign; in that year, Grenada had been granted elected members in the council. Their arguments and aims were quite as moderate as in the 1890s, no doubt to avoid provoking determined white resistance after the unrest of 1919-20. The middle-class leadership organized a Legislative Reform Committee (LRC), but TWA played an important role in the reform campaign: Howard Bishop went to London in 1921 and conferred with Colonial Under-Secretary E. F. L. Wood and with Labour Party MPs. Through his contacts with Labour MPs, questions were asked in Parliament about conditions in Trinidad, and these MPs pressed for a commission to visit the West Indies to make recommendations on constitutional reform. As a result Wood was sent to the West Indies in 1921-2.

The various interest groups focused on the Wood Commission, which was in Trinidad early in 1922. Significantly, the Chamber of Commerce and the Agricultural Society, representing businessmen and planters, both opposed any change in the existing contitution; local whites had withdrawn from the movement for representative institutions and probably feared that the coloured and black middle class would gain most from reform. The Indian leadership was also doubtful. The East Indian National Association, which claimed to speak for the wealthiest Indians from the south, opposed any change, arguing that an elective system would harm Indians because of their relative lack of education. Instead Indians should be given more nominated representatives to protect their interests. The other major group, the East Indian National Congress, whose leader was a member of the LRC, advocated elected members and communal or ethnic representation for Indians to avoid their being outvoted, for this group anticipated that relatively few Indians would qualify to vote.

Interestingly, the LRC opposed communal or ethnic representation, and Wood was told that they would prefer the retention of the wholly nominated council rather than any communal system of voting. This indicated their anxiety about the possibility of several Indians being elected to a reformed council. Communal representation would weaken the influence of the coloured and black professionals, while strengthening the middle-class Indian leadership. Indeed, the middleclass political leadership of both major races seemed to fear each other more than the dominant whites who ran the existing system: rather than risk a loss of influence to the other's advantage, they preferred to maintain the status quo. However, Wood rejected communal voting, and this should be seen as a concession to the coloured and black leadership, though he justified it on the grounds that communal voting would perpetuate differences 'which it should be the object of statesmanship to remove' in order to produce 'a homogeneous community'; Indians should be encouraged to share in the main current of political life.

Wood recommended the introduction of elected members in a mixed legislative council, which should consist of seven electives (one for Tobago), six nominated Unofficials and twelve officials, with the governor exercising both an original and a casting vote to ensure an official majority. The details of franchise and constituencies should be left to a local franchise committee, which recommended fairly high property qualifications for voting and even higher qualifications for election. Men who qualified had to be over 21 to vote, but women had to be over 30. The voter had to satisfy the registering officer that he or she understood spoken English, but there was no literacy test for voting. Only men literate in English who possessed considerable real estate or earned a fairly high income could be candidates for election. This meant, of course, that working-class or even lower-middle-class men (such as made up TWA's membership) could not be candidates, and many could not even qualify to vote. This narrow franchise, recommended by the local committee and accepted by the Colonial Office, reflects the conservative views of the LRC and was a disappointment to TWA, which was not represented on the committee. Perhaps it was also a response to Wood's hint that no action should be taken which would disturb the confidence of foreign capitalists, who had invested in the oil and asphalt industries, in the stability of the local government.

Only about six per cent of the total population qualified to vote under the new constitution for Trinidad's first national elections in 1925, after 128 years of British colonialism. Nevertheless the reformers were satisfied; the reform provided a legitimate political forum for middle-class elected members to initiate public debate on issues vital to the people, and to formulate programmes of political, social and economic reform. The masses could not vote in the period 1925-46, but the periodic elections created political excitement and an awareness that they were closer to political power than ever before. The unenfranchised majority influenced elections by disrupting meetings, heckling opponents and cheering popular candidates, especially in Port of Spain, and through the leadership and organization provided by TWA, the people gained experience in political organization and electioneering. This is the real significance of the 1925 constitutional reform, limited though it was. It accustomed the people to political organization and the electoral system, and it greatly increased their political awareness in the years between 1925 and 1937.

The TWA leadership decided to take advantage of the new constitution by putting up Cipriani for the Port of Spain seat. He enjoyed the backing of an organized party and a political paper, the *Labour Leader*; he had very vocal support from the Port of Spain workers as well as widespread support from middle-class voters. He won his seat with an overwhelming majority, and held it virtually unchallenged until his death in 1945. Cipriani's election marks the beginning of his ascendancy over the Trinidad labour movement.

Cipriani was born into a white French Creole family of Corsican descent in 1875. They were land-owners and businessmen, and Cipriani went into racehorse owning and training. His early life was not especially remarkable but, with the outbreak of the First World War, he was one of the first West Indians to enlist in the armed forces. He rose to the rank of captain in the BWI Regiment. Because he defended his men against discrimination by the military authorities they idolized him, and when he came home in 1919 he brought with him the affection and respect of the ex-servicemen; in that year he was elected president of the Soldiers and Sailors Union, an organization set up to promote the interests of the demobilized men. His wartime experiences had given Cipriani a social conscience and a new political awareness; he joined TWA, and in 1923, already aged 48, he accepted the presidency. The TWA leadership knew what it was about in offering him the top post: he was extremely popular, he had outstanding gifts of oratory and personal magnetism, he was a sincere advocate of all TWA's industrial demands. As a white Creole, he might be expected to bridge the gap between blacks and Indians and encourage the recruitment of Indian members. Whiteness was highly valued in the colonial society, and Cipriani's colour enhanced his charisma. Working-class blacks and Indians were flattered that a white man should champion their cause, and it was also felt that he would be better able to negotiate with British officials than a black man, especially after the repression of 1919-20. Under Cipriani and Howard Bishop, TWA entered a period of rapid growth.

In 1925 TWA's membership was predominantly black and urban, and the *Labour Leader* projected a strong interest in Garveyism and Pan-Africanism, as well as socialism. Sections and branches were established - perhaps as many as forty-eight in Trinidad and thirteen in Tobago existed by 1928 - and representatives from all the branches met four times a year to decide policy for the whole organization, although increasingly the main body in Port of Spain dominated decision-making. If Cipriani can be believed, TWA had 33,000 members in 1928, and it had begun to make significant progress in mobilizing Indians. In the 1925 elections only one Indian had been elected, Sarran Teelucksingh, and Cipriani persuaded him to join TWA as a vice-president. In 1928 another successful Indian candidate, Timothy Roodal, was also appointed a vice-president, and TWA supported F. E. M. Hosein's candidacy in the same elections. In this way, almost by chance, TWA gained important Indian members. A key recruit was Krishna Deonarine, later Adrian Cola Rienzi, elected president of the San Fernando branch in 1925. With the support of these influential Indian members, TWA's potential to develop as a genuine multi-racial party had increased; but its membership always remained predominantly black.

Once in the council, Cipriani's role was to articulate TWA's reform programme and, if possible, to secure legislation in the workers' interests. He took up most of the major TWA demands. In 1926 he helped to secure a workmen's compensation Ordinance; it excluded most of Trinidad's workers, since it did not cover agricultural workers, domestics, shop assistants or clerks, but it was a real gain for the industrial workers to whom it applied and it was an important achievement for TWA. Another major issue was the eight-hour day for all workers. Cipriani took it up, and a select committee was appointed that recommended a forty-five-hour week for clerks and a forty-eight-hour week for labourers in agricultural and industrial concerns (except labourers in sugar factories during crop and domestics); work in excess of eight hours was to be paid at overtime rates. The government stalled, and it was not until 1930 that an Ordinance was enacted which merely restricted hours of work for clerks in provision shops. This was a tactical move, involving compromise on a limited issue in order to shelve the larger one - the eight-hour day for all categories of workers. Indeed, Cipriani virtually abandoned the eight-hour day for industrial and agricultural workers whose working conditions were most oppressive. A limited victory came in 1927, when agitation by TWA and a petition from Cipriani and four other elected members led to legislation prohibiting employment of children under twelve. Despite these gains, one has to conclude that Cipriani's performance in the council was not very effective in terms of achieving practical legislative reforms of real benefit to the working class of Trinidad and Tobago.

Yet Cipriani played a very significant role in articulating grievances and politicizing the people by his speeches in the council. For most of the years between 1925 and 1938, he was the only legislator who consistently defended the workers' interests and attacked the employers and the government. Capital was heavily over-represented in the council in this period, with nominated Unofficials drawn from businessmen, planters, managers of oil companies and wealthy lawyers. Between 1925 and 1940, out of a total of fourteen nominated Unofficials, there were four lawyers, two planters, two representatives of the oil industry and six businessmen, many of whom had interests in oil and sugar. Typical representatives of capital in the council during this period were James Forbes (1938-46), president of the Chamber of Commerce, manager of the Cocoa Planters Association and director of an oil company; and F. G. Grant (1930-46), director of Gordon Grant & Co., member of the Cocoa Planters Association, director of a sugar company, president of the Chamber and with family interests in oil. Besides the nominated Unofficials, many of the other elected members sided with the employer class. For years Cipriani formed almost a one-man opposition to the government, and he introduced a note of controversy and attack into a council dominated by businessmen and employers. He used the council as a public platform to attack the government and voice the workers' grievances and demands. Even if his tangible achievements in terms of legislation were few - and it could hardly have been otherwise, granted the composition of the council and the constitutional constraints - Cipriani's role as a legislator contributed significantly to the political awareness of the people.

Recognizing the limitations of the legislative approach, Cipriani and TWA attached much importance to developing close links with the British Labour Party. In 1925 Cipriani visited London and met with Labour Party officials. They greatly impressed him, and he was confident of the party's commitment to the cause of the colonial masses. Labour MPs promised to take up Trinidad issues in Parliament. From 1925 Cipriani considered himself a socialist in the British Labour tradition. TWA also formed links with similar organizations in the Caribbean, and in 1926 Cipriani and Howard Bishop attended an inter-West Indian conference of labour leaders, organized by the British Guiana Labour Union in Georgetown, and played a prominent part in the proceedings. Cipriani's faith in the Labour Party was deepened by his attendance in 1928 at the second British Labour Commonwealth Conference in London, and he tried to model the policy and organization of TWA on those of the Labour Party. His disillusionment - and that of TWA members - was correspondingly great when the Labour government, in power in 1929-31, failed to change colonial policy along the lines of Labour pledges and programmes. None of the benefits that Cipriani had anticipated from a Labour government materialized, and in 1931 the Labour Colonial Secretary explicitly rejected constitutional change for Trinidad on the grounds that the colony was not ready for further advance towards self-government. For TWA, and above all for Cipriani, this was a betrayal of faith, and he sadly told the council

'Those who have the best interests of the working-class at heart are bitterly disappointed at the attitude of the Labour Government towards the working classes in these colonies . . . whether it be Conservative, Liberal or Labour, the situation is exactly the same.' Yet Cipriani continued to cling to the party, perhaps because he recognized that the alternative strategy was the politics of the street, which he had always repudiated.

The Turbulent Thirties

By 1931-2 there were signs that Cipriani's ascendancy over the labour movement was weakening, and that TWA was a less effective and united organization than it had been in the 1920s. One crisis involved a 1931 Bill to make divorce legal. The TWA leadership had decided to remain neutral, and to allow the government and the Catholic Church to fight it out; but at the last moment Cipriani was persuaded by the church and the French Creoles to oppose the Bill. This split the TWA, alienating the intelligentsia and weakening public confidence in Cipriani, who had apparently capitulated to the reactionary Catholic element. It also alienated Teelucksingh and Roodal, who both voted for the Bill, and jeopardized Indian support for TWA. Howard Bishop criticized Cipriani on the issue in the *Labour Leader*, and it closed early in 1932, apparently as a result.

TWA was also divided over the Trade Union Ordinance of 1932. After many years of intermittent pressure from the Colonial Office to enact legislation making trade unions legal, the local government finally enacted a law that empowered the government to register (or refuse to register) trade unions, which would then be legal. But this law failed to grant them the legal protection they enjoyed in Britain; in particular, it did not legalize peaceful picketing nor protect unions from legal actions for damages arising out of strke action. Far from helping the growth of trade unionism in Trinidad, this Ordinance frustrated the development of organized labour until after the 1937 riots. TWA sought advice from the British Trades Union Congress (TUC) on whether to register under this Ordinance. After two years of consultation, Cipriani finally decided not to register as a union, and instead the Association was formally renamed the Trinidad Labour Party (TLP) in 1934 to indicate that it had become a political party instead of a 'workingmen's association'. This decision was opposed by several of Cipriani's colleagues, who felt that TWA should have registered and then agitated for the amendment of the law. Perhaps Cipriani believed that politics was more important than the development of trade unionism, or he viewed the emergence of new leaders and new labour unions as a threat to his leadership of the workers, or he simply had faith in the TUC's advice. In any case, there was increasing dissatisfaction within TWA/TLP over Cipriani's authoritarian leadership, exemplified by his handling of both the divorce issue and the Trade Union Ordinance. The authority of the Port of Spain leadership was being challenged by the branches, and younger leaders were resentful of Cipriani's intolerance of criticism from within the party.

But the most serious challenge to Cipriani and TWA/TLP was their failure to bring about practical improvements in the living and working conditions of the people, at a time of depression, unemployment and low wages. As economic conditions deteriorated, workers became increasingly disillusioned with Cipriani's leadership. The more desperate and militant among them turned to mass demonstrations and hunger marches, to Cipriani's dismay. Some of the urban unemployed demonstrated in Port of Spain in 1933, but by 1934 conditions were worst in the sugar districts. Managers had drastically reduced employment and extended tasks to maximize profits. Unemployment and low wages were aggravated by a severe drought in 1934, which delayed the planting of rice after the sugar crop, an occupation that had absorbed some of the retrenched sugar workers. Shopkeepers began to refuse to extend credit for 1934 because workers had been unable to clear their debts from the year before. For those labourers without rice lands or garden plots, the situation was desperate.

In July 1934 sugar workers staged mass demonstrations in Couva, Chaguanas, Tunapuna and San Fernando, and went on a hunger march from Caroni to Port of Spain. The unrest spread all over the sugar belt, involving some 15,000 plantation labourers, many of them women. Overseers, managers and policemen were attacked, company buildings set on fire, shops looted; it was the spontaneous violence of desperate people close to starvation. The disturbances were not organized, and no leaders were publicly identified. TWA played no role in the unrest. The workers refused to consult with Cipriani, and when he visited the sugar belt trying to get them to go back to work, they mostly ignored him. In fact, the unrest demonstrated the workers' growing impatience with Cipriani's tactics; it damaged him and TWA/TLP. The demonstrations were put down by the police without any loss of lives, though many were arrested and fined or imprisoned. Virtually no interest group in the colony showed any concern for the labourers' situation. The government-appointed Commission of Enquiry, which did not include any representatives of the Indian plantation workers, made no recommendations for increasing jobs or improving their living conditions. It was left to the governor to point out that callous retrenchment and overtasking by the sugar companies were the major causes of the riots, yet the only positive steps he could recommend were the distribution of the princely sum of £150 in relief for destitute workers and the irrigation of rice lands to enable them to plant rice. But the unrest was a watershed in Indian participation in labour movements in Trinidad, preparing the way for the 1937 riots, and it marked the beginning of radical labour politics in the second half of the 1930s.

The episode also served to highlight the whole question of wages. After a four-year delay, in 1935 the government introduced a Bill enabling the governor to fix a minimum wage rate in any occupation where wages were deemed unreasonably low. In 1936 a Wages Advisory Board was appointed to recommend suitable minimum wage rates. By using highly questionable calculations and cost of living indices, this Board reached the extraordinary conclusion that the cost of living for the average worker was lower in 1935 than in 1920, and that minimum wages should be lower than those suggested in 1920; it recommended 46 cents per day in the country and 69 cents in Port of Spain. Of course many agricultural workers earned far less than these wages, low though they were, yet the Board refused to recommend minimum daily rates for agricultural labourers on the grounds that agricultural wages depended on prices for export crops, which were beyond the control of the local employers. Cipriani agreed (reluctantly) to sign this dishonest and callous report, and his action further disillusioned the workers with his leadership. Even then, no minimum wage legislation followed, and the operation of the Ordinance was postponed indefinitely. The government's failure to enact minimum wage legislation seemed to demonstrate that it had no real interest in the workers' welfare, even in their survival.

Sugar workers resorted to the politics of the streets in 1934; the following year it was the turn of the oil workers. In March 1935 workers at Apex Oilfields went on strike. The Fyzabad branch of the TLP had sought Cipriani's support for a strike when Apex failed to redress workers' grievances, especially low wages, long hours, wage deductions for late-coming and poor conditions. Cipriani refused to sanction strike action, but the workers went ahead, downed tools, and organized a hunger march to Port of Spain, under the leadership of two members of the Fyzabad TLP executive, T.U. B. Butler and John Rojas. This strike saw the emergence of Butler as a working-class leader. Cipriani disavowed the strike and refused to negotiate with Apex on behalf of the strikers. Without effective organization, the strike petered out and the workers settled for a two per cent increase. But it was a challenge to Cipriani and TLP; Butler had openly attacked Cipriani as a fence-sitter who would not support the workers' demands. From then on Butler began to mobilize oil workers in the south as the unchallenged labour leader in the oilbelt.

Cipriani's working-class support was slipping away, but he consistently refused to sanction extra-constitutional politics or violence, preferring to lose members to other groups. In the 1930s, as economic conditions worsened, a number of new groups emerged which began to mobilize workers and others for political action. In 1934 the National Unemployed Movement (NUM) was formed in Port of Spain by Jim Headley, who had been active in trade unionism in the USA, Dudley Mahon and Elma Francois, a former TWA member. This group organized public meetings, demonstrations and hunger marches, and mobilized many of the urban unemployed. A more influential body emerged out of NUM at the end of 1934: the Negro Welfare, Cultural and Social Association (NWA). Its leaders included Elma Francois, Jim Barrat, Christina King, Clement Payne, Rupert Gittens and Bertie Perceval. Its base was Port of Spain, where it held public meetings and private discussions, established cells in factories and districts, put out pamphlets and tried to organize hunger marches. The NWA leadership was closely in touch with the international labour movement, and they tried to publicize international issues like the struggle against fascism in Europe. Their stand on the equality of the sexes was very advanced, and women filled top leadership roles: Francois was a founding member and a leading speaker.

The NWA leadership attacked Cipriani and the TLP for failing to support the workers' demands. Francois denounced Cipriani as 'Britain's best policeman in the colonies', and NWA attracted many ex-members of the Port of Spain branch of the TLP. It was socialist in ideology, and its working-class leadership was intelligent and capable. Gradually its activities were extended from Port of Spain to northern Trinidad generally. The year 1936 marked the high point in its work. It staged a massive demonstration on the Italian invasion of Ethiopia and held meetings all over northern Trinidad. The leaders, recognizing that Butler was the undisputed labour leader in the south, tried to link up with him, and during 1936 NWA co-operated with Butler and his south-based movement.

NWA was eventually eclipsed by Butler's successes in the south and by the emergence of an orthodox trade union movement after the 1937 riots. Its effectiveness was also reduced by constant police harassment. The NWA leadership faced frequent arrests and convictions on sedition charges, as well as a daily struggle to survive. Arthur Calder-Marshall, the British socialist writer who visted Trinidad after the riots, described a NWA meeting at which Elma Francois was trying to raise funds for an appeal on behalf of Jim Barrat, in jail on a sedition charge; she was virtually starving, having devoted herself almost exclusively to agitational work. In his autobiography Albert Gomes writes that he served his 'political apprenticeship' with NWA in the 1930s; though he noted that they were doctrinally dogmatic, holding aloof from other groups that were not ideologically 'pure', he was deeply impressed by their courage and self-sacrifice. The leaders were all 'miserably poor', Gomes writes, facing permanent insecurity and often actual hunger for their ideals. These dedicated working-class leaders of the 1930s have been largely forgotten, yet their role in politicizing the workers of northern Trinidad, especially in Port of Spain, was critically important, and NWA did much to prepare the way for the 1937 riots.

Another new group that challenged Cipriani and the TLP was the Trinidad Citizens League (TCL), formed late in 1935 by a few young leaders disillusioned with Cipriani, notably Butler and Rienzi. Rienzi had left the TLP in that year after Cipriani denounced him as a communist; Butler had been expelled when he defied Cipriani to lead the Apex march and strike. By 1936 the TCL, based in the south, had emerged as a serious rival to TLP. It addressed itself to problems of working-class existence, incompetent administration and corruption, and it petitioned for a commission to investigate the general state of Trinidad. Although the TCL did not remain in existence for long, it helped to politicize people in the south, and it forged an important alliance between Butler and Rienzi.

Cipriani's ascendancy over the labour movement was further challenged by the spread of black nationalism and race consciousness. Garvey's ideas had been influential ever since 1919, and contacts with black US organizations and literature were extended in the 1920s and 1930s. NWA had links with George Padmore, the Trinidadian Pan-Africanist who was based in London in the 1930s, and some middle-class blacks became interested in black nationalism. In 1937 a NWA leader, Rupert Gittens, founded the Club L'Ouverture to promote the interests of blacks in Trinidad and to disseminate knowledge about, and pride in, Africa. It was a kind of literary and debating society, whose members were mostly middle-class blacks, and it helped to educate urban blacks about race issues and to promote race pride.

But it was the Italian invasion of Ethiopia in 1935, and the failure of the western democracies to support the Ethiopians, that really stimulated black nationalism in Trinidad and the West Indies. Calder-Marshall said - with some exaggeration - that 'Britain's betrayal of Abyssinia was nearly as much to blame for the riots in Trinidad and Jamaica as the high cost of living', and there is no doubt that West Indian blacks reacted strongly to the invasion of the ancient African kingdom. In Trinidad, dockers refused to unload Italian ships, and a Port of Spain store, whose owner was agent for an Italian shipping line, was forced to take down its agency sign. NWA organized a large demonstration and the crowd handed in a petition to the Italian consul. Later an open-air service was held to commemorate Haile Selassie's coronation. A 'Friends of Ethiopia Committee' was set up in Port of Spain, with links with similar organizations elsewhere in the Caribbean. As late as 1938, Calder-Marshall reported that Trinidadians were still following events in Ethiopia with 'fervent interest'.

The Ethiopian invasion stimulated race pride among many middle - and working- class blacks, and there was a similar (if less marked) surge of Indian race consciousness in the 1930s. Visits by missionaries and cultural leaders from India, such as Mehta Jaimini, and the successes of the independence movement in India, stimulated a new interest in the motherland and in Indian culture, languages and religions. These developments made many articulate Indians begin to think in terms of separate Indian organizations. The development of race consciousness among sections of both major ethnic groups helped to make the 1930s a complex and turbulent era in the history of Trinidad.

These were the years, moreover, in which Trinidad experienced something of a cultural renaissance, a literary and artistic movement that tried to create an authentic West Indian cultural expression. This movement was led by a group of young Trinidadian writers and intellectuals whose work marks the real beginning of West Indian creative writing. The leaders were Albert Gomes, Alfred Mendes, R. A. C. de Boissière and C. L. R. James, and the group met regularly in the 1930s, especially at Mendes's house, to discuss art, literature and politics. In 1929-30 Mendes and James brought out the first of the 'little magazines', *Trinidad*. Only two issues appeared, containing stories, poems and articles. Then Gomes came back from the USA in 1930 and founded *The Beacon*, which he financed and edited; twenty-eight issues appeared between 1931 and 1933. This magazine became the focus, Gomes wrote, 'of a movement of enlightenment spearheaded by Trinidad's angry young men of the Thirties. It was the torpor, the smugness and the hypocrisy of the Trinidad of the period that provoked the response which produced both the magazine and the defiant bohemianism of the movement that was built around it.'

The magazine published excellent short stories, especially by Mendes and James, and its creative writing reflected concern for the poor and oppressed in West Indian society, a new social realism that helped to produce the 'yard literature' of early West Indian writers like James (*Minty Alley*, 1936), Mendes (*Pitch Lake*, 1934, and *Black Fauns*, 1935) and de Boissière (*Crown Jewels*, 1952, and *Rum and Coca Cola*, 1956). The *Beacon* writers were enthusiastic about the Russian Revolution and socialism; communist literature was illegally smuggled to Gomes by European seamen whose ships called at Port of Spain. This group explored the problem of West Indian identity, and its writers were among those Trinidadians trying to instil a sense of race pride among Afro-West Indians. *The Beacon* published frank articles on race relations, and its writers criticized blacks for their sense of inferiority and their rejection of Africa and African cultural forms. The magazine was also interested in India and Indo-Trinidadians, and for a time there was a regular 'India section' with news on India and the nationalist struggle. A number of Indo-Trinidadians wrote for *The Beacon*, influencing people of other races to have a more sympathetic and perceptive view of their situation.

The Beacon was stridently anti-Catholic, and the Catholic establishment mounted a campaign to get advertisers to boycott it. It was also anti-colonialist and anti-government, and Gomes was frequently visited by the police - looking for illegally smuggled literature or for material deemed to be seditious. The magazine always had a strong political interest, and it attacked in its editorials and articles poor social services and poverty, it protested the persecution of the Shouter or Spiritual Baptists+, it advocated unemployment insurance and better conditions for shop girls, and it condemned barrack housing. Indeed, *The Beacon* served as a launching pad for a number of future politicians: Gomes himself, Ralph Mentor, C. A. Thomasos and James. *The Beacon* was conceived, in part, as an organ of political education dedicated to the attack on Crown Colony government.

But *The Beacon* had a chequered career, with financial problems, police harassment and boycotts by advertisers, and it closed in 1933; James left Trinidad in 1932, Mendes in 1933. The group remained active, however; Jean de Boissière, a prominent member, brought out magazines like *Picong* and *Callaloo*, and in 1937 Gomes published an anthology of Trinidadian writing called *From Trinidad*, which featured a number of the *Beacon* group. Indeed, this group of writers and intellectuals helped to create a new social, cultural and literary consciousness in Trinidad and the West Indies, which laid the foundations for the flowering of Caribbean creative writing in the postwar period. Their work also contributed to the politicization of Trinidadians in the turbulent 1930s.

---

1. See Chapter 8 for TWA's early history.

2. Members of a group that combined Christian and African forms of worship and was characterized by noisy, emotional prayer meetings and services.

TEN

The Emergence of Modern Trinidad, 1936-50

Economic Crisis and the 1937 Riots

The fundamental cause of the widespread strikes and riots in June 1937 was the deteriorating economic condition of the majority of the workers in Trinidad and Tobago. By 1937 much evidence had accumulated of worsening living conditions among nearly all sectors of the labouring population. A number of medical reports testified to the widespread malnutrition and deficiency diseases among workers, especially in sugar. The infant death rate in 1934 was as high as 127.44 per thousand; in some rural districts up to 80 per cent of the population were infested with hookworm; malaria was prevalent everywhere. Bad health conditions were the result of endemic diseases, malnutrition, overcrowding, bad housing and improper sanitation. The poor relief statistics for 1934-6 revealed the extent of destitution, both in the towns and the countryside. Poverty was the cause of extensive malnutrition and debilitation, aided by poor dietary habits, themselves the result of low earnings. Both cocoa and sugar plantations laid off labour after 1929, so that unemployment and underemployment had increased considerably by 1937. The mass of evidence given to the 1937 Forster Commission and the 1938-9 Moyne Commission shows clearly that for the labouring population, mere subsistence was increasingly problematic.

Worker housing was deplorable. On the sugar estates the old barrack ranges were mostly in a state of extreme dilapidation, lacking even elementary sanitary provisions. The Forster Commission, which investigated the causes of the 1937 riots, concluded that the condition of most agricultural workers in Trinidad 'justifies the view that many managements display a surprising indifference to the welfare of their labour'. Housing on the oilfields was also very poor. Fyzabad, said the Forster Commission, was 'a village which has grown up on the edge of the oilfields without any apparent regulation or control or observance of elementary rules as to structure, space, or sanitation'. Similar examples of bad housing in the oilbelt were to be found at Frisco Village, Point Fortin and Cochrane Village, Guapo. Some of the worst examples of worker housing were in Port of Spain, where the Commission saw barracks 'indescribable in their lack of elementary needs of decency', with rooms renting at 12-15 shillings per month. A medical witness described John John as 'an entangled conglomeration of unsightly ruinous huts and privy cesspits placed helter-skelter on a sloping, steep and slippery hillside - a danger to health, life and limb, for the local residents and a menace to the surrounding city population'.

Grinding poverty was the normal experience of ordinary Tobagonians in the 1930s. The sister island continued to be neglected by the colonial authorities; efforts by the elected council members for Tobago since 1925 to gain some rudimentary amenities, such as electricity, adequate medical services or a deep-water harbour, met with failure. Many Tobagonians gave some wage labour to the cocoa and coconut estates, which had replaced the sugar plantations, and wages were abysmally low. In 1937-8 the average daily wage for picking cocoa was only 30 cents. For pruning 100 trees, a skilled job, the labourers received 60-70 cents. With labour costs as low as this, Tobago cocoa planters continued to enjoy reasonable profits even though prices were very poor. On the coconut estates, men were paid 60 cents for picking 1,000 nuts, while children received two cents for every 100 nuts gathered from the ground. The workers who split the nuts and extracted the copra were even worse paid than the pickers. Existence on these starvation wages was tolerable only because most Tobagonians had garden plots, and rural families were largely self-sufficient in food. But life for the Tobago peasants in the 1930s was terribly hard. The Tobago writer Eric Roach writes that subsistence farmers, cultivating a barren soil, 'wrestled with the earth with their bare hands for sustenance'. In bad seasons they boiled 'bush', drank 'hot water tea', and hunted for crabs, iguanas and manicous. Both hookworm and malaria were endemic in Tobago in the 1930s, and the entire island was served by one hospital in Scarborough, built in the mid-nineteenth century, and two district medical officers, whose treatment of poor black patients was usually perfunctory. Yet Tobagonians perhaps had fewer grievances than the workers in Trinidad: it was fairly easy to own land and thousands were in fact peasant proprietors, and there were no real slums, no barracks on the estates. Tobago was an island of peasants; semi-illiteracy, poverty and hard work had always been their fate, and they were perhaps less inclined to resent these conditions than the more sophisticated workers of the larger, more developed island.

It was the oil workers in particular who had special grievances. Oil was an expanding industry paying handsome returns to British investors. The two major oil companies in Trinidad declared dividends of 35 per cent and 25 per cent for 1935-6, and even the smaller companies were doing reasonably well. Their high profits were the result in part of very low taxes and royalties, but chiefly of low wage rates. In 1936 the average oil worker was earning less than in the 1920s, since the companies had reduced working hours to minimize costs. Reduced earnings coincided with consid-

Plate 7 Tubal Uriah 'Buzz' Butler, labour leader of the 1930s to 1950s

erable inflation between 1929 and 1937. The rising cost of living while wages were not adjusted, in an industry known to be prosperous, was the major grievance of the oil workers, who had no recognized machinery of collective bargaining to articulate their demands or discuss conditions. They resented discrimination against experienced black workers, and they were well aware of the high standard of living enjoyed by white managers and employees. Some of these were South Africans, employed especially by Trinidad Leaseholds Ltd, whose attitude to the black workers was particularly objectionable. Further, the workers suffered from chronic job insecurity: they were liable to instant dismissal without compensation, and the companies had various devices for victimizing and blackballing workers, so that a man dismissed by one company often found it difficult to find a job with any other. Workers were not compensated for less serious industrial accidents, they received little or no extra pay for overtime, Sunday or holiday work, and they were given neither pensions nor gratuities on retirement.

The oil workers, then, had particular grievances besides the universal problem of low earnings and high prices; and they were concentrated together in large numbers on the oilfields, a modern industrial proletariat of skilled workers who were easier to organize and mobilize than the agricultural labourers, whose conditions were certainly even worse. Between 1935 and 1937 they were mobilized by T. U. Butler, who had emerged as a labour leader after the 1935 Apex strike. Butler was a Grenadian who had come to Trinidad in 1921 to seek work in the oil industry, like so many of his compatriots; in 1929 he had been permanently lamed in an industrial accident that made him unfit for further employment in the industry. He became deeply involved in the Baptist Church, and founded his own Butlerite Moravian Baptist Church, which became an important centre of his activities in mobilizing workers for industrial and political action. It provided a base and a source of contact with oil workers. Butler's involvement in the Baptist Church influenced his political style, his Messianic oratory, his intense religious feeling and his use of biblical rhetoric. In 1936 Butler left the TLP to found his own party, but his influence in 1936-7 was personal rather than party-based.

Butler was a genuine and powerful working-class leader, but he was not an ideologue, nor a political radical. He was essentially concerned with the alleviation of working-class grievances. Like Cipriani, he was loyal to the British empire and had faith in British justice; he felt that he was defending the rights of British citizens in Trinidad who had been betrayed by the unBritish behaviour of local employers and officials. He was conducting, he said, 'a heroic struggle for British justice for British Blacks in a British country'. His fiery rhetoric and his close links with the people made him the unchallenged leader in the oil districts, where the Grenadian and 'small-island' immigrants were concentrated. In the first months of 1937, Butler criss-crossed the oilbelt, holding public meetings and mobilizing the workers, appealing both to race feeling and to their particular industrial grievances. His authority was limited to the south; in north Trinidad, especially Port of Spain, NWA tried to mobilize the workers and the unemployed. The NWA leaders linked up with Butler in 1936, but the partnership was uneasy; NWA was socialist and anti-colonial, while Butler believed in the essential goodness of the British government. Perhaps more important, Butler was always an individualist, a charismatic figure who repudiated organization and collective leadership, while NWA was committed to careful organization and a secular ideology. Nevertheless, the agitational work of NWA helped to ensure that people in north Trinidad would respond to the strike that the oil workers began in June 1937.

Butler turned to strike action only when he became convinced that further appeals to the oil companies and the government were useless, and he envisaged a peaceful sit-down strike; he cautioned against demonstrations, looting or violence. But the point was that a strike in the critical oil industry, however peaceful, could not be tolerated by the local government, which would not hesitate to use the forces at their disposal to crush it. Immediately after oil workers at Forest Reserve struck on 18 June, police reinforcements were sent to the oilbelt, and it was decided to arrest Butler on charges of inciting people to commit breaches of the peace.

The attempt to arrest Butler on 19 June triggered off widespread riots and strikes, first in Fyzabad, then rapidly escalating into an island-wide movement. Between 19 and 21 June, the rioting was confined to the south, with serious disturbances at Fyzabad, Point Fortin, San Fernando, Penal and St Madeleine. On 22 June disorder spread to Waterloo and Woodford Lodge estates, Port of Spain, Rio Claro (where five people were killed by the police) and Dinsley Village. In Tobago rumours abounded, and the resident white males were issued with arms; but there were no real incidents and no loss of life. In all, two policemen were killed (Corporal Charlie King and Sub-Inspector Bradburn, both at Fyzabad on 19 June) and nine policemen and Volunteers wounded, while twelve civilians were killed and fifty wounded by police action. The unrest cut across race lines, and affected every sector of the economy. The basic impulse was for better wages and working conditions, and the rioting expressed the pent-up grievances and resentments of workers whose economic situation had deteriorated over the preceding years and who had no legitimate channels for the peaceful resolution of industrial problems.

It was left to the various interest groups in the community, and the government, to respond to the workers' outburst of June-July 1937. The established labour leaders alienated themselves from the workers by condemning the strikers. Vivian Henry, secretary of the TLP, published an open letter repudiating 'mob rule' by 'irresponsible strikers' and urging a return to 'constitutional agitation'. On 25 June Cipriani returned from London (where he had been attending the Coronation of George VI) and denounced the strike, dissociating the TLP from the unrest, and advising workers to adopt only constitutional and legitimate methods. Giving evidence to the Forster Commission, Cipriani stated that the violence was caused by groups with 'Communistic tendencies'. Cipriani's innate conservatism, accentuated perhaps by his age (for he was 62 in 1937), had caused him to lose touch with the workers' changing needs and aspirations.

Predictably enough, the business community, and especially the oil industry, immediately began to pressure the government into crushing the strikers by an overwhelming show of force. Their view was that 'agitators' had irresponsibly stirred up trouble and endangered capital and property in the island. George Huggins, for instance, told the Colonial Office that capital might be withdrawn from Trinidad if 'life and property' were not protected by the stationing of British troops in the island, and similar views were expressed by a delegation from the West India Committee which met the Secretary of State early in July. In both Houses of Parliament questions were asked about the riots; in the Lords the Duke of Montrose, chairman of a Trinidad oil company, drew attention to the need to organize a defence force to protect the oilfields in any emergency. He stated that 'the trouble had nothing to do with wages and living costs, but was purely the result of communistic propaganda - the work of Communists who had been touring the islands stirring up racial conflict and urging the natives to grab all the wealth'. The chairman of Caroni Ltd went even further, insisting that the riots represented 'an attempt at revolution by a minority of extremists. There was no question of unemployment, underpay, or undernourishment.' For the business community in Trinidad, and particularly for the British capital interests involved, the issue was clear-cut: capital had been jeopardized by labour unrest and the strikes had to be crushed by full-scale repression.

At first, however, the local government was not prepared to recommend such a course. The governor, Sir Murchison Fletcher, was honest enough to recognize that economic hardship and low earnings were the real causes of the strikes: he blamed the oil companies for failing to pay better wages and for racial discrimination against black workers. On 9 July Fletcher and the acting Colonial Secretary, Howard Nankiwell, castigated the oil and sugar companies in famous speeches to the legislative council. Fletcher stressed the general poverty and low earnings of the workers, praised Butler as a sincere (if misguided) man whose pleas had been ignored, and advised the employers that they would 'find in tact and sympathy a shield far more sure than any forest of bayonets to be planted here'. Nankiwell was even more forceful. He stated unequivocally that 'industry had no right to pay dividends at all until it pays a fair wage to labour and gives the labourers decent conditions'. Both acknowledged that the government was partly to blame in failing to legislate for minimum wages and labour reform, and Fletcher felt that the riots were a 'salutary purge' that would lead to much-needed reforms. For once the two senior representatives of British colonialism in Trinidad took seriously their trusteeship role, and emerged as champions of the working class, refusing to throw their weight behind the capitalists who were calling for repression.

Fletcher's strategy was to bring the country gradually under control through the police and the Volunteers (aided by British marines who landed on 22 and 23 June), while negotiating separately with various sectors of the strikers, inducing as many as possible to go back to work. A mediation committee, with Nankiwell as chairman, was set up to receive representations from employers and workers in industries affected by the strikes and to make recommendations to the governor. A law was rushed through the council enacting an eight-hour day and a minimum wage for public works employees, while Fletcher personally negotiated with the dockers. By the start of July armed forces had secured the all-important oil installations and had 'cleaned up' centres of resistance like Fyzabad. Gradually workers returned, and by 6 July the *Trinidad Guardian* considered that the strikes were over. Negotiations began with the oil workers, who formed a union (on the advice of A. C. Rienzi, acting as Butler's representative while he was in hiding) and insisted that the mediation committee should negotiate only with the union executive. The committee under Nankiwell was prepared to accept the union as the legitimate bargaining agent, much to the dismay of the Petroleum Association, the employer group, which was anxious to prevent unionization. The oil companies pressured the Colonial Office, and their first victory was to get London to suspend the mediation committee (dominated by the liberal Nankiwell) pending the report of the Forster Commission which had been appointed to investigate the causes of the riots and to make recommendations.

For both Fletcher and Nankiwell had alienated the business community and the British capitalists, who felt that they had capitulated to the workers and had failed to suppress disorder. By October 1937 these interests were alarmed: workers were threatening renewed industrial action because the major employers in oil and sugar had refused to meet their demands, and because Butler had been put on trial for sedition when he voluntarily gave himself up. The principal organs of capital in Trinidad - the Petroleum Association, the Sugar Manufacturers Association and the Chamber of Commerce - demanded adequate defence against disorder and the suppression of 'agitators'. Under heavy pressure, Fletcher capitulated; he reversed his former policy, requested British troops (which he had always felt to be unnecessary), and criticized Nankiwell as biased towards labour and therefore useless as a mediator. Fletcher had abruptly switched from a policy of conciliation to a policy of repression. His turn-around convinced the Colonial Office that Fletcher was too unreliable and vacillating to continue in office. The Colonial Office's major concern was to safeguard the vital oil industry by swiftly restoring industrial peace and smooth labour relations, and the Secretary of State concluded that Fletcher was too indecisive, too unstable, to carry out this task effectively. He was recalled to London and forced to resign in December 1937; in May 1938 Nankiwell was transferred to another colony. For the British government, the priority was to normalize conditions in the oil industry as soon as possible - for Trinidad oil was vital to British security at a time of threatening international crisis - and Fletcher and Nankiwell were expendable.

The Forster Commission Report was published in February 1938, and it was welcomed by capitalist interests as a 'law and order' report. Although the Commission agreed with Fletcher that the unrest was the result of low wages and poor working conditions, it strongly criticized the government for failing to repress disorder at the outset. It recommended a labour department to conciliate and arbitrate industrial disputes, with discretionary powers to register unions; it should have the power to refuse registration to trade unions when 'the credentials of persons seeking to register a Union are unsatisfactory'. It further recommended that an industrial court should be set up, and that the workers' compensation law should be amended to include agricultural labourers. On more general issues, the Report made no recommendation about wages and only on housing did the Commission make any serious concession to labour; even here its recommendations hardly went beyond previous legislation empowering the government to order the demolition or repair of estate or oilfield housing.

But labour disturbances broke out elsewhere in the West Indies in 1937-8, and the British government became increasingly alarmed at the evidence of colonial instability at a time of threatening world war. The West India Royal Commission, headed by Lord Moyne, investigated conditions in the whole British Caribbean in 1938-9, and its major recommendations formed the basis of British policy towards the region in the post-1939 period. The Commission recommended a significant British effort in promoting 'development and welfare' by injecting considerable sums of money through a new organization in the West Indies, headed by a comptroller for development and welfare. In 1940 the Colonial Development and Welfare Act provided £5 million per annum for the whole British empire for a period of ten years; a second Act in 1945 extended the period to 1956 and provided for a total expenditure of £120 million. The Moyne Commission also recommended major programmes to improve health services, to eliminate slums and to build new low-income housing. In the economic field, Moyne recommended agricultural diversification and the rehabilitation of cocoa. Significantly, the Commission advised moderate constitutional change in the direction of self-government, and legislation to enable 'responsible' trade unions to function properly. There was nothing particularly new in the Moyne recommendations, but they formed the basis for British policy after 1939: social welfare, limited constitutional change, and encouragement of an orthodox trade union movement. After Fletcher's resignation, his successor, Sir Hubert Young, who came to Trinidad with the reputation of being a strong 'law and order' man who had suppressed disturbances in Africa, moved quickly to implement reforms. A Town Planning and Housing Commission was established to oversee slum clearance and rebuilding; plans were implemented to improve the health services, particularly with respect to the elimination of malaria and hookworm, and the improvement of infant and child health; and in 1939 a social welfare department was established in Trinidad to extend and reform the existing social services.

The Growth of Trade Unionism

Perhaps the most important result of the 1937 riots, however, was the establishment of an organized trade union movement on British lines, and this development had been recommended by both the Forster and the Moyne Commissions as the best guarantee of orderly labour relations in the future. The years between 1937 and 1950 saw the emergence of modern trade unionism in Trinidad and in the West Indies as a whole.

Immediately after the strikes of June 1937, workers recognized the need for labour organizations to represent their interests with employers and the government. In the critical years of 1937-9 it was Rienzi (see photo, p.230) who organized the oil and sugar workers into unions, with the help of a group of dedicated colleagues. Between July and September 1937 Rienzi held meetings with oil and sugar workers, and from these meetings emerged the decision to organize unions in both industries and to register them under the 1932 Ordinance so that workers would gain the right to carry out collective action. Rienzi felt that the organization of properly constituted unions would also strengthen the hands of a government which, under Fletcher and Nankiwell, was markedly sympathetic to the workers. The Oilfield Workers Trade Union (OWTU) and the All Trinidad Sugar Estates and Factory Workers Trade Union (ATSEFWU) were registered, respectively, in September and November 1937, and Rienzi was elected president-general of both. Rienzi and his colleagues - who included E.R.Blades, John Rojas, MacDonald Moses, and Ralph Mentor - were also influential in organizing the Federated Workers Trade Union (FWTU), registered in September 1937, which mobilized railway and construction workers. By the end of 1937, besides these three leading unions, three others had registered: the Seamen and Waterfront Workers Trade Union (SWWTU), the Amalgamated Building and Woodworkers Union, and the Public Works Workers Trade Union. Trade union organization was further encouraged by Sir Arthur Pugh, who represented the British labour movement on the Forster Commission; he addressed union meetings and opened branches while he was in Trinidad during the last months of 1937.

Both the Colonial Office and the local government accepted, after the riots, that proper trade unions could prevent further labour unrest and contribute to peaceful industrial relations. The encouragement of trade unionism by the government was recommended by three important commissions in 1938-9. The Forster Commission, as we noted, believed that the absence of organized means of collective bargaining was a major cause of the riots, and that a trade union movement, guided by the government and accepted by the employers, was the best way to secure industrial stability and 'the removal of extremist tendencies'. In order to 'guide' the fledgling unions, and to 'protect them from the errors of inexperience', a labour department should be established to carry out conciliation work and to oversee the union movement. These recommendations were echoed by the report (May 1939) of Major Orde-Browne, the new labour adviser to the Secretary of State who investigated labour conditions in the Caribbean in 1939. Finally, the Moyne Commission (which included two representatives of British Labour, Sir Walter Citrine of the Trades Union Congress, and Morgan Jones, a Labour MP) criticized West Indian governments for failing to enact and implement labour legislation, and advocated the immediate enactment of laws to give unions the legal status and privileges that British unions enjoyed. These recommendations reflect the new conviction in London that a trade union movement, properly 'guided', was the most promising post-riot strategy to restore order and guarantee the safety of British capital in the colonies.

But this conviction was certainly not shared by the employers, nor (at first) by the local government. Both the oil and sugar barons were dismayed by the organization of OWTU and ATSEFWTU; they felt that Rienzi was a dangerous communist, and they refused to co-operate with the unions he led, even though the mediation committee was prepared to deal with them; as we noted, they pressured London to suspend the committee. Intense hostility from the employers was the major obstacle faced by the early unions, as the Moyne Report noted, even though the employers always professed publicly to welcome 'responsible' trade unionism. The employers resisted the unions in every way possible, and the early organizers faced relentless victimization and persecution; as a result, noted the British writer Arthur Calder-Marshall who visited Trinidad in 1938, their attitude towards their union work was almost religious. In the early days, too, union organizers were constantly harassed by the police, who scrutinized their every move. It took a long time for the Trinidad officials to rid themselves of the notion that trade unionism was seditious. Labour demonstrations were often prohibited, and trade unionists were sometimes prevented from travelling to other colonies on union business. Calder-Marshall described how the OWTU leadership in 1938 was constantly shadowed by police spies. After a meeting with the industrial adviser and representatives of the oil companies, the OWTU executive went to a city restaurant for a meal and the establishment was 'swarming with policemen' within minutes. Calder-Marshall pointed out the absurdity of this kind of behaviour when it was official government policy to foster trade unionism.

Despite opposition from the employers and harassment by the police, the trade union movement was steadily consolidated between 1937 and 1939. In March 1938 A. V. Lindon, a British official in the Ministry of Labour, was appointed industrial adviser for Trinidad, following the recommendation of the Forster Commission. His mandate was to arbitrate disputes, to guide the developing trade unions, to encourage sound collective bargaining and to prepare for the establishment of a labour department. Lindon was successful in helping to foster trade unionism on British lines, and the Orde-Browne Report gives him credit for the fact that unionism in Trinidad was more advanced, in 1939, than in any other colony. But Calder-Marshall, who had won the confidence of the union leaders during his 1938 visit, reported that they were mistrustful of Lindon's motives. He advocated trade unionism based on the principle of co-operation between capital and labour, and the union leaders felt this amounted to 'the co-operation of Labour with Capital in the interests of Capital'. When Calder-Marshall interviewed Lindon, he represented himself as the instructor of ignorant union leaders who were too inexperienced to know what they wanted. Whatever the limitations of Lindon's approach, there is no doubt that he and his department were responsible for new labour legislation in 1938-9 and for some important industrial settlements between employers and unions.

In 1938 the Trade Disputes Ordinance was enacted. Rienzi, now an elected member of the legislative council as well as president of OWTU and ATSEFWTU, helped to draft the law, which provided machinery for settlement of disputes after collective bargaining had broken down. An arbitration tribunal could be set up by the governor, to comprise either one arbitrator appointed by him, or one arbitrator and an equal number of assessors representing the parties to the dispute. In 1938, seven disputes were referred to Lindon, and only one was arbitrated under the Ordinance. This was the dispute over wages and conditions in the oil industry which had been pending since July 1937. The tribunal chairman issued an award in January 1939: a retroactive wage increase of one cent per hour, overtime pay and one week's paid leave each year for workers with twelve months' service. This was a modest award, and a disappointment to the workers, but the OWTU leadership accepted it as a step forward in its battle for legitimacy as the sole bargaining agent for the oil industry. And at the end of 1938, SWWTU and the Shipping Association successfully reached agreement under Lindon's chairmanship; this was the first collective bargaining agreement to be completed in the British Caribbean.

In the sugar industry, by contrast, Rienzi and his colleagues were less successful in securing agreements. At the start of 1938 ATSEFWTU opened negotiations with the Sugar Manufacturers Association (SMA) for an all-round increase of ten cents per day for field workers, and increases for factory workers of 15-20 cents. The SMA was recalcitrant, Lindon intervened, and the dispute was about to go to arbitration under the Ordinance when the Usine St Madeleine branch of the union forced the situation by strike action, which the union executive was obliged to endorse. The strike collapsed in sixteen days, partly because of pressure from cane-farmers whose livelihood was threatened by a strike at the height of the crop season. Hundreds of workers were victimized, and the SMA refused to consider the union's renewed attempt to go to arbitration. It was a setback for ATSEFWTU, and it illustrates the point that in the circumstances of 1937-8, the acceptance of arbitrated awards was a sounder tactic than strike action, granted the superior power of the colonial government, and the pressures that employers could exert against strikers. It was not until 1945 that the SMA finally agreed to a negotiated settlement with ATSEFWTU.

The trade union movement expanded rapidly after 1938, under the leadership of Rienzi, Moses, Mentor, Rojas and Blades (OWTU); Quintin O'Connor, Rupert Gittens and Albert Gomes of the Trinidad & Tobago Union of Shop Assistants and Clerks; C.P. Alexander of SWWTU; and E.M. Mitchell, A.P. Roberts and S. Patrick of FWTU. By the end of 1938 ten unions had registered, more than in any other Caribbean colony. It was Rienzi, in particular, who saw the need for co-ordinating the union movement, especially since there seemed to be a dichotomy between the south-based unions that he led and the unions based in Port of Spain. He established the Committee of Industrial Organization as a co-ordinating committee, and he helped Rojas to organize the Transport and General Workers Union, which they envisaged as an umbrella union that would bridge the north-south divide. In 1939 a Trade Union Congress was established with Rienzi as its first president. In 1942, the government belatedly amended the 1932 Trade Union law and implemented Orde-Browne's recommendation that peaceful picketing be legalized and that unions be granted immunity from actions for damages arising out of strikes.

In these years, the British labour movement played a key role in guiding the leadership of the Trinidad trade unions. Both the Colonial Office and the British TUC actively encouraged the Trinidad unionists to model their unions on 'sound', constitutional, British lines. Their advice was to avoid politics or extremism and to work closely with the industrial adviser and the local government. Citrine was especially influential. When he was in Trinidad with the Moyne Commission he was actively engaged in advising the unions and in recommending the formation of a Trade Union Congress. Largely through him, the British TUC mounted a comprehensive programme of assistance to the West Indian labour movement. Most of the leaders enthusiastically co-operated with the British. Albert Gomes, an important figure in the Port of Spain-based unions at this time, especially the FWTU, writes that 'the advice and guidance which the British TUC provided at this critical stage may well be historically an instance of colonial paternalism at its best'. Gomes considered that the TUC's advice helped to prevent or modify inter-union strife and personal rivalries, and he and O'Connor cooperated closely with Lindon; they found that the best method of dealing with recalcitrant employers in the early days was through the Labour Department, though it was often hard to restrain workers from strike action. The results, Gomes writes, justified their policy, for they built up FWTU into a large, viable union. By 1940 most of Trinidad's union leaders were committed to British union goals and methods. The 'responsible' type of union leadership that the Colonial Office and the British labour movement favoured had developed, and the trade union movement was consolidated and institutionalized.

The establishment of US bases in Trinidad during the Second World War (1939-45) influenced union development. Thousands were employed at the bases, and they experienced new US personnel practices that treated workers like adult human beings. In general, the 'American occupation' influenced the aspirations of Trinidadian workers for more dignified treatment and better working conditions. On the other hand, the government used the war as an excuse to repress political and union activities. Unions were harassed, union meetings were spied on and the government tried to prevent outdoor union meetings, with the co-operation of Cipriani as mayor of Port of Spain. Unions were pressured into agreeing not to strike for the duration of the war. Gomes and O'Connor were among the leaders who opposed the government's efforts to crack down on union activities, through *The People*, which Gomes edited during part of the war, and through the city council, public meetings and the FWTU, which they led. The governor wanted to detain Gomes and O'Connor under the emergency wartime regulations, but he was advised (writes Gomes) not to give them the honour of martyrdom. But two Irish women who had become active in trade unionism in Trinidad were detained, and one of them, Kay Donellan, who had edited the OWTU newspaper, hanged herself while in jail. And Butler was detained throughout the war; his activities in the oilbelt between May and November 1939 were judged to be dangerous to the security of the oil industry, which was vital to Britain's war effort.

The end of the war in 1945 was the signal for new developments in the labour movement.The no-strike agreement came to an end, and Butler was released in 1945. Many thousands of workers were displaced by the completion of the bases after 1944, and these workers had enjoyed relatively decent wages and modern personnel practices. Further, the end of the war was a time of rapid inflation, and by December 1946 the cost of living index was 214, as compared with 1935 as the base year (100). Workers were restless and dissatisfied, and they welcomed Butler on his release as a hero. Butler's defeat in the 1946 elections - he rashly opposed Gomes for a Port of Spain seat, in a part of the country where he had little support - made him available for union agitation while increasing the frustrations of his followers. Butler's issues were the cost of living, unemployment, racial discrimination in industry, neglect by the government and the apparent inactivity of the recognized trade unions. He launched his British Empire Workers Peasants and Ratepayers Union and campaigned against OWTU in the oilbelt. He succeeded in winning a large number of oil and asphalt workers away from OWTU, and also made some progress with sugar workers.

Employers in oil and sugar refused to recognize Butler's union, or agree to a poll of the oil workers, and the government supported their stand. Butler turned to direct action and called on oil workers to strike in December 1946; OWTU countermanded his instructions. A significant number of oil workers responded to the strike call at first, but within a few days the great majority of the strikers had returned to work. Naturally this increased the Butlerites' sense of frustration, tensions rose, and two oil-wells were set on fire. The government introduced an Emergency Powers Ordinance to control the movement of people in the oilbelt, and Butler and five of his colleagues were ordered to leave the county of St Patrick, the main oil district. Meanwhile unrest spread to Port of Spain, where workers went on strike, and rioting took place in the city when hundreds of Butler's followers staged a protest march to the Red House (January 1947). Later in 1947 sugar workers went on strike for higher wages; this was not sponsored by ATSEFWTU but by Ranjit Kumar, an elected member of the council who was allied to Butler's movement.

The years 1946-7, therefore, witnessed considerable labour unrest, caused by rising prices, unemployment and low wages, as well as inter-union conflict accentuated by Butler's campaign against the recognized trade unions. The government, along with the recognized unions, regarded Butler as a threat to orderly trade unionism, and it invited a British trade unionist, F. W. Dalley, to investigate and report on the state of trade unionism in the island. Dalley's 1947 Report was very hostile to Butler, whom he described as 'a curious phenomenon whose egocentricity and biblical references made him a 17th century man instead of a modern union leader'. Dalley urged Trinidad unionists to distance themselves from Butler: 'Butlerism and responsible trade unionism are incompatible.' The Report was endorsed by the Trinidad TUC, and this widened the rift between Butler and the orthodox trade unions. Nevertheless, by the late 1940s trade unionism on modern lines was well established in Trinidad, and the labour movement would play an important role in the politics of the postwar period.

Trinidad and the Second World War

The Second World War had a considerable impact on the socioeconomic development of Trinidad, and the island played a significant role in the Allied war effort. In 1940, British Prime Minister Winston Churchill agreed to lease areas in the West Indies as naval bases to the USA in exchange for fifty old US destroyers, and Trinidad was chosen for major naval and air bases. Governor Sir Hubert Young conducted negotiations with the US authorities in 1940. They insisted on two large, separate areas: the North West Peninsula, including the Five Islands, for a naval base, and the Valencia-Sangre Grande area (Wallerfield) for a military and air base. It was clear to Young that the Americans had already decided on these two areas and were not prepared to consider his alternative proposal of a single large base in the Caroni swamp, which he envisaged could be drained quite easily. Young was acutely aware that a base on the North West Peninsula would have been greatly resented by the local population, both the residents in the area and the far larger numbers who for decades had been accustomed to spend holidays there. He warned that serious friction with the local population might result from accepting the US proposals, but Young was overruled, and he was eased out of the governorship. He was replaced by a more flexible diplomat, Sir Bede Clifford, who was given the task of establishing smooth relations between the British and US authorities on Trinidad during the war.

The Bases Agreement, establishing large US leased areas at Chaguaramas and Wallerfield, was signed in 1941, and all the residents on the North West Peninsula were compulsorily bought out. Trinidad played an important role in the war: it was the convoy assembly point for the dispatch of tankers from the Caribbean oil ports across the Atlantic to North Africa and Europe. The Gulf of Paria was used by US carriers and airplanes for their final exercises before going to the Pacific battleground via the Panama Canal, and planes for the Eighth Army in North Africa were ferried through Trinidad. Vessels and civilian planes from South America had to stop at Trinidad for clearance to proceed to North American and European destinations; this involved a large censorship department serving as cover for British and US agents searching for Latin Americans engaged in smuggling and espionage to Germany through Spain and Portugal, both neutral countries. Because Trinidad was the assembly point for the vital oil tankers, the waters around the island were infested with German submarines and they sometimes surfaced and shelled reconnaissance planes based on the island; occasionally they landed at lonely beaches in the eastern Caribbean to exercise their crews, and the US Air Force stationed some 'blimps' (airships) at Trinidad for inspection and reconnaissance.

Despite these exciting wartime events, the majority of Trinidadians were too preoccupied with survival to feel deeply involved in Britain's struggle against Germany. Albert Gomes reports that cinema audiences cheered film appearances by Hitler, and people felt secretly pleased when Britain suffered reversals in the early years of the war. Of course Trinidad was not directly endangered in the way that Britain was, and people were disillusioned by the government's repression of political and union activity under the pretext of the war. On the other hand, the construction of the US bases had a tremendous socio-economic impact. Tens of thousands were employed, at wages higher than any known before in Trinidad. Living costs rose sharply, thousands abandoned sugar, cocoa and the established industries, and a great deal of money circulated, creating a boom-time atmosphere in which prostitution and organized vice flourished under people like Boysie Singh, a well-known mobster in the 1940s, and gang conflict and violence increased. Further, the 'American occupation' demolished the myth of white superiority; Trinidadians saw white Americans perform hard manual labour, and laughed at the antics of drunken 'bad behaviour' sailors. The automatic deference to a white face became a thing of the past; as one writer put it, 'the humility of a subject people disappeared'. On the other hand, Trinidadians were impressed by the efficiency of the high-level technology that the Americans brought with them. The American Navy Construction Brigade (Sea Bees) undertook major public works in Trinidad, including the north coast road to Maracas Bay, which Clifford got them to construct as 'compensation' for the loss of the North West Peninsula. The Americans were admired for their competence, their modern personnel practices and their aura of easy money, but their racial attitudes were cruder and more obvious than the subtler racism of the British. These mixed influences generated by the US presence in the island after 1940 helped to prepare Trinidadians for the new era of mass electoral politics after the war.

Constitutional Change and Electoral Politics

One of the major recommendations of the Moyne Commission had been gradual constitutional advance for the West Indies. The Commission envisaged a fairly slow process in which the official element in the council would be reduced while the number of electives was increased, and the franchise extended to greater numbers. These were the lines along which constitutional change proceeded in the 1940s. In 1941 the first two recommendations were implemented: nine officials were withdrawn from the council and the number of electives was raised from seven to nine. This meant that the council now consisted of the governor, three ex officio members, six nominated Unofficials and nine electives. The governor's casting vote gave the non-elected element a majority of one; and since the governor had lost his official majority, he was given the 'power of certification': a reserve power enabling him to give the force of law to any measure rejected by the council which in, his view, was necessary for good government. In the executive council, which advised the governor on policy, the number of elected members was increased to two in 1941 and four in 1944, while the number of nominated Unofficials was reduced from three in 1941 to one in 1944. In the latter year the executive council consisted of the governor, three ex officio members, one nominated Unofficial and four elected members of the legislature. But the ultimate responsibility for government still rested with the governor, who was not obliged to take the advice of the executive council. It was a difficult, transitional stage in Trinidad's constitutional development towards fully responsible government.

The Moyne Commission had advised that the all-important question of widening the franchise should be entrusted to a local committee, and in 1941 the franchise committee was appointed. This body, consisting of thirty-three local notables including three representatives of the unions - Rienzi, Gomes and Mentor - became the centre of political activity until it reported in 1944. A number of groups agitated for universal suffrage and fully responsible government: the Port of Spain city council under the left-wing mayor Tito Achong; the People's Party of Trinidad and Tobago; the TUC; the Trinidad and Tobago Socialist Party; and others. But the committee was dominated by a strong conservative wing, headed by the chairman, Sir Lennox O'Reilly. The critical motion recommending universal suffrage for all adults over 21 was carried by a bare majority of one, and the sixteen who had voted against the motion, including O'Reilly, submitted a 'rider' advocating property and income qualifications for voting. Neither the governor nor the Secretary of State was prepared to override the majority vote, however, and so the recommendation for universal adult suffrage was accepted. Candidates for election had to be men or women literate in English with an income of not less than $960 per annum or property worth at least $5,000. The three union members protested against these property and income qualifications for membership of the council, but London accepted them.

The most intense debate centred on the majority's recommendation that voters should be able to understand spoken English to qualify to vote. Rienzi interpreted this (no doubt correctly) as a deliberate effort to disenfranchise older Indians, most of whom had been denied the opportunity of obtaining formal education in the English language. Rienzi's view was accepted by the Secretary of State, who instructed the governor to use his reserve power, if necessary, to force through legislation granting universal suffrage without the language test, contrary to the recommendation of the committee. The Order in Council that incorporated the new constitutional changes (1945) extended the vote to all adults over 21 without any language qualification. Trinidad had entered the era of mass electoral politics, and 46 per cent of the total population registered as voters for the 1946 elections, the first to be held under universal adult suffrage.

Elections were postponed during the war, but the anticipated introduction of universal suffrage after the war's end set the stage for new political groups that were mostly linked to trade unions or generally sympathetic to the Labour cause. In 1941 Rienzi and OWTU launched the Socialist Party of Trinidad and Tobago (SPTT), which, Rienzi hoped, would link up northern and southern unions and would campaign for 'immediate self-government with adult franchise'. Although this party failed to integrate the northern unions into an island-wide political organization, its candidate won the Victoria seat in the legislature in 1941. A new south-based party was the West Indian National Party (WINP), formed late in 1942 by David Pitt and Roy Joseph, although it did not become really active until 1944. WINP gained important adherents in Gomes and O'Connor, both of FWTU. Its programme was radical: self-government for a federated West Indies, immediate responsible government for Trinidad, and eventual state ownership of the oil and asphalt industries. The WINP leaders seemed uneasy at the strength of Rienzi and OWTU in the south, and they agitated for Butler's release, an event that could only have weakened Rienzi's power base in the south and embarrassed the OWTU executive. In fact, Rienzi's ascendancy over labour politics in Trinidad, which had been so notable in 1937-42, began to weaken in 1943. In that year he accepted a seat in the executive council, and this decision was unpopular with some of his colleagues and rivals. In November 1943 Rienzi's nominees for the San Fernando borough council were defeated, and the WINP leadership was hostile to Rienzi and OWTU; so were NWA (which still survived) and the Butlerites. Rienzi recognized that the political tide was turning against him, and he had been disturbed by the apparent racism of the franchise committee majority in recommending a language qualification that would have affected Indians in particular. Late in 1943 Rienzi decided to opt out of politics, resigning his trade union offices and his seats in the executive and legislative councils. When he accepted a government post early in 1944, many union leaders and rank and file felt betrayed and abandoned; yet we can agree with a recent historian who concludes that, by 1944, Rienzi 'had safely delivered the trade union movement through the crisis of its birth'.

As the end of the war approached, political organization and electioneering stepped up. The old TLP was still alive. Cipriani died in 1945, and Gerald Wight took over its leadership. But TLP was a spent force: it contested a few seats in 1946 and failed to win even one, and a number of TLP leaders including Wight left to form the business-oriented Progressive Democratic Party (1945), which contested the 1946 elections with equal lack of success. The SPTT was south-based and sponsored by OWTU and TUC. After Rienzi's retirement it was led by Rojas, Mentor and MacDonald Moses, all members of the OWTU executive. WINP was closely linked to FWTU, and Gomes and O'Connor were on its executive, although its leader was the south-based doctor, David Pitt. Another important group was Butler's new party, the British Empire Workers and Citizens Home Rule Party (BEW&CHRP), which grouped together his supporters in a loose organization. Early in 1946, just before the elections, the leftist lawyer Jack Kelshall tried to amalgamate a number of Labour-oriented groups into the United Front (UF). Eight out of nine seats were won by party candidates, indicating that the day of the independents was passing.

Perhaps the most striking feature of the 1946 elections was the fragmentation of the Labour vote. Universal suffrage meant that workers would form the great majority of the electorate, yet a number of unions or Labour-based parties competed for their votes. Nearly all the contending groups presented a vaguely socialist programme, especially the UF and SPTT, but the Labour vote was hopelessly divided and no single group emerged a clear winner. It is certainly significant that so many of the successful candidates were active trade unionists or Labour sympathizers: C. C. Abidh (SPTT), Gomes (UF), Roy Joseph (UF), Victor Bryan (SPTT), Patrick Soloman (UF), Timothy Roodal (BEW&CHRP) were all elected. But the leaders of the three most successful parties, Kelshall of UF, Butler of BEW&CHRP and Rojas of SPTT, were all defeated by rival Labour candidates. The UF won three seats, the Butler party three and the SPTT secured two; one independent, Ranjit Kumar, was elected. The Tobago seat was won by A.P.T. James, at this time allied with the Butler party. James, a self-made man whose colourful personality and close links with the people made him immensely popular in Tobago - which became, politically, almost his personal fiefdom - had worked as a stevedore at the Pitch Lake and had then set up as a contractor. He became involved in trade unionism and then entered politics, belonging to a number of parties and groups during his political career. Essentially non-ideological, his overriding commitment was to the development of his native island.

It was a confusing election, reflecting the undeveloped state of party politics in Trinidad, the importance of personality and leadership struggles, and the divisions in the society. The fragmentation of the Labour movement that was so marked a feature of this election- the first to be held with universal suffrage - meant that middle-class politics would dominate the scene in the years after 1946.

The 1946 constitution did not satisfy the progressive, nationalist politicians, and agitation began almost immediately for further change: 'reform became outdated from the moment it was given'. The nine elected members could not act as a unified group. For a start, four of them (Gomes, Joseph, Abidh and Roodal) were appointed to the executive council, which meant that they were in a sense part of the government and usually supported the governor and the ex officio and Unofficial nominated members, leaving the five remaining electives to form a kind of opposition bloc. Then the legislative council still had a non-elected majority, so even if a single party had won all nine seats, it still would not have controlled the council. These constitutional limitations, which were justified by Britain on the grounds of the inexperience of the Trinidad electorate and the new elected members, hindered party organization and political development, and it was generally recognized that adult suffrage would have to be followed by further changes. In response to a motion by Roy Joseph, a constitutional reform committee was set up early in 1947 to recommend changes. It consisted of elected and nominated legislators and local notables, with O'Reilly (again) as.chairman. It was heavily weighted in favour of conservatives. According to Patrick Soloman, a progressive intellectual and politician, sixteen out of twenty-five were clearly supporters of the status quo, while the remaining nine included some who only paid lip-service to self-government, and he included Gomes and O'Connor in this group because they signed the Majority Report (1948) which did not recommend responsible government. Gomes had reversed his stand: in 1946 he had called for responsible government, by 1948 (now a member of the executive council) he claimed that to abandon the nominated system would be disastrous for progress and stable government. Soloman himself, A.P.T. James and Ralph Mentor all resigned before the committee had finished its work because they saw they could not secure a majority in favour of responsible government.

The Majority Report recommended a legislative council presided over by a Speaker with neither an original nor a casting vote, and consisting of three ex officio members, five nominated Unofficials and eighteen elected members. At last, the elected members would have a clear majority in the legislature. As for the executive council, the Report recommended that it should consist of three ex officio members, three nominated Unofficials and six electives: an equal balance between nominated and elected elements. The Secretary of State rejected this suggestion, which was clearly too cautious, and sanctioned an executive council with an elected majority (three ex officio, one nominated, five elected). The five elected members would be elected by the whole legislative council and could be removed by a two-thirds majority of the legislative council. Further, the five elected members of the executive council could be charged by the governor with the administration of a department or portfolio. The executive council was not a Cabinet, but it was partly responsible to the legislative council, and it had an elective majority; if the five electives voted togther they could control policy, subject to the governor's reserve powers, and the use of these powers was not envisaged as a likely event. In effect the Majority Report recommended a transitional, quasi-ministerial constitution that gave elected members, for the first time, a clear majority in both councils. The Colonial Office accepted the Report, and a new constitution based on it became law in April 1950.

Inevitably, the 1950 constitution was strongly attacked by the radical and nationalist groups. Soloman submitted an important Minority Report in which he attacked the committee as heavily over-representative of the conservative element and called for a wholly elected single-chamber legislature, and an executive council chosen by the legislature from its members with full ministerial responsibility, with the majority party in the legislature providing a Prime Minister and a Cabinet (or executive council). In other words, he recommended fully responsible government and the abolition of the nomination system. The Labour movement, on the whole, attacked the 1950 constitution; Rojas, then president of the TUC, called it a 'colossal fraud', but the unions decided against calling a general strike in protest. The leading architect and defender of the constitution was Gomes. He recognized that it was a 'tricky transitional constitution', but he did not support unequivocal self-government for Trinidad alone partly because of his commitment to the goal of a federated West Indies, partly because his early radicalism had faded with the decision to enter the executive council in 1946. He knew it was a dangerous decision, for a seat in the executive council identified the elected member with the government while he had little real power to influence policy, but Gomes felt that he could not evade an opportunity to learn the processes of government and to face the realities of the West Indian situation. Between 1946 and 1956 Gomes was almost certainly the single most influential politician in Trinidad.

Just as happened in 1946, politicians and organizations geared up for the 1950 elections; now eighteen seats were at stake. As before, several Labour-oriented groups competed for the electorate. After the collapse of WINP and the UF, shortly after the 1946 elections, Soloman had founded the Caribbean Socialist Party (CSP), a loose collection of individuals rather than an effective party. The old TLP, somewhat revitalized by Raymond Hamel-Smith, contested the election, but the new leadership failed completely to recreate the party as a vibrant electoral organization. A third Labour-oriented group was the TUC, which fought the election. Efforts to fuse the TLP, CSP and TUC into a united coalition in order to avoid the fragmentation of the labour vote failed; it was 1946 all over again.

Meanwhile, Butler's party had strengthened itself by forging an alliance with a number of Indian politicians, like Mitra and Ashford Sinanan and Ranjit Kumar. The Sinanan brothers had been associated with Butler since 1937, and in the 1946-7 strikes Mitra had served as legal counsel for several arrested Butlerites. In fact, while opportunism played a part in this alliance, the Butler movement was more successful than any other political organization in this period in achieving effective co-operation between blacks and Indians. Finally, the Political Progress Group (PPG) led by Gomes was middle-class and business-oriented; its backers were mostly white businessmen and planters.

The 1950 elections again demonstrated the fragmentation of Trinidad politics. No united progressive coalition emerged; 141 candidates, ninety independents and fifty-one with some kind of party affiliation, vied for eighteen seats. The Butler party, the only one to contest all eighteen seats, won six. The successful candidates included Butler himself and four Indian politicians, and the party gained two more supporters when James, again the successful Tobago candidate, and another Indian contestant announced that they would support Butler in the legislative council. The CSP, TLP and PPG each won two seats, while six independents were returned.

Butler's party, then, was the largest single group in the legislature after the 1950 elections, but it comprised only eight out of a total of twenty-six (eighteen elected, three ex officio, five nominated Unofficials). This enabled Governor Sir Hubert Rance to manoeuvre among the members of the legislature to ensure that no member of the Butler party would be elected to the executive council. No doubt the ex officio members and the nominated Unofficials, representing a conservative element, joined with elected members of moderate views to choose executive council members whom they regarded as 'safe' and acceptable both to the governor and to the Colonial Office. Butler was felt to be too unpredictable, too crude, too unsophisticated to hold a ministerial position, and the Indian politicians who were his colleagues were generally mistrusted by the conservative element. The result was that not a single member of the Butler party was chosen to sit on the executive council. Instead, the five elected members comprised three independents, one member of the CSP and one member of the PPG, and these members were assigned portfolios as 'ministers' responsible for their departments. A clever piece of constitutional manoeuvring had allowed the governor and the local conservative elements to keep the Butler party out of the executive council between 1950 and 1956, and these years would see the eclipse of Butler and his movement. As Eric Williams writes, Butler failed 'in the sense of mobilizing the mass movement that he had helped to develop and guiding it along the inevitable organizational channels for the capture of political power'.

ELEVEN

Oil and the Twentieth-Century Economy, 1900-62

The History of Oil Production in Trinidad

In the nineteenth century Trinidad's economy was overwhelmingly agricultural, with the major export crops of sugar and cocoa accounting for the bulk of the colony's revenues and employing most of its labour force. But in the present century, oil has increasingly dominated the economy. More than any other factor, it is the development of an oil industry that made twentieth-century Trinidad relatively prosperous.

The existence of oil in Trinidad had long been known or suspected by geologists and scientists, but the oil-bearing districts in the southern part of the island were virtually unopened before 1900, still mostly covered with thick tropical forest, inhospitable and fever-ridden; and the oil industry was in its infancy before the development of the internal combustion engine in the 1890s. The first oil-well in Trinidad - perhaps the first successful oil-well in the world - was drilled by the Merrimac Oil Company of the USA at La Brea in 1857. Oil was struck at a depth of 280 feet, but difficulties in getting capital, as well as the limited demand for oil in the 1850s, brought the venture to an end with the liquidation of the company around 1859. In the following decade Walter Darwent floated the Paria Oil Company in 1865, and drilled wells at Aripero and San Fernando in 1866-7. At least three struck oil, and by 1867 production was about 60 gallons a week. Another company, the Trinidad Petroleum Company, drilled at La Brea in 1867 and struck oil at 250 feet. By 1868 a few wells were in operation around the Pitch Lake, and crude oil had been shipped to the USA and Britain. But a combination of primitive equipment, shortages of capital, heavy soils and transport difficulties forced Darwent to suspend his activities in 1868; he died at La Brea in that year, 'the first martyr to the oil industry in Trinidad', and his death marked the end of the early explorations. Drilling did not resume until the opening years of the twentieth century.

It was the development of the internal combustion engine and the car in the 1890s and 1900s that gave a decisive impetus to the oil industry worldwide. In Trinidad, the true pioneer of oil began his activities in these decades. Randolph Rust was an Englishman who arrived in Trinidad in 1881 as a young man and lived in the island for the rest of his life. Rust acquired an estate at Guayaguare in 1883; this area was virgin forest in the late nineteenth century. Teaming up with Edward Lee Lum, a Trinidadian-Chinese businessman who also owned land in the district, Rust sought to interest local entrepreneurs in floating a company for drilling in the Guayaguare area. When he failed to get support from local capitalists, partly because of the cocoa boom, he sought and obtained Canadian capital, and the Oil Exploration Syndicate of Canada was established. Rust was given a 50-square mile lease in the area, and the first well was drilled in May 1902; oil was struck at between 40 and 1,015 feet, and chemical analysis revealed it to be of excellent quality. Eight more wells were drilled between 1902 and 1907; most yielded oil, and Well No.3 was the first to be drilled by a rotary drilling rig. In these pioneer days, the major problems encountered by Rust and his colleagues were shortage of capital, appalling transport difficulties in an area still largely covered by tropical forest, the lack of trained staff and dangerous health conditions: malaria and yellow fever were both endemic. Rust was a tireless publicist for the Trinidad oil industry in these years. He persuaded the governor to visit the Guayaguare works less than a month after the first strike, and he lobbied both in Trinidad and in London for support from British entrepreneurs and from the government, which, he believed, would have to provide the necessary infra-

Plate 8 The Pitch Lake

structure, such as roads, railways and port facilities to serve the oil districts.

After 1904 the British government began to take an interest in developing the Trinidad oil industry because of plans to convert the navy to oil-powered ships. A British engineer, A. Beeby-Thompson, was sent to Trinidad in 1905 to prospect for a British company around Guapo, and between 1907 and 1909 he drilled several successful wells in the Guapo-Point Fortin area. His successes led to a conference in 1909 at Downing Street, attended by Beeby-Thompson, the Governor of Trinidad, and representatives of the Admiralty and the Colonial Office. As a result, British capital was invested in increasing amounts after 1909, and a British company, Trinidad Oilfields Ltd, was established in 1910. By 1911-13 the La Brea-Guapo-Point Fortin area was a modest but growing exporter and producer of oil: a small refinery and wooden pier had been built at Point Fortin, and in 1911 a second refinery at Brighton began operations. By then southern Trinidad was becoming a port of call for ships needing fuel, for these were the years when most ships, including the British navy in 1910, were converting from coal to oil. The industry moved inland to Palo Seco, Roussilac, Siparia, Erin and Tabaquite between 1911 and 1919, as areas farther removed from the sea were opened up. Six wells were drilled at Barrackpore in 1913-14 and twelve were opened at Tabaquite during the same years.

In 1913 two major companies entered the oil industry: United British Oilfields of Trinidad (UBOT), a subsidiary of Shell, and Trinidad Leaseholds Ltd (TLL), which took over six smaller companies. UBOT was based at Point Fortin, and it was from its small refinery here that a tanker took a first shipment of 6,000 tons in 1914 to the British navy. TLL began drilling at Forest Reserve in 1913, struck oil the next year, and by 1914 this company had a refinery at Pointe-à-Pierre, with a connecting pipeline from Forest Reserve. These two companies were to dominate the industry, but several others flourished, and by 1919 there were five refineries, and production had reached 1.9 million barrels annually; about 66 per cent of crude production was being locally refined. In fact, the oil industry was well established in Trinidad by the end of the First World War.

The first three decades of the twentieth century belonged to the hardy pioneers of the oil industry. Technology and equipment were primitive by later standards, and blow-outs, gushers and even oilfield fires were frequent occurrences. Until the late 1920s spectacular gushers were common. Accidents were frequent: the log for Rust's Well No. 3 at Guayaguare reads 'March 23, 1903: work stopped. Boiler exploded'. Fires were a constant danger. In 1929 a fire at a runaway well at Dome Field near Fyzabad killed several people including the Trinidadian in charge of the well and

Plate 9 Preparing clearance for staff camp and further drilling, mid 1914

the Indian family who owned the land. Labourers were usually bare-footed, there were no helmets, and in general safety was given low priority by the rugged pioneers who opened up the oilfields. These districts were extremely inaccessible, and heavy machinery and equipment had to be manhandled through dense forest. Rust wrote in 1910 'the lack of roads and railways was something marvellous . . . it was one terrible fight against nature'. Heavy equipment was heaved into place by human muscle, the forest was cleared by axemen, well sites and roads were graded by a 'Tattoo Gang'* - men and women who dug and moved tons of earth using forks, shovels and wooden trays carried on the women's heads. Miles of forest roads were dug and hundreds of well sites were levelled by these forgotten Trinidadians, who deserve to be remembered as pioneers of the oil industry just as much as Rust and the other entrepreneurs involved.

By about 1930, however, the oil industry was changing: the day of the self-taught pioneer was passing and the industry was increasingly dominated by the technicians and the scientists. New methods of rotary drilling - first used by Rust as early as 1902-3 - were introduced by UBOT in particular, and the new techniques of using heavy drilling fluids and the 'Blow-Out Preventer' helped to control blow-outs and gushers, and to make possible much deeper wells. Between 1924 and 1930 the average depth of an oil-well in Trinidad increased from 1,386 feet to 2,284 feet, and depths of over 4,000 feet became common. Exploration became more scientific: up to 1930 or thereabouts, most wells were 'wildcats', drilled without a complete geological exploration of a locality on or near surface seeps or gas vents. Geophysical methods of probing underground structures began in 1931, and were increasingly elaborated in the following years, making the location of new, high-yielding fields much more precise.

As the industry expanded, roads, buildings and settlements were constructed in previously inaccessible areas of southern Trinidad. Point Fortin became the first centre of oilfield operations as a port and a developing township: in 1907 Trinidad Oilfields Ltd set up base at La Fortunée estate, Point Fortin, in what became Trintoc's industrial area, and buildings and clay roads were built in a region that had been wild bush and abandoned estates. After UBOT took over in 1913, a refinery, a jetty, houses, railways and pipelines were constructed and a crude but flourishing town sprung up. Point Fortin was, in fact, 'the town that oil built', growing up in the space of fifty years from a forest clearing with a few rough huts to a modern town of about 30,000 people (1907-57). In the other oilfield areas, houses, roads, railways and pipelines were built, and gradually the southern half of the island was opened up and made accessible.

The oil industry enjoyed a boom period between 1914 and 1924.

The considerable increase in production in these years was largely the result of the successful exploitation of Forest Reserve by TLL, which built a 26-mile pipeline to connect the field to its refinery at Pointe-à-Pierre, which had a capacity of 3,500 barrels per day as early as 1916. Another important company was Apex Trinidad Oilfields, which began drilling near Fyzabad in 1920, with conspicuous success; while Kern Trinidad Oilfields exploited fields at Guapo. The old Guayaguare fields were reopened by TLL in 1925, and many south-western fields - Palo Seco, Siparia, Fyzabad, San Francique - were developed in this period.

At this time the administrative and technical staff was mostly British and European, the drillers tended to be Americans, and the semi-skilled or unskilled labour Trinidadian or 'small-islander'. P. E. T. O'Connor, from a local French Creole family, was the first Trinidadian university graduate to enter the oil industry when he joined Kern in 1923. At Kern the staff in the 1920s was British and American, and O'Connor tells us that the social life of the oilfield staff camps was organized on a strictly 'whites only' basis, for the oil industry had accepted the racial segregation that was typical of Trinidad society until after the Second World War. By the 1920s the oil companies had begun to train local blacks as technicians, but many of them, resenting salary discrimination in favour of US drillers and technicians, left Trinidad to take part in the Venezuelan oil boom of these years, for in Venezuela they were treated on a more equitable basis with other expatriates. O'Connor notes that it was not until the 1950s that significant numbers of Trinidadians entered supervisory positions in the oil industry.

At the end of the postwar boom years, a period of consolidation and steady technical development followed. Many of the smaller, weaker companies failed, and a few large concerns, notably UBOT, TLL and Apex, dominated the industry in the period between 1924 and 1937. By 1929, with the growing demand for gasoline for motor cars, new processes for producing gas were added to the Pointe-à-Pierre refinery. But oil prices slumped in 1930-1 as a result of overproduction. Drilling was suspended on some fields and men were laid off, but crude oil production increased steadily, from a total of 5.4 million barrels in 1927 to 20 million in 1939. In fact the major companies made good profits throughout the depression years of the 1930s, and as we noted in Chapter 10, the two major companies declared dividends of 35 per cent and 25 per cent in 1935-6. Low wages and a number of objectionable labour policies by the major oil companies led directly to the strikes of 1937, but 'normality' was soon restored, and the Second World War ushered in a second boom period. Trinidad's oil was vitally important to Britain's war effort; in 1938 the island accounted for 44.2 per cent of British empire production; the figure had risen to 65 per cent by 1946. In comparison with other sources, Trinidad's oil was far less vulnerable to enemy action so long as the British and US fleets dominated the Caribbean and the Atlantic, and British war planners placed considerable emphasis on the need to expand and defend the local oil industry. To meet the growing demand for aviation fuel, the world's first iso-octane fuel plant was built at Pointe-à-Pierre in 1938, producing 10,000 barrels per day for the Royal Air Force, and in 1940-1 virtually a new refinery was built at Pointe-à-Pierre for the British Ministry of Aircraft Production, which TLL bought at the end of the war. With a greatly increased refining capacity, crude was first imported for refining in 1940; the importation of crude oil and the extension of refining proceeded rapidly during and after the war.

When the war began, in fact, the oil industry had come to dominate the economy of Trinidad and Tobago. Oil accounted for only ten per cent of exports (by value) in 1919, but by 1932 the proportion was fifty per cent and by 1943 (in the middle of the war) the figure had reached a staggering eighty per cent. The narrowly based, primary agricultural economy of the nineteenth century had been transformed, and by 1940 Trinidad was virtually a one-export economy. Yet the numbers employed in oil, while they increased steadily, remained small in comparison with those absorbed by the traditional agricultural sector. Oil employed 800 in 1912, 3,280 in 1925, 8,000 in 1939 and 15,000 in 1944, at the height of the wartime boom. The oil workers comprised a very small percentage of the labour force during this period, and agriculture continued to employ the great majority of Trinidadians in the first forty years of the century. The Olivier Commission of 1929-30, for instance, estimated that at least 40,000 people were then directly employed by the Trinidad sugar industry as labourers and cane-farmers.

Traditional Estate Agriculture in the Twentieth Century

By the early years of the twentieth century, the Trinidad sugar industry had recovered from the depression of the 1880s and 1890s, and the years during and immediately after the First World War were prosperous for sugar. The war led to a marked decline in beet sugar production by European growers, and a rising demand for cane sugar. In Trinidad production rose from 43,000 tons in 1913 to a peak of 72,016 in 1917. Prices rose sharply in 1918-20 and production was increased. But prices for sugar - like so many other agricultural commodities - collapsed in the early 1920s. By then beet sugar production had recovered and was rapidly expanding, stimulated by special bounties, while cane production continued to grow steadily. The result was world overproduction and large surpluses that forced down prices throughout the 1920s, despite a temporary recovery in 1922-4. Prices reached their lowest point in 1929-30 and some estates were abandoned. Labourers were laid off, wages were reduced, and by 1934, as we noted in Chapter 9, conditions were desperate for the majority of sugar workers.

Yet the 1920s and 1930s were not, on the whole, disastrous years for the Trinidad sugar industry. Production continued to grow, if slowly. In 1928 production reached 81,600 tons and by 1936-7 a peak of 154,000 tons was attained. This growth in production was not the result of any extension of acreage, but of continued amalgamation of smaller estates, new cane varieties, greater use of inorganic fertilizers, better methods of land preparation, a systematic campaign against the froghopper pest after 1926, and better extraction rates. The period saw improvements in field operations: mechanized ploughing and land preparation began on the estates and was considerably used by 1929-30. In fact the Soulbery Report (1948) described the years 1927-37 as a time of progress for sugar, and during these years sugar was again Trinidad's major export crop. In order to protect West Indian producers from falling prices in the 1920s, the Olivier Commission (1930) recommended a generous British preference for colonial sugar, and by 1939 this preference amounted to forty per cent of the price received by colonial growers, while Canada also gave a preference to West Indian sugar. But world over-production, the basic cause of low prices, continued, and efforts were made in the 1930s to reduce output by international agreements. The Chadbourne Agreement in 1931 sought to restrict production by participating countries, but it failed to stabilize the market because the countries that were not participants continued to increase their production. In 1937 an International Sugar Agreement (ISA) was negotiated by which the chief producers agreed to limit exports by a quota system, which had the effect of limiting the further expansion of West Indian production. In any case, the outbreak of the Second World War in 1939 led to the suspension of the ISA.

Whatever the state of the international sugar market, the 1920s and 1930s were difficult years for the sugar workers of Trinidad. As commissioners and historians have made clear, the planters were able to increase their production and exports and maintain their profit levels by cutting their labour costs to a minimum. Labourers were retrenched or offered only a few weeks' work, tasks were arbitrarily increased and earnings fell. The result was a marked increase in destitution, malnutrition and disease among sugar workers in the 1930s, attested to by a number of medical reports and by the rapid increase in the number of people seeking poor relief: in the Ward of Victoria, 22,021 people were relieved as paupers in 1935, an increase of over 4,000 since the previous year. Conditions were especially bad in the sugar belt by 1934, when sugar workers carried out mass demonstrations and riots ensued (see Chapter 9).

Cane-farmers were also affected by the depression years. By

1921 a total of 26,425 farmers produced over fifty per cent of the canes ground. Cane-farming was more economic for the estates than estate production because the cost of production was lower, as a result of using unpaid family labour. In the 1920s and 1930s the large sugar companies made systematic efforts to exploit and manipulate the farmers. When prices dropped after 1920, the planters combined to form the Sugar Manufacturers Association (SMA), and the SMA instituted a system of territorial division by which only one factory could operate scales in a particular farming district; in other words, the system eliminated competition between factories for farmers' canes, and removed the last bargaining counter that the farmers had possessed. Farmers' prices were determined by a sliding scale, which, as Scottish planter Norman Lamont wrote, had 'too much of a disposition to slide down when prices were low, and an extraordinary reluctance to slide up when prices were high'. Further, most farmers leased land from the major companies, and their tenure was often insecure; the companies could evict a tenant for failure to cultivate his canes 'in a proper and husbandlike manner' after only three months' notice.

The cane-farmers might have tried to protect themselves by forming a strong organization, but this was very difficult: the social and cultural gulf between Creole and Indian farmers could not be easily bridged, and there were also economic divisions between the large farmers, who often had a privileged relationship with the companies, and the majority of the smaller farmers. No strong farmers' group emerged in this period. Kelvin Singh concludes his study of the cane-farmers in this period by noting that the system had been so organized (by the sugar companies in alliance with the government) that a high proportion of the production costs was borne by the farmers. In times of low prices, farmers would be paid according to a scale that would be uneconomic to them but would leave a margin of profit to the companies. If it was necessary to curtail production because of quota obligations, the small farmer would suffer; if increased demand stimulated greater production, the farmers could be compelled to sell specified tonnages to particular factories. The system had been manipulated in such a way as to enable the companies to profit from the labour of a small farming class.

For the cocoa industry, the 1920s and 1930s were a time of disaster, coming after fifty years of prosperity, the 'golden age' of cocoa (1870-1920). Like sugar, cocoa enjoyed a tremendous boom during and immediately after the First World War and prices peaked in 1919-20. Production expanded rapidly, estates were bought for fabulous sums, cultivation was extended to areas that could only be profitable when prices were very high. Most well-to-do Trinidadians were interested in cocoa to a greater or lesser extent. Disaster struck in 1920 with a precipitate collapse in prices: from $23.90 per fanega in 1919-20 to $9.50 in 1920-1.+ The collapse was the result, essentially, of an enormous increase in world production between 1910 and 1920 (chiefly in West Africa and South America) and of a marked change in the relative importance of 'fine' and 'ordinary' types of cocoa: the fine types, grown in Trinidad, were no longer by 1920 the base of most cocoa products, but were merely added in small amounts to improve the flavour of the ordinary types. Worse still, the basic factor of world overproduction continued for several years after 1920, since areas planted during the era of high prices after 1914 came into production in the 1920s. Almost overnight a buoyant, prosperous agricultural industry was plunged into panic and gloom.

Inevitably the labourers were the principal victims. Planters curtailed costs by reducing wages from about 60 cents per day to 40 or 45 cents. Virtually all medical facilities previously extended to workers were withdrawn; estate housing was allowed to fall into dilapidation; workers were laid off. Although conditions were not as bad as on the sugar plantations in the 1920s and 1930s, there is no doubt that cocoa workers and peasants suffered from low earnings and increased unemployment in these years of 'hard times'.

Yet the government's reaction was not to intervene to protect the labourers, but to mount an elaborate rescue effort to shore up the larger cocoa planters. These were mostly French Creoles, though many English whites and others had also gone into cocoa in the early twentieth century boom. The local ruling class and the government were concerned that the collapse of an industry in which so many upper-class whites were deeply involved would fundamentally upset the established socio-economic relations of the colony. And so the local government moved with unaccustomed speed to protect the planters from the consequences of adverse market forces and their own lavish expenditure and deep indebtedness.

Many of the planters held their estates on mortgages and were liable to immediate foreclosure, and the government feared a scramble by mortgagers to foreclose. It rushed through the Mortgages Extension Ordinance (1921) which placed a moratorium on all existing cocoa mortgages for six months, and the operation of this law was extended until 1925. At the same time the Agricultural Relief Ordinance provided for aid to cocoa planters from government funds, for carrying on cultivation and meeting interest payments and necessary personal expenses. Most of the funds granted under this Ordinance in 1922-5 were channelled to large planters. Then in 1925 the government established the Agricultural Bank to lend money to cocoa planters as long-term mortgages. It is significant that the government only agreed to set up an agricultural credit bank - long advocated by liberal officials and planters, such as Chief Justice Gorrie in the 1890s - when the white elite was in difficulties, and as C.Y. Shephard makes clear, the Bank was designed 'to provide credit facilties for a special class of investors', the large cocoa planters.# The government was determined to use all its political resources to prevent the collapse of the large cocoa plantations.

Prices recovered somewhat in 1924-5, and between 1924 and 1930 they hovered somewhere between $19 and $23 per bag, not a disastrous price by any means. But they began to fall again in 1928 and had reached $9 per bag by mid-1932; the lowest point came in 1933, with a price of $5.77 per fanega. Cocoa planters were in a state of panic by 1930, despite all the financial aid extended to them. For one thing, poor management and extravagant living aggravated the basic problem of low prices: as Cipriani told the council in 1930, the cocoa planters were 'bon vivants, they had lived off the fat of the land, and they wished to continue living off the fat of the land in spite of the depression'. Another major difficulty, this time beyond the planters' control, was the rapid spread of witchbroom disease, first discovered in Trinidad in May 1928. By 1932, 126,900 acres of cocoa were affected, and every cocoa district had shown signs of the disease. The planters felt that they could not survive without further financial aid, and the Cocoa Relief Ordinance enacted at the end of 1930 authorized crop advances to cocoa planters from government funds of up to $7 per fanega to be reaped from the estate, so long as advances were not made to estates that were still profitable or were clearly uneconomic. In 1932-3, moreover, the government was authorized to raise large loans on the London market, and most of the money raised was channelled to the Agricultural Bank for lending to cocoa planters.

So the cocoa planters had obtained long-term government-backed mortgages (through the Bank) and short-term crop advances at lower interest rates than they could have obtained from local private capitalists. Yet the fundamental problem of planter indebtedness was not solved, and cocoa prices remained low; the average price between 1932 and 1935 was only $6.35 per fanega. Many planters found it difficult even to pay the low interest on Bank advances and by mid-1934 arrears of interest on Bank loans were mounting. Yet another scheme was devised to help the planters: the disbursement of free grants totalling $2.5 million over four years for cocoa rehabilitation: replanting with better-yielding seedlings or cuttings, and measures to control witchbroom. This scheme was approved by the Colonial Office - partly because London feared labour unrest if cocoa estates were abandoned and labourers thrown out of work - and implemented between 1936 and 1940. The Colonial Office was anxious to prop up the cocoa estates to avoid massive retrenchment; the local government was prepared to go to virtually any lengths to assist the white elite in their hour of distress. Most of the money lent or given to cocoa producers between 1920 and 1940 went to the large planters, not to the many small proprietors, and the government did nothing to stop the planters reducing wages, curtailing fringe benefits and laying off workers during these years.

While oil in Trinidad helped to diversify and modernize the economy, the smaller sister island remained overwhelmingly agricultural in the first decades of the present century, and rural poverty continued to be the experience of the vast majority of Tobagonians, estate labourers and peasant farmers. By the turn of the century, estate-based sugar production for export had virtually disappeared, though sugar continued to be grown on a small scale into the 1930s; Orange Hill was one of the last surviving sugar estates. Cocoa and coconuts replaced sugar as Tobago's major export crops, grown on estates and by peasants. By the 1930s most of the planters producing these crops on estates were Creole whites, or British expatriates, perhaps in all fifty or sixty resident white families. Cocoa was still king in Tobago in the 1930s, despite collapsing prices, and it was grown all over the hilly little island. The contract system was used to build up estates. Wage labourers, as we saw in Chapter 10, were miserably paid, and as a result of cutting labour costs to a minimum the planters were able to make substantial profits even with the low prices; although, as two perceptive US writers who stayed in Tobago in 1938-9 noted, they complained endlessly of ruin while giving lavish entertainments, running cars (a luxury in Tobago at that time), taking holidays in Europe and educating their children in Britain. By the 1930s coconuts were Tobago's second most important export crop, and several large estates were situated along the coast. Here, too, labour costs were very low, prices were fairly good; but the expansion of coconuts was limited by the hilly terrain of most of the island.

Although many cocoa and coconut estates existed, Tobago was predominantly a peasant economy. As the sugar industry collapsed, the labourers and sharecroppers bought or rented small plots of estate land all over the island, and a vigorous peasantry had been established since the early years of this century. A variety of food crops was cultivated, livestock were raised and the produce was sold locally in Trinidad. It was transported by horse, donkey and mule cart, and shipped to Trinidad by small schooners, often owned by Tobagonians. Part-time wage labour was given to nearby cocoa or coconut estates. The villagers lived in crude wattle or clapboard cabins, with thatched or (increasingly) tin roofs, each hut having its plot or garden; the village was virtually self-sufficient in food and often each individual family satisfied most of its own daily needs. Agricultural methods were primitive: ploughs were not used on the stony soil; the hoe of slavery days was the chief implement for turning the earth, and the fields were cleared by fire-stick cultivation.** To clear bush and put a new field under corn, peas, cassava or sweet potatoes, all the adult men of the village community would cooperate in giving unpaid labour to the owner of the field, in the

Tobago custom of 'len' hand'. The community was closely knit in its shared life of poverty and labour. The aged lived on aid from their family or friends; charity came naturally to people whose religion was the simple, fervent Christian faith of barely literate folk, who combined formal membership in the Anglican, Methodist, Moravian or Baptist churches with dimly remembered African rites and customs. Doctors hardly ever entered these villages: people either died, or sought the healing medicine of the obeahmen, although by the 1930s not all the villagers still respected their craft. The Tobago writer Eric Roach, in a striking phrase, characterized village life in the Tobago of the 1920s and 1930s (when he was a boy) as 'a morass of illiteracy, servitude, poverty and folk customs'.

Little changed in these peasant communities, and poor transport and communications reinforced their isolation. Regular steamship services to Trinidad did not begin until 1910. Before then, mail was taken to Toco by donkey and then sent by row boat to Tobago, and it was often lost at sea. Tobago had no electricity until as late as 1952. Roads and bridges were neglected, at least until the late 1930s when Governor Fletcher was one of the first governors to take an interest in Tobago's development. Still, the peasantry experimented with new crops. In 1930 peasants growing limes established the Tobago Lime Growers Association, which set up a factory to produce lime juice at Scarborough, and did quite well until competition with Mexican producers in the mid-1950s forced the factory to close. There were other co-operative efforts by the peasants, which were always ridiculed and opposed by the resident planters; the small cultivators of the Windward Districts established a co-operative cocoa fermentory at Pembroke. Using unpaid family labour, growing most of their own food, inured to poverty, the Tobago peasants were able to survive the difficult years of the 1930s.

These were hard times for the great majority of Trinidadians and Tobagonians, the labourers in cocoa, sugar and oil, the peasant farmers and the unemployed. The fragile colonial economy could not escape the effects of the worldwide Great Depression, aggravated by more localized difficulties. Not until the coming of the Second World War did the economy begin to recover, and then to move forward decisively.

We saw that the war ushered in a boom period for oil production. It was a vital wartime industry, and heavy capital expenditures were made between 1938 and 1942 to upgrade Trinidad's refinery capacity and develop plants to produce high-grade aviation fuel. Output reached 20 million barrels by 1941, and by 1943-4 some 15,000 people were employed in oil. By then oil accounted for fully 80 per cent of Trinidad's exports. After the war's end the oil industry would enter a period of spectacular expansion.

By contrast, traditional estate agriculture suffered setbacks during the war. In the sugar industry, bulk purchasing arrangements by the wartime British Ministry of Food meant guaranteed prices and large quotas for West Indian sugar. But the sugar industry in Trinidad suffered a disastrous decline in production: it fell from 131,609 tons in 1941 to an average annual production of 74,000 tons between 1943 and 1945. It was not until 1946 that production exceeded 100,000 tons again. The major reason for this rapid fall was a chronic shortage of labour: thousands of sugar workers and farmers deserted the industry to seek jobs on the US bases that were constructed between 1941 and 1944. At the peak period the bases employed about 30,000, a considerable number in a labour market where only about 200,000 were wage earners. Organized lorry transport took workers from the sugar districts to the bases. The numbers employed in sugar dropped from about 25,000 in 1939-40 to only 16,700 in 1943, and many of those who stayed were the older, less efficient workers, so that tasks had to be reduced and wages increased. Further, US personnel in the island put a great deal of money into circulation, allowing many former sugar workers and farmers to make an easier living by supplying their needs for services like transport, food and housing. Cane-farmers were not only attracted by jobs on the bases; they also diverted much of their land to food production because the government offered good, guaranteed prices for most food crops. The result was a drastic labour shortage and a fall in the amount of the farmers' canes: while 571,000 tons of farmers' canes grown by 19,300 farmers were ground in 1938, the figure in 1944 was only 228,247 tons produced by a mere 9,300 farmers. Much cane was left unreaped (perhaps 35 per cent of the total crop in 1943), cultivation was neglected, replanting was halted almost completely, and by 1944 the industry was facing collapse in the sense that replanting and cultivation were being neglected to the point that production in future years was seriously jeopardized. The crisis was compounded by bad weather and ravages by the froghopper pest between 1938 and 1943.

At the height of the crisis, in 1943, the Benham Committee was appointed to investigate the situation and make recommendations for guaranteeing the survival of sugar; as the Committee pointed out, when employment at the bases began to decline and fewer Americans were stationed in Trinidad, the island would badly need a strong sugar industry as a major source of employment and income. The Committee recommended government assistance for estates and farmers, in the form of a guaranteed minimum price for cane in order to encourage planting, and a planting subsidy of $40 for each acre replanted in 1943. Both these recommendations were implemented from 1944 onwards, and the industry began to recover. Towards the end of the war less emphasis was placed on food crop production and replanting resumed, encouraged by the subsidy in 1944-5 which led to better crops in 1946-7; by 1948 most estates had managed to rehabilitate their cultivation. The largest companies were able to push ahead with modernization plans despite the wartime crisis. Caroni Ltd, established in 1937 as a subsidiary of Tate & Lyle from the merger of Caroni and Waterloo estates, constructed and opened in 1940 a new, modern factory at Brechin Castle and closed down the old Brechin Castle and the Caroni Village factories. By 1948 the industry had recovered from the crisis, and the late 1940s and above all the 1950s were prosperous years for sugar in Trinidad.

The other major export crop, cocoa, had been in crisis ever since 1920, despite all the assistance from the government. The subsidy scheme implemented between 1936 and 1940 was replaced - on the recommendations of the Moyne Commission and of a local committee - by a Rehabilitation Scheme that envisaged the expenditure of $4 million over a ten-year period (1940-9). Under this scheme, which was operated by a Cocoa Board and financed by a cess of $2 per 100 lb of cocoa exported, subsidies were granted to planters to enable them to replant with seedlings and cuttings, which were known to be from high-yield strains, on good soils suited to cocoa. The Board set up propagating stations for the development of high-yield plants and distributed cuttings and seedlings to planters. In addition, subsidies were granted for witchbroom control. Where the Board determined that soils were unsuitable for cocoa (for a great deal of unsuitable land had been planted in cocoa during the pre-1920 boom), subsidies were given to help planters to establish alternative crops like coffee and citrus or to go into mixed farming. This long-term rehabilitation scheme, after a slow start, proved moderately successful in increasing yields.

In the war years the cocoa industry came under special wartime regulations. The British Ministry of Food took 3,000-4,000 tons at a fixed price, and the rest was marketed in North America as and when shipping was available. The average price during the war was $14 per fanega, a tremendous improvement over the 1932-5 period, but cocoa planters also faced severe labour shortages and few planters could maintain traditional cultivation standards. On one 2,000-acre estate the whole labour force in 1943 numbered twenty-six. Operations were reduced to harvesting and processing, with an inevitable decline in production as a result. Exports dropped from 42.5 million lb in 1938 to a mere six million in 1946. But things improved at the end of the war, and demand increased steadily with peacetime conditions. As a result prices were fairly good after 1946, and the rehabilitation scheme enabled the cocoa industry to take advantage of them by increasing yields.

During the war the government made a major effort to boost local food production, including rice growing and fishing, in view of the disruption of shipping and the scarcity of imported supplies. A Food Controller was appointed and a marketing organization was established, to meet wartime needs. The government guaranteed prices for most food crops, and the result was a tremendous increase in food production - at the expense, as we have noted, of the traditional export sector. The total acreage under food production in 1945 was two and a half times the amount in 1939. In addition, local industries processing food and manufacturing such things as soap, cooking oil and margarine received a great impetus, and so did the manufacturing of clothes, shoes, cigarettes and building materials. In fact it was a period of compulsory import substitution, a time when skilled craftsmen and small businessmen had a chance to do well. And the construction and servicing of the US bases meant a greatly expanded market for many small businessmen and artisans.

Above all, the bases created thousands of jobs; in 1942-4 perhaps as many as 15-20 per cent of the entire labour force found work at the bases, along with many 'hangers-on', and the wage rates were far higher than those paid in sugar, cocoa or government public works. The provision of food, housing , transport and recreation - not to mention sexual services - for the Americans enabled thousands of Trinidadians to increase their incomes by 'working for the Yankee Dollar'. These free-spending US servicemen played a major role in galvanizing the whole Trinidad economy and accustoming thousands of people to decent wages and modern labour conditions.

Postwar Economic Development

The postwar period (1946-62) was one of general economic growth for Trinidad and Tobago. The oil industry in particular surged ahead, and the dominant position of this sector in the whole economy was strengthened. Trinidad became a classic petroleum economy, dangerously dependent on oil for export earnings and for government revenues.

Oil production grew rapidly in this period, reaching a record of 55 million barrels in 1966. The growth in output was the result, primarily, of the exploitation of marine fields. Land production peaked around 1958 at 36 million barrels and then began to decline. Because of geological conditions, the average production of land wells in Trinidad is very low in comparison with other producers: in 1965 the average daily production of the land wells was only 27.7 barrels, but when marine wells were added the figure went up to 41.5 barrels. Both British Petroleum (BP) and Shell, two of the major companies, discontinued land drilling in the early 1960s. Marine exploration began in about 1943, and in 1948 the first submarine leases were made; by 1963 about 1.8 million acres of marine leases had been granted. In the 1940s the coastal waters around Brighton were explored, first by wells 'deviated' (extended) from the shore, and then from offshore platforms. Soldado was discovered in 1954; by 1961 it had surpassed the Fyzabad-Forest Reserve area to become

Trinidad's major producing field. Shell, BP and Texaco set up Trinmar in 1962 to operate Soldado and other marine areas, and by 1965 Trinmar was responsible for 32 per cent of the country's total oil production. In all there were 250 marine wells by 1966, producing 47,500 barrels per day. Clearly, the future lay with the marine-producing fields.

The other major growth area was the development of Trinidad's refining capacity, geared to refine imported crude from Venezuela, the Middle East and West Africa. Refining throughput increased phenomenally from 15 million barrels in 1937 to 137.2 million in 1965. During the war a large new refinery was built at Pointe-à-Pierre, and it used its excess capacity by importing crude from Venezuela, where production greatly exceeded refinery capacity. After 1948, when new laws allowed the importation of crude duty free under certain conditions, the imports of crude and the extension of refining proceeded rapidly. A Fluid Catalytic Cracking Plant was built by Pointe-à-Pierre in the early 1950s by TLL, and by 1956 this company was producing 32,000 barrels and refining 80,000 barrels per day. When Texaco acquired TLL in 1956, a major programme of refinery extension was carried out, for Trinidad was strategically placed to refine Texaco's Middle Eastern crude and to supply its North American and Caribbean markets by cheap water transport. From 1957 Texaco embarked on a very heavily capitalized programme of expansion of refining and marine production. By 1965 Texaco was producing 70,000 barrels and refining 345,000 barrels per day. At Pointe-à-Pierre Texaco developed a major port to serve the expanding refinery complex and the steady growth in crude imports, which totalled in 1965 over 93 million barrels; in that year over 272,000 barrels of crude were imported each day, and an average of five tankers were handled daily. By then Pointe-à-Pierre was the largest port in Trinidad, whether by tonnage, or by value of imports and exports. The other major refinery was the complex at Point Fortin, owned by UBOT/Shell. It was modernized in the early 1960s, so that its production in high octane gas, kerosenes and jet fuels; by 1965 its throughput was 50,000 barrels per day.

This tremendous expansion after the war, involving large capital investment, was accompanied by a tendency to concentrate ownership in the hands of a few major companies. BP absorbed a number of smaller concerns: Trinidad Petroleum Development in 1956, Kern and Apex in 1961. In 1956 Shell bought out its subsidiary, UBOT, based at Point Fortin. In that year, too, Texaco bought TLL for $310 million, as well as a few smaller oil companies and a one-third interest in offshore development (with Shell and BP). It was Texaco that led in refinery expansion after 1956, and Texaco became Trinidad's largest producer and refiner of oil and the major oil employer. It led in the footage drilled per year and the number of wells: between 1957 and 1962 Texaco drilled

649 wells. Behind Texaco were Shell and BP, and these three companies dominated the industry in the early 1960s, producing 98 per cent of the country's oil in 1965: the day of the small company was over.

In the period between 1945 and 1962, the oil industry, in the words of an economist, 'was the prime mover in the economy...the dominance of the industry in the economy, in the external trade and in the financing of government expenditure makes it inevitable that oil should hold this position'. Oil accounted for over 80 per cent of exports in this period, and it was largely responsible for Trinidad's relatively healthy balance of trade; indeed, the island had become virtually a one-export economy. Oil contributed very heavily to government revenues, through taxes, royalties and other payments including customs duties and harbour dues. In these years, the division of profits between the government and the companies was approximately 50:50, with some fluctuations; for instance, in 1958 the government took 51 per cent in total payments, the companies pocketed 49 per cent. In that year the oil industry contributed 41.5 per cent of total government revenues. Between 1951 and 1964 the industry contributed about 30 per cent of the GDP and it was largely responsible for the steady growth of the GDP in these years. The heavy contribution of oil to government revenues has helped to finance expenditure on public works and social services since the war, and the oil industry has played a major role in developing a skilled labour force and a class of technicians.

But because oil is heavily mechanized and capital intensive, the total labour force has always been small in comparison with other major sectors. Employment in oil rose from 15,000 in 1944 to 19,000 in 1954, and then began to decline to 14,000 in 1964. The productivity of this fairly small labour force was high because of the large investment in capital equipment, and the industry paid salaries and wages that were significantly higher than those paid by other major industrial sectors. Oil disbursed $22 million in wages in 1949 and $100 million in 1962, but it employed only about 5 per cent of the total labour force in 1965. Economists agree that this was a major structural weakness of the modern Trinidad economy, for the burden of providing employment fell on the weaker sectors of the economy.

Oil dominated the whole economy between 1945 and 1962, but agriculture continued to make an important contribution to employment and export earnings. By 1948 sugar had recovered from the wartime crisis, and the years that followed were years of expansion. Prices were high at the end of the war and continued to be fairly good in the 1950s; the Commonwealth Sugar Agreement (1951) provided for a long-term quota system that stabilized the market and offered good prices for about two-thirds of Trinidad's exports. Production and acreage increased, to an average

130,000 tons per annum in 1945-50 and 217,900 in 1958-63.

The amalgamation of estates and the concentration of ownership - a tendency that began in the nineteenth century - were pushed to their logical conclusion in this period. While in 1948 there were ten sugar factories operated by nine firms, by 1962 there were six factories operated by three firms, and four of them were owned by a single company, Caroni Ltd. The two giant sugar companies of the postwar period were Caroni and St Madeleine Sugar Company. Caroni was established in 1937, merging the Caroni, Brechin Castle and Waterloo estates, as a subsidiary of Tate & Lyle. The new company embarked on a major programme of factory modernization. Between 1939 and 1952 three of its factories were scrapped - Brechin Castle, Caroni and Waterloo - and all its canes after 1952 were ground at the new Brechin Castle factory, opened in 1940 and considerably extended in the following years. In 1956 Caroni acquired Gordon Sugar Estates Ltd, with around 4,000 acres, and the Brechin Castle factory was further extended to bring its annual production to around 40,000 tons of sugar.

The St Madeleine Sugar Company greatly extended the old Usine St Madeleine at the end of the First World War, and in 1923 a refinery for the production of granulated sugar was added to the factory. In 1949 the company bought Reform Estates from Gordon Grant and Co.; then in 1957 it became a subsidiary of Tate & Lyle, and finally in 1961-2 a subsidiary wholly owned by Caroni Ltd. Around that time, too, Caroni acquired Woodford Lodge Estates Ltd with its factory in Chaguanas. By 1962, therefore, Caroni had acquired all the land under cane except for that owned by two small companies (Forres Park Ltd and Orange Grove) and by independent farmers. The company owned over 73,000 acres and operated four factories, and was producing some 90 per cent of all the sugar produced in Trinidad. So the process of amalgamation and consolidation had gone as far as it could, and when Trinidad attained independence its sugar industry was dominated by a single company owned by the great British sugar combine, Tate & Lyle.

With the stable market and reasonable prices that obtained in the 1950s, the large companies were able to embark on major programmes of expansion and development. Factories were modernized, cultivation processes were increasingly mechanized, modern road transport tended to replace the older railways, new types of canes were planted, tractor-drawn trailers were used for transporting canes, a new bulk-loading facility was constructed at Goodrich Bay, an experimental station for research was established jointly by Caroni and St Madeleine Sugar Company, and new worker housing schemes were launched. These developments made possible a significant expansion in production and exports between 1948 and 1962.

But the progress of the cocoa industry in the same period was far more modest. The Cocoa Rehabilitation Scheme, begun in 1940, made possible extensive replanting with high-bearing strains of cocoa. By 1957 about 8,000 acres had been completely, and 15,000 acres partially, replanted. Prices were generally good between 1946 and 1964, and exports rose steadily from the low point of 6.5 million lb in 1946. By 1956 exports had reached 22 million lb, although they declined again to 13 million in 1962. Cocoa producers faced increasing difficulties in attracting labour, and many estates were abandoned because their owners were unable to offer competitive wages. In the economic conditions of the postwar period, it was clear that the cocoa industry could not recover its pre-1920 prosperity, but it continued to make a modest contribution to export earnings and to employment.

But the most striking developments in the postwar economy were not in agriculture. Apart from the tremendous expansion of the oil industry, the most important departure was the emergence of a significant manufacturing sector. Nearly every West Indian government since the war had tried to establish industries, and Trinidad was no exception. The Moyne Commission rejected the idea that West Indian governments should get involved in conducting or financing industries, but the wartime conditions did stimulate the growth of a number of small industries in Trinidad, particularly factories processing foods and food products. In 1947 the government appointed the Shaw Committee to recommend an economic policy, and it advised that the incentives granted to new hotels since 1946 should be extended to manufacturing industries, together with tax reliefs. A board should be established to explore the possibility of establishing new industries and to examine applications for assistance. An Economic Advisory Board was set up in 1948, and in 1950 the Aid to Pioneer Industries Ordinance and the Income Tax (In Aid of Industry) Ordinance were enacted. These laws defined a pioneer industry as an industry that was new and/or had potential for further development, and provided for exemptions from income tax for five (possibly ten) years, an accelerated depreciation allowance at the end of the 'tax holiday', and duty-free importation of materials and machinery for the construction of the factory plant for a five-year period. This marked the beginning, in Trinidad, of the policy of 'industrialization by invitation': a systematic effort to attract foreign capital to establish manufacturing industries through tax concessions and other privileges. It was hoped that this policy would generate considerable new employment to absorb surplus rural labour, and produce a local entrepreneurial class that would gradually involve itself in the manufacturing sector.

It was the quasi-ministerial regime of 1950-6 that really initiated the new policy, and Albert Gomes, as Minister for Labour,

Commerce and Industry, was at the centre of the new effort to develop secondary industries and hotels. The policy was continued and expanded by the People's National Movement (PNM) government that took office in 1956. In 1959 industries were allowed to import duty-free a wide range of raw materials, chemicals, supplies and semi-manufactured goods for use in industry, and special concessions were given to industries where the capital investment was very high - as for cement, fertilizers and petrochemicals. In 1959, too, the Industrial Development Corporation (IDC) was established to deal with all applications for pioneer status and for tax concessions, and to promote the development of industries, including hotels.

There is no doubt that the pioneer industry programme had, by 1962, succeeded in establishing many new industries in the country, mostly foreign-owned. By 1963 a total of ninety-nine pioneer industries were in operation, representing a capital investment of about $85 million, and forty more were being constructed or planned with an estimated investment of $173 million. Most of this capital (about 80 per cent) was American and British. But the number of jobs created by the programme was insignificant in relation to the growth in the labour force. By 1963 only 4,666 direct jobs had been created by the pioneer industries, and another 2,255 were expected to be created by the factories then under construction or in the planning stage. Yet the labour force, between 1950 and 1963, had increased by perhaps 100,000. Clearly, during this period the new manufacturing sector had not generated anything like enough jobs to deal with unemployment. These industries were capital-intensive and highly mechanized, and a very large investment was required to generate one direct job, although it is true that 'spin-off' jobs were created by industrial development. Furthermore, the pioneer industries were predominantly foreign-owned up to 1962; in 1959 only 16.3 per cent of the capital investment in these industries was locally owned. By and large, the expected development of a local entrepreneurial class involved in manufacturing did not materialize in this period, and the industrial programme increased the country's dependence on foreign capital, technology, markets and expertise. The new industries did not contribute significantly to foreign exchange earnings, nor were there many linkages with the domestic economy. At the same time the government lost revenues as a result of the tax concessions, and the provision of infrastructural supports for the new industries was a drain on the government's resources. In fact, after twelve years of operation, the industrialization programme had not, by 1962, begun to fulfil the expectations of its promoters, in terms of generating significant increases in employment and contributing to the structural transformation of the economy.

But the postwar years saw significant economic growth in the country. Between 1951 and 1961 the real GDP (gross domestic product) increased at an average annual rate of 8.5 per cent (adjusted for inflation), a rate that compared very favourably with other developing countries. Much of this growth, however, was due to the expansion in oil, and oil continued to dominate exports. The contribution of agriculture to the GDP declined particularly tree crops like cocoa and citrus, but other important sectors increased their contributions, especially manufacturing, construction (a key sector because it generated considerable employment and used mainly local raw materials) and services. There was also significant growth in the financial sector (banking, insurance, finance). But a weakness in the economy was that the foreign-owned commercial banks and insurance companies invested over sixty per cent of their assets abroad: they collected local savings and lent them to foreigners to assist the economic development of other countries. Their loans policies militated against the development of locally owned industries or commercial farming and, in general, failed to mobilize local resources for productive economic enterprises.

Although industrialization was the major thrust of the postwar period, some efforts were made to develop tourism, valuable as a significant source of foreign exchange and employment. From 1946, tax incentives were offered to entrepreneurs investing in hotel construction, and the government of 1950-6 extended further concessions and incentives. The first PNM government (1956-61) continued this policy. A Hotel Development Corporation was established in 1957 to loan money for the construction and expansion of small hotels; Crown Point Hotel, in Tobago, was completed in 1958. In 1959 the government's new IDC took over the function of encouraging hotel construction and expansion, and a Tourist Board (1958) assumed responsibility for the promotion of tourism. North coast roads were constructed in the late 1950s in both Trinidad and Tobago, to improve access to scenic beaches, and tourist facilities at Maracas Bay in Trinidad were provided. Trinidad's major hotel, the Trinidad Hilton, was begun in 1959 as a profit-sharing enterprise between the government and the international Hilton chain. In this period, too, Piarco Airport was developed to accommodate jets, and the little Crown Point airstrip in Tobago was improved and extended. It was not the policy of the PNM government to become a significant hotel proprietor or the major source of capital for hotel expansion; instead, incentives were offered to private investors, foreign and local, under the same conditions as to pioneer industries. The Tourist Board was expected to publicize the country as a tourist attraction, develop sites and beauty spots, register hotels and guest houses, and encourage private enterprise to develop tourist facilities.

Tourism did not play an important role in the development of the Trinidad economy after 1946 - Trinidad, after all, had oil - but it became increasingly significant for Tobago. As early as the 1930s, resident white planters were beginning to invest in hotels and guest houses, such as the Bacolet, Speyside and Robinson Crusoe hotels, or to seek posts as hotel managers. Others rented their estate houses to winter visitors, or built bungalows and cottages to rent to tourists. In the 1950s hotel construction began to accelerate, partly as a result of government aid, and tourism gradually began to replace agriculture as Tobago's major economic activity and source of employment.

Up to the 1950s, however, the development of Tobago was almost totally neglected by the authorities in Port of Spain, despite the efforts of A.P.T.James, Tobago's sole elected member in the council between 1946 and 1961. It was partly as a result of his persistent advocacy that electricity was brought to the island in 1952, a new water scheme at Hillsborough replaced the old (1926) supply, and a deep-water harbour and wharf were opened at Scarborough. At last Tobago was entering the twentieth century. Although Tobago electors rejected the PNM in 1956, remaining loyal to James, the first PNM government paid special attention to the development of the island Ward. Chief Minister Eric Williams took personal responsibility for Tobago affairs, noting in 1957 that 'Tobago had exchanged the neglect of U.K. Imperialism for the neglect of Trinidad Imperialism'. In his view, 'Tobago is a test case ... its development is necessary to illustrate to the West Indies and the world outside our capacity for self-government and taking care of our own affairs.' A five-year plan for Tobago was inaugurated, envisaging expenditure of $9.6 million for infrastructural development, especially roads. In 1958 the government separated Tobago's expenditure from Trinidad's in the country's estimates, and accepted the advice of a development and welfare report that 'Tobago is a distinct community with a history and life of its own and must not be regarded as a mere appendage of Trinidad.' No wonder that the Tobago electors, impressed by the apparent sincerity of the government's commitment to develop the island, rejected James in 1961 and returned the PNM candidates.

By 1962, in fact, the state had begun to take a more active role in the economy, and systematic development planning was begun by the first PNM government. While in the period between 1951 and 1959 the expansion of the oil industry was the generator of growth in the whole economy, after 1959 the public sector played a leading role in promoting growth. In these years the non-oil sectors were significantly less dependent on oil for growth, and sectors like manufacturing, construction and public services grew faster than oil. These trends suggested that structural transformation of the economy was beginning by independence, but many of the characteristics of the typical petroleum company economy still persisted. There were wide income disparities between the sectors and between the occupational groups, with employees in the oil and manufacturing sectors earning far more than their counterparts in agriculture and services. Oil still dominated exports, and manufacturing had failed to develop as an important foreign exchange earner. Further, there were few linkages between the oil and manufacturing sectors and the domestic economy, which retarded growth; and the importation of foreign services and capital increased over this period. Unemployment and underemployment also increased, as the population continued to grow rapidly and as agriculture and oil employed decreasing numbers, while manufacturing created relatively few new jobs.

When Trinidad and Tobago entered the era of independence, the national economy was considerably stronger than that of most developing countries, but there were fundamental weaknesses that hindered economic growth and better living standards for the people. The task after 1962 would be to mobilize domestic savings for investment, to create a more dynamic entrepreneurial class, to establish industries that were labour-intensive and which utilized local materials, to develop a more diversified agricultural sector, and to reduce income disparities between sectors and between occupational groups. This would involve the whole population in a national effort for development, but it would be especially the responsibility of the party, government and leader which took the country into the era of independence.

---

1 See P. E. T. O'Connor, *Some Trinidad Yesterdays* (Port of Spain, 1978). The word 'tattoo' is Trinidad Creole for the armadillo, which digs in the earth.

2 Prices were sometimes quoted per fanega (110 lb) and sometimes per bag (165 lb, or one and a half fanegas).

3 See C. Y. Shephard, *The Cacao Industry in Trinidad* (Port of Spain, 1932).

4 Fire-stick cultivation ('slash and burn') is the practice of burning stumps and undergrowth in order to clear bush for cultivation.

TWELVE

Free at Last? 1950-62

In the years following the Second World War, Britain began - slowly and painfully - to disengage from her empire. First in India, then in the other colonial possessions, under heavy pressure from anti-colonial movements in Asia and Africa, the imperial power set into motion a long and tortuous process of political decolonization. These years were a time of transition from colonialism to self-government and, inevitably, it was a confused and difficult period in the history of Trinidad and Tobago.

Finding a Cultural Identity

Political decolonization was accompanied by a remarkable cultural renaissance, an upsurge of popular creativity that developed a new cultural identity which was Creole and national in orientation. We saw in Chapter 9 that Trinidadian intellectuals and writers in the 1930s had begun to work towards a truly West Indian literature, and had advocated that local authors and artists should look to their own society for their inspiration. Albert Gomes, Edric Connor, Alfred Mendes, C.L.R. James, Hugh Wooding and Eric Williams were among the patrons and supporters of this outburst of creativity in art, poetry, fiction, drama, music and dance. One of the leading figures in this renaissance in Trinidad (and in the West Indies as a whole) was Beryl McBurnie, who began research on West Indian folk dances in the late 1930s and opened, in 1948, the first Little Carib theatre in a shack situated in her own backyard in Woodbrook, a middle-class suburb in Port of Spain. Here she organized and presented folk dances based on Trinidad and Tobago's rich multi-cultural heritage, jeopardizing her standing in the city's coloured middle class (to which she belonged by birth) by her active participation in African dances and her co-operation with young dancers of all ethnic backgrounds. For this was a time, as Gomes points out, when most middle-class blacks were still ashamed of African-derived cultural forms and the music and dance of working-class West Indians. Gomes himself publicly defended and supported the Shouter or Spiritual Baptists, the Shango or Orisha faith, calypso and steelband, and was an active patron of the arts in the 1940s and 1950s. McBurnie was undeterred by criticism and misunderstanding. Her interests extended to African, Indian, French and Spanish traditions in dance and music; she presented steelbands on stage in the very early days of the pan (steelband music) movement, and in 1949 she staged a parang concert featuring the traditional Christmas music of Trinidad's Spanish-descended community. McBurnie and Gomes, in quite different ways, were each in the vanguard of the postwar renaissance, which also produced brilliant Trinidadian novelists like Vidia Naipaul and Samuel Selvon.

But the major cultural developments of these years centred on the working-class ghettos of Port of Spain, where the calypso was developed as an important art form, and the steelband made its spectacular appearance. Calypso emerged in its modern form around the turn of the century, with lyrics in English accompanied by European musical instruments like the flute, guitar, cuatro and bass. By the 1920s regular performances were staged, in the weeks before Carnival, in 'tents', which by that time were becoming bigger, more comfortable and better organized, to attract middle-class patrons. Many calypsos commented on local and international events, others dealt with the relations between the sexes. In the first three or four decades of the century, the 'oratorical' calypso was popular; this featured long, elaborate sentences and impressively erudite words in which the singer showed off his prowess in the English language. Masters of this genre were Roaring Lion (Hubert de Leon) and Atilla the Hun (Raymond Quevedo). Another type was the 'ballad' calypso, pioneered by Chieftan Douglas (Walter Douglas) in the 1920s, which narrated a story in simpler language and shorter lines. Traditionally, calypso was used to attack injustice and pull down the mighty, and this tendency was especially strong in the 1930s and 1940s, when singers assailed colonialism and the sins of officialdom. In the 1930s censorship was implemented; singers were required to submit their songs for official scrutiny before a performance. This censorship was, of course, bitterly resented and attacked (though it never effectively inhibited political or 'sexy' calypsos), especially by singers like Atilla and King Radio (Norman Span), and it was ended in the later 1940s, partly as a result of Gomes's influence.

The Second World War and the 'American occupation' greatly stimulated the development of calypso. In the first place, singers began to make records in the USA for a rapidly expanding market there and in Europe, forcing them to improve their techniques and polish their lyrics and melodies. Calypso became internationally popular. Over five million records of Lord Invader's *Rum and Coca Cola*, itself dealing with the effect of the US presence on Trinidadian women, were sold in various pirated versions. In the ghettos of Port of Spain, partly as a result of US influence through films and the servicemen in the island, a whole sub-culture emerged, dominated by the Saga Boy: the glamorously dressed, flashy stud who controlled his women through his sexual prowess and probably lived off their earnings. Many calypsos celebrated this underworld. Of course the Saga Boys resented the US servicemen, who took away 'their' women through the superior attraction of the Yankee Dollar, and a whole crop of calypsos was sung on this theme, and on the Saga Boys' revenge when the Americans left and the good-time girls had to creep back to their former lovers; Sparrow's *Jean and Dinah* (1956) was only the most famous of many.

Sparrow himself, easily the dominant calypso personality since 1956, superbly expressed the new surge of black nationalism and pride. While Atilla and Lion, in the 1940s, had lambasted Crown Colony government in its dying stages, Sparrow celebrated the rise of Creole nationalism and the PNM. He was a supporter of the PNM and its leader, Eric Williams.

Leave the damn doctor
And don't get me mad
Leave the damn doctor
Or is murder in Trinidad.

And he expressed the new, post-1956 black pride and aggression:

Well the way how things shaping up
All this nigger business go stop
I tell you soon in the West Indies
It's please, Mister Nigger, please.

In the hands of Sparrow (Francisco Slinger) and his colleagues and rivals, calypso was taken to new levels of sophistication and wit, becoming an important cultural form as well as a major channel for political and social comment and protest.

The development of the steelband - music produced by beating carefully tuned oil drums - was an even more striking achievement. Pan (steelband music) was born in the working-class ghettos of Port of Spain, notably John John, Rose Hill, East Dry River, Gonzales, Hell Yard and New Town, in the late 1930s. The actual origins of the steelband - the question of which individual or band first used steel drums or tins to beat out a recognizable tune, and when - are surrounded by confusion and controversy; any positive statement on the subject would be unwise. The main lines of the story are, however, quite clear.

In the first three or four decades of this century, the main form of popular music to accompany Carnival bands on the streets was the tambour/tamboo-bamboo band; percussion was provided by striking lengths of bamboo on the ground and by hitting shorter pieces against each other. Around 1937, tamboo-bamboo band members in various Port of Spain yards tried to create more strident sounds by using metal objects - dustbins, buckets, biscuit tins, pitch oil pans, car hubs - which produced a strong metallic ring when struck. At Carnival time between 1937 and 1940, bands appeared on the streets beating these metal objects. Carnival was banned as a security measure for four years during the war, and in these years band members, confined to their yards, experimented with metal instruments to produce a drum or tin that could give different notes and thus be used to play a recognizable tune. Almost certainly the leading innovators were Winston 'Spree' Simon of John John and Neville Jules of Hell Yard; both have been credited with playing the first proper tune.

All this feverish experimentation burst out into the open on VE (Victory in Europe) Day in May 1945. In a spontaneous upsurge of popular joy, bands took to the streets with their new instruments, made from biscuit tins and sawn-off oil drums. Port of Spain went wild to the new, strident sound; steelbands mushroomed all over the city and spread to other towns. The process of experimentation continued, carried out mostly by men with no musical education. Besides Simon and Jules, other steelband pioneers in the 1940s were 'Fish-Eye' Olivierre of Hell Yard, Ellie Manette, Sonny Roach, Patsy Haynes, Oscar Pile, Anthony Williams and Bertie Marshall. These men (and others) developed different kinds of pans capable of producing a considerable variety of notes, worn hung around the neck and beaten with rubber-tipped sticks; increasingly complex and sophisticated melodies were played.

But the early steelbands were greeted with considerable hostility. The panmen were mostly slum-dwellers, working-class men with little formal education; middle-class residents objected to the noise from the pan yards and associated the men with hooliganism and rough behaviour. In fact, the 1940s and 1950s were years of intense rivalry between bands, similar to the gang fights of the second half of the nineteenth century, and fights at Carnival time were frequent and sometimes serious. Magistrates handed out stiff sentences to panmen accused of fighting or other offences; respectable people, including most middle-class blacks, saw the bands as a menace to society. They failed to see that the steelband movement could play a crucial role in promoting social stability, by providing an outlet for the creative energies of underprivileged, often unemployed ghetto youths. By the late 1940s, however, some prominent Trinidadians were beginning to sense the social and artistic potential of the steelbands. McBurnie and Gomes both extended their support to the panmen, and McBurnie put the Invaders band on stage at the Little Carib. The government appointed a committee to investigate the whole steelband phenomenon in 1949, and in that year too a Steelband Association was formed. Influential people began to protect steelbandsmen from persecution, and gradually - very gradually - attitudes changed. In 1951 a national steelband, the Trinidad All Stars Percussion Orchestra, was chosen to perform at the Festival of Britain, and it was triumphantly successful; in 1952 steelbands were invited to participate in the prestigous Music Festival, hitherto devoted solely to European musical forms. Gradually, in the later 1950s, band conflict declined and the stigma of hooliganism faded, although pan remained essentially the music of working-class Afro-Trinidadians. But the steelband was on its way to becoming an important part of the national culture and a genuine musical achievement.

The Labour Movement Loses the Initiative

This renaissance in music, art and literature was the cultural counterpart of the process of political and constitutional decolonization. In 1950, a modified form of Crown Colony government still existed, but universal suffrage had been granted in 1946, and a proliferation of groups and politicians competed for the new electorate in the elections of 1946 and 1950. It was the heyday of the individualist in politics, the independent, the 'broker politician' wheeling and dealing between various interest groups, manipulating the voters and the divisions among them in his own interests, seizing every chance in the confused transition from one system of political authority to another. What had not yet emerged was a cohesive, nationalist party with considerable support from the middle class and the labour movement, the kind of party that had already developed in Jamaica and Barbados, the kind of party to which the imperial government would be prepared to hand over political power. The central development in this period of Trinidad's history is the eclipse of the labour movement in politics and the rise of a Creole nationalist party that would carry the black middle class into power in 1956 and take the country into independence in 1962.

There were many reasons for the political weakness of the labour movement in the years after 1950. Butlerism was a spent force by then. In 1950, as we have seen, Butler's party was excluded from the executive council even though it had gained the largest number of elected seats in the legislature. Deprived of patronage and the fruits of power, the party fell apart; in any case, it had never been a cohesive, organized body, but rather the vehicle for the messianic ambitions of the leader, who always despised organization and collective leadership. Butler spent much of his time during the 1950s in Britain, and his absences weakened his position and led to leadership conflicts. When he came home to fight the 1956 elections, he was totally unprepared for the spectacular performance of the PNM, and his old-fashioned biblical harangues seemed dated to crowds who had become accustomed to the incisive, academic discourses of Eric Williams, the PNM leader. He was still personally popular in the oilbelt, where he won his seat, but as a political leader he had been completely eclipsed by the new Messiah. By 1961 he could poll only 517 votes in his old La Brea stronghold; he had become a political anachronism, and many of his followers moved to support the PNM as the new champion of the black masses.

Moreover, the various groups that had advocated working-class, leftist positions in the 1940s were in disarray by the mid-1950s. Socialists from the NWA joined with a younger generation like Lennox Pierre and John La Rose to form the West Indian Independence Party (WIIP) in 1952. This was a socialist party that developed close relations with John Rojas of OWTU and Quintin O'Connor of FWTU, as well as other trade unionists, and was suspected of being 'communist inspired'. The government took fright especially since WIIP had links with Cheddi Jagan, the Marxist who was elected to office in British Guiana in 1953, and put heavy pressure on the OWTU and FWTU leadership to disengage from WIIP. Both Rojas and O'Connor were prevailed on to leave WIIP, and the party withered away by about 1956. The eclipse of Butlerism, the demise of WIIP, and the weakness of other left-wing groups occurred at the historical moment of the emergence of the PNM; the way was open for a nationalist movement led by middle-class politicians.

Furthermore, organized labour had its own divisions and weaknesses, which forced it to play a secondary role on the political stage in the 1950s. Inter-union rivalries and disputes were intense in this period, aggravated by politicians who used the unions as bases for their own careers. These difficulties were especially marked in the sugar industry, 'perhaps the most striking illustration of the deleterious effects of recognition conflict and trade union rivalry in the Caribbean', to quote the words of Zin Henry. The oldest sugar union, ATSE&FWTU (All-Trinidad) had been founded in 1937, but it was not until 1945 that the SMA recognized it as the bargaining agency for the workers in sugar. Even then, collective bargaining was not satisfactory, and recognition was withdrawn in 1948 when a period of strikes and acute inter-union rivalry began with Butler's attempts to displace All-Trinidad with his own, loosely organized union. The older union was resurrected and revitalized by McDonald Moses, but he resigned when he failed to secure election to the legislature in 1950, and the union again fell into decline. Two rival unions were founded by Lionel Seukeran and Mitra Sinanan, both aspiring politicians and members of the legislature; and the SMA refused to recognize any of the four competing unions.

Between 1953 and 1955 attempts were made to federate two of the unions - All-Trinidad and the Sugar Industry Labour Union (SILU), Sinanan's union - with an agreement that the former would organize the southern estates and the latter the estates in northern and central Trinidad. The presiding genius of this federation was Bhadase Sagan Maraj, a member of the legislature who was elected president of All-Trinidad in 1953, and he emerged as the strong man in the sugar belt. In 1954-5 recognition was granted to the All-Trinidad-SILU federation, but this step did not end inter-union rivalry. Two Boards of Enquiry were established in 1955, and in 1956-7 the British TUC intervened by sending an emissary to try to bring the factions together. As a result, in 1957 All-Trinidad was recognized as the sole bargaining agency under Maraj's leadership, but instability and rivalry continued on a reduced scale. Trade union development in the sugar industry was impeded by political intrigue, personal rivalries, divisions between Indian field labourers and black factory workers, the failure of the union movement as a whole to support the major sugar union, and the problems always encountered in organizing underemployed, seasonal, poorly educated estate labourers. But if the sugar industry provides the most striking example of rivalries between union leaders in this period, the problem was general throughout the Trinidad labour movement in the 1950s.

Ideological and political conflicts further weakened the unions. Some important unions were conservative in their political thinking, such as the powerful SWWTU under its founder-president Cecil Alexander, while the OWTU and FWTU leadership tended to more radical positions. In particular, leaders of these two unions were closely linked to the left-wing WIIP, although both Rojas and O'Connor tried to separate their political activities from their union leadership. But the connection seemed ominous to the government, and to the more conservative unionists, and Fred Dalley, the British trade unionist who had investigated the Trinidad labour movement in 1947, was invited to come for a second visit in 1953-4 to help to disengage Rojas, O'Connor and their colleagues from WIIP. His report (1954) stated unequivocally that WIIP was 'communist inspired and directed', and that the OWTU and FWTU leaders were acting irresponsibly by their active participation in the party. Both Rojas and O'Connor resigned from WIIP, which existed only on paper by 1956.

Cold war conflicts of the postwar world further divided the Trinidad labour movement. In 1946 the Trinidad TUC, grouping all the major unions, had joined the World Federation of Trade Unions (WFTU) on the urging of the British TUC. But in 1949 the British and western unions left WFTU, believing that it had become merely an arm of Soviet (Russian) foreign policy, and set up the International Confederation of Free Trade Unions (ICFTU) as a rival, anti-Soviet organization. The Trinidad union leaders refused to follow suit; Rojas and O'Connor, who controlled the TUC, argued that they would not be pushed into withdrawing from WFTU either by the colonial government or by the British TUC. Under the leadership of Cecil Alexander of SWWTU, six unions split off from the TUC to form a rival body, which affiliated in 1951 to the western-aligned ICFTU. This left OWTU and FWTU under Rojas and O'Connor still affiliated to the socialist WFTU. Heavy pressure was put on them – Dalley's second visit was part of this campaign - and in 1953 they agreed, reluctantly, to withdraw from WFTU. This marked the defeat of the leftist labour leaders in Trinidad, and the unions became less political after 1953 (for a time).

Plate 10 Adrian Cola Rienzi, labour and political leader of the 1930s-40s
Plate 11 Albert Gomes, Minister of Labour, Commerce and Industry, 1950-6
Plate 12 Dr Rudranath Capildeo, leader of the Democratic Labour Party in the 1960s
Plate 13 Dr Eric Williams, Chief Minister, Premier and Prime Minister of Trinidad and Tobago (1911-81)

In 1957 the two rival federal bodies united to form the National Trade Union Congress, representing all the major unions, but by then the labour movement had lost political leadership and initiative to a party that avoided formal links with the unions. In fact, the divisions in the union movement, the decline of Butlerism, and the disintegration of left-wing groups, combined to clear the way for a middle-class, nationalist party.

And the way was made even smoother by the weakness of the quasi-ministerial regime of 1950-6. The five ministers, dominated by Albert Gomes as Minister of Labour, Commerce and Industry, had to operate within a difficult constitutional framework (which Gomes himself had helped to create). Each came from a different party or group, yet they had to maintain a semblance of collective leadership and responsibility. There was no chief minister or premier; they shared power with the governor and the top officials, especially the financial secretary; they had no choice but to pursue policies acceptable to the Colonial Office and the local government. Radical politics were ruled out; the ministers tried to keep the peace, pursue a policy of economic development, and make expedient concessions to each important vested interest or group. In his autobiography Gomes admits all the disadvantages, but claims that the regime ensured political stability and laid the foundations for the economic policies that the PNM continued, and perhaps we may agree with Selwyn Ryan's conclusion that it 'performed moderately well' granted the constitutional and political constraints.*

But the regime soon alienated important groups and the population as a whole, making its electoral defeat in 1956 relatively easy. As Gomes tells us, he pursued as minister policies that frustrated and embittered his former trade union colleagues. He came to believe that his government's policy of attracting foreign capital for industrialization depended on restraining the unions and keeping industrial peace. Strikes were never made illegal, but Gomes kept a tight rein on union activity. He tried to pre-empt strikes by forcing each side to make concessions before a crisis situation had been reached, and labour leaders were convinced that he favoured capital more often than labour. Even more serious was the regime's failure to project an image of unity, integrity and reforming zeal. Several notable scandals highlighted corruption in high places, and no serious efforts were made by the ministers to expose or correct such activities, despite a 1954 motion in the legislature (which was defeated) to censure the government for its failure to do so. This aura of graft and corruption seriously damaged the regime, and provided devastating ammunition for the PNM in 1956. In general the 'Gomes ministry' seemed too fragmented to be effective; it spoke with five different voices, it lacked a clear, legitimate national leader, it could not provide the electorate with a vigorous, reform-minded government. These weaknesses represented a golden opportunity for a new party starting off with a clean slate, a nationalist programme and an undisputed leader; and constitutional changes in 1955-6 further encouraged the emergence of a new political movement.

At the end of 1954, Gomes moved for a select committee on constitutional reform, the Sinanan Committee, and as a result, in April 1955 the legislative council agreed to postpone elections (due in September 1955) until a new constitution had been implemented. There were three major reasons for the government's anxiety to postpone the elections. First, the Gomes ministry wanted to put their house in order before facing the electorate. Second, the British government was concerned to get a final agreement on the Federal constitution before any change of government in Trinidad; opposition to Federation, articulated mainly by Indian politicians who understandably feared that Indo-West Indians would become a small powerless minority in a federation, was gaining strength. Finally, the strongest single party in 1955 seemed to be the People's Democratic Party (PDP), led by Maraj and based on the rural Hindus, and neither Britain nor local interest groups welcomed the possibility of a PDP government. Critically, the postponement of the elections gave the Creole progressives and nationalists time to organize, and hence it sealed the fate of Gomes and his colleagues.

A new constitution became law in 1956 on the basis of the Sinanan Committee's recommendations. The legislative council was to consist of only two ex officio members (the Colonial Secretary and the Attorney-General), five nominated members and twenty-four electives. A speaker to be elected by the council would preside, without a casting vote, and the legislature would elect a chief minister who would serve as leader in both the legislature and the executive council. This last body would consist of seven ministers with portfolios, elected from the legislature and led by the chief minister. A minister of finance would replace the official financial secretary. Only the two ex officio members of the legislature would sit on the executive council. But the governor still presided, and the portfolios were to be allocated by him after consultation with the chief minister. This constitution, providing for something close to a Cabinet, opened up the possibility of party government, if a single party gained a clear majority of the elected seats. The governor, Sir Edward Beetham, recognized that the new constitution would only work properly when stable parties were formed, and he was accordingly prepared to do what he could to accommodate a well-organized party that might win a majority of the elected seats in the elections which had been re-scheduled for September 1956. In this sense, the 1956 constitution, and Beetham's attitude to it, were developments that helped to make possible the PNM's capture of power.

The People's National Movement

The PNM was the creation of a group of middle-class professionals, mainly but not exclusively black, who rallied round the dominant personality of Eric Williams (see photo, p.230) in 1955-6 to establish a party that could take the Creole middle class into power. Williams had come home to Trinidad in 1948 as deputy chairman of the Research Council of the Caribbean Commission, after a successful career in Britain and the USA as a university teacher and historian. The brilliant black scholar, occupying a highly visible and prestigious post, soon began to attract attention, and he involved himself in a number of cultural, educational and semi-political activities. By 1950 he was already well known, and he had formed an important relationship with a group of progressive teachers, the Teachers' Educational and Cultural Association (TECA), founded in the 1940s and led by men like D. W. Rogers, W. A. Alexander, Donald Pierre, John Donaldson and Fitz Maynard. It was TECA that published, in 1950, Williams's *Education in the British West Indies*. In the following years Williams steadily built up a wide circle of admirers by public lectures, often on aspects of West Indian history: Williams soon recognized that his presentation of the Caribbean historical experience roused tremendous pride among his black listeners and helped to stimulate mass adulation of himself, and he exploited his historical knowledge to the hilt. He became the centre of various informal study groups in which well-educated nationalists met to talk politics and listen to his discourses, such as the 'Bachacs', while his public speeches made him well known to the people. By 1954, in fact, Williams had developed a popular reputation, a wide circle of middle-class admirers, and a coterie of close friends and disciples, many of them members of TECA.

In 1954-5 Williams emerged on to the centre stage. Towards the end of 1954 he engaged in a series of formal debates with Dom Basil Mathews, a well-known Catholic educator, on Aristotle and education, and the tremendous public response probably made him see the possibilities for political action. During the course of 1955 Williams's friends began to organize in earnest. A semi-secret cell of disciples, consisting of about twenty professionals and called the Political Education Group (PEG), was organized around Williams to discuss courses of action, and by the middle of 1955 the group was agreed on the need for a political party under Williams's leadership. Meanwhile, TECA set up the People's Educational Movement (PEM) as an ostensibly non-partisan platform through which Williams could build up a mass following by public lectures. By 1955 Williams's relations with his employers, the Caribbean Commission - strained for several years - had reached their lowest point, and he knew that his contract would not be renewed. It was as a speaker for the PEM that he made his famous speech, in June 1955, on his relations with the Caribbean Commission, announced his dismissal, and told the public:

'I was born here, and here I stay, with the people of Trinidad and Tobago, who educated me free of charge for nine years at Queen's Royal College and for five years at Oxford, who have made me whatever I am ... I am going to let down my bucket where I am, now, right here with you in the British West Indies.'

It marked his formal launching into politics.

For the rest of 1955 Williams spoke on PEM platforms all over the country, outlining his major political ideas. In July he opened the University of Woodford Square, the major public square in the heart of Port of Spain ('Now that I have resigned my position at Howard ... the only university at which I shall lecture in future is the University of Woodford Square, and its several branches throughout the length and breadth of Trinidad and Tobago'), a brilliant move which symbolized his commitment to mass political education and enlightenment. Williams's speeches on constitutional reform led to an organized campaign to collect signatures to his petition calling for a bicameral legislature with a nominated senate to represent the 'special interests' and a wholly elected Lower House, and this campaign was the first real test of his people's organizational skills. By October nearly 28,000 signatures had been collected, and the PEG/TECA nucleus had established a volunteer network of supporters and activists that would play a critical role in the 1956 election victory.

By the end of 1955 all the essential preparations for launching a party had been completed. In London, Williams discussed the draft party constitution and manifesto with George Padmore, C.L.R. James and Arthur Lewis, and in January 1956 the new party was formally launched. Significantly, it was called the People's National Movement. It was not a Labour party, not a party of any section but a national organization; not indeed a party so much as a movement, or, as the Charter called it, 'a rally, a convention of all for all, a mobilization of all the forces in the community, cutting across race and religion, class and colour, with emphasis on united action by all the people in the common cause'. The Charter emphasized that the new movement would have, as its major task, the work of mass political education, but it immediately swung into action for the election campaign. The PNM had eight crucial months in which to build its following and establish an electoral machinery, and in these months Williams persuaded several popular businessmen, professionals and politicians to be PNM candidates, including Gerard Montano of San Fernando, Patrick Soloman (who had left politics after his election defeat in 1950), Winston Mahabir, a San Fernando based doctor, and Learie Constantine, famous cricketer and public figure.

Williams and his colleagues were determined not to make any 'deals' with the labour movement or with established politicians. The new party did not seek formal links with the trade unions, unlike similar national parties elsewhere in the West Indies. For one thing, the leaders felt that, as a national party, the PNM should not identify too closely with the predominantly black labour movement. Further, the unions were already well established by 1956, with influential and ambitious leaders, and the PNM had no intention of being 'captured' by them. In no sense was the PNM's ideology leftist or socialist, and the party was envisaged as a broad national movement that would somehow incorporate both capital and labour. The PNM was able to do without union affiliates partly because, as we saw, the labour movement lacked political cohesiveness, partly because Williams's charisma had created a mass following independent of the unions. And the PNM leadership steadfastly rejected any electoral alliances with existing politicians or groups. Of course the PNM wanted Indian support, but Williams refused to be party to any deal with the powerful Indian politicians, especially Maraj, or indeed with the representatives of any of the ethnic or economic interest groups. One of the formal requirements for membership in the party was that the candidate should not be a member of any existing political organization. In this way, the new party avoided entangling alliances with the old-guard politicians, many of them discredited in the public mind.

The political scientists Ivar Oxaal and Selwyn Ryan have shown that the PNM's organization and leadership patterns were greatly influenced by those adopted in the PEG/PEM period between 1954 and 1956. Admission to the group was only as a result of personal endorsement and sponsorship by an already trusted member, and this 'old guard' of the coterie close to Williams in 1954-6 tended to monopolize the influential positions in party and in government for many years after the 1956 victory. It is very significant that even in this early period, the leader defined policy almost alone, and every member was expected to be personally loyal to him and to support his current thinking on any given issue. Moreover, the growth of the PEG nucleus 'by invitation only' meant that the early PNM membership - and therefore a high proportion of leadership positions - proceeded along a network of personal relationships, and this ensured that the initial recruitment of leaders would be mainly from the black or coloured middle class, though some effort was made to recruit people of other ethnic groups to balance the leadership. But the essential fact is that the PEG group became the nucleus of the PNM leadership, and this group was solidly middle class and predominantly black. Below the top leadership, the lower level party activists were mainly lower-middle-class blacks, often prominent in their localities. The PNM victory represented a long-delayed move by the black middle class, the heirs of the nineteenth-century reformers, into the seats of power.

The 1956 campaign was bitterly fought; the PNM injected a note of excitement and controversy into the electioneering. Against the new party was ranged a number of political groups. The Party of Political Progress Groups (POPPG), led by Gomes, was a loose collection of politicians who spoke for the interests of business. Although its platform was very similar to the PNM's, it was identified in the public mind with the Chamber of Commerce, the French Creoles, the Catholic Church and the forces of reaction in general, and it never succeeded in throwing off this fatal image. Cipriani's old party, the TLP, now under Victor Bryan, claimed to be the true Labour party, and attacked the PNM as middle-class and intellectual. But the TLP had virtually no support outside Tobago and the eastern counties, where James and Bryan himself enjoyed almost unchallenged influence among the rural voters. Three parties claimed to present socialist platforms: the Caribbean National Labour Party was the organ of the OWTU and a few other unions, led by Rojas; WIIP fought a low-key campaign, contesting only one seat and disappearing after the election; and the Butler party struggled manfully against the new black Messiah. Although Butler won his seat in the oilbelt, the Butler movement, always disorganized, was clearly a spent force by 1956.

But the party that the PNM identified as its major opponent was the PDP, established in 1953 under Bhadase Maraj. This party was essentially the political arm of the Hindu community; for the rural Indian masses, Maraj filled much the same role as Williams for the black masses. Because Maraj combined the leadership of the major sugar union, the Maha Sabha (the organ of the majority Sanatanist Hindu group) and the PDP, he was clearly a serious threat to the PNM; he could, presumably, deliver the votes of the rural Hindu community. The PNM's tactic was to isolate the PDP by portraying it as a reactionary, communal Hindu organization, hoping to drive a wedge between the orthodox rural Hindus and the reformist or secular-minded Hindus, the Muslims and the Christian Indians, to prevent the PDP rallying the Indian population as a whole. Williams attacked the PDP and the Maha Sabha savagely, often unfairly, and he succeeded in winning significant support from Muslims, Christian Indians and urbanized Hindus. Muslims like Kamalludin Mohammed and Ibbit Mosahib, and Christian Indians like Winston Mahabir, were given conspicuous leadership positions in the PNM to encourage this tendency. There is no doubt that the PNM's tactics succeeded brilliantly in isolating the PDP in the rural Hindu districts: it contested only fourteen seats and won only five, all in the sugar belt.

After the most exciting campaign in Trinidad's short history of electoral politics, the results were a narrow victory for the new party: the PNM won 39 per cent of the votes and thirteen out of twenty-four seats. The PDP won five seats with 20.3 per cent of the votes; the old TLP and the Butler party each won two seats, while two constituencies went to independents. Geographically, the PNM swept the urban and suburban areas, but in the rural districts the old, traditional loyalties were too strong for them, though the party ran quite well in Tobago (narrowly won by TLP's James) and in the rural eastern and north-eastern counties. The PNM did badly in the rural Indian areas, where the PDP won its five seats, and in the oilbelt, Butler's stronghold. And the trend was clearly towards a division of the votes on race lines. The PDP did not contest the seats where Indians were in a small minority, and it only won seats that were overwhelmingly Indian. In these seats the PNM put up Indian candidates who were all defeated, while in the racially mixed seats like Tunapuna PNM candidates won by narrow majorities. The bitter anti-PDP, anti-Hindu campaign that the PNM had mounted clearly helped to heighten racial fears and to institutionalize patterns of voting and political mobilization along racial lines.

But one crucial fact was clear: the PNM, with thirteen out of twenty-four elected seats, was the majority party in the legislature. Yet when the two ex officio and the five nominated members were counted in, the party could command only thirteen out of a total of thirty-one members, short of an absolute majority. At this point the attitude and actions of Governor Beetham became critical. Anxious to support what he saw as a stable, disciplined party led by responsible and educated professional men, Beetham persuaded the Colonial Office to allow the PNM to form the government. He agreed that the PNM could appoint two party members to nominated seats, and he pledged that the two ex officio members would vote for the government. This gave the PNM a clear majority: the party could command seventeen out of thirty-one members of the legislature. All seven ministers appointed to the executive council were party members, and the PNM leader duly took office as chief minister. At last a single party controlled both the legislative and executive councils, and could govern through what was, in fact if not yet in law, a Cabinet responsible to the legislature. Although independence was six years away, the Colonial Office had effectively handed over political power to a nationalist movement that was dominated by the Creole middle class.

And to make the transfer of power as smooth as possible, Williams was quite willing to make gestures of reconciliation to the traditional elite after the bruising campaign, in which the PNM had been bitterly attacked by the Catholic Church, the Chamber of Commerce and other spokesmen for the old power elite. He nominated a prominent white businessman to the legislature (Cyril Merry), he included two more in the executive council (Gerard Montano and John O'Halloran), and he pointedly refused to nominate any trade unionist to the executive council or to a nominated seat in the legislature.

During the campaign, Williams had explicitly rejected socialism; he had indicated his support for foreign capital investment, welcoming the Texaco takeover in 1956, and his economic policies - modelled on the Puerto Rican experience and involving the attraction of foreign capital for industrialization through tax concessions - were endorsed by many local businessmen. No effort was made to build up a trade union wing to the party. Those who looked for radical policies from the new government, therefore, were very wide of the mark. But the business and planter elite refused to see this; they responded to the PNM victory less in terms of economic interest, more as a status group resentful at the erosion of their traditional ascendancy by a party led by black, middle-class men. Despite the accommodating gestures of the new government, the years that followed the elections saw a new kind of political polarization: the PNM versus the traditional elite in alliance with old-guard politicians and Indian leaders. The result was a climate of political bitterness that climaxed in the elections of 1958 and 1961, and heightened tensions between Creole and Indian politicians, between the new men of power and the old.

To confront the PNM, various opposition groups recognized that they would have to unite. The occasion was the establishment of federal parties in preparation for the first federal elections in 1958. Alexander Bustamante of Jamaica came to Trinidad in 1957, seeking a Trinidad affiliate for his Federal Democratic Labour Party, and after negotiations with opposition politicians, the Trinidad Democratic Labour Party (DLP) was set up in July 1957, merging the PDP, TLP and POPPG. The provisional leader was Victor Bryan of the TLP, for both Maraj (PDP) and Gomes (POPPG) were felt to be too controversial; the leaders were anxious to create an opposition that would not be exclusively Indian-based. Since the PNM had ignored the Indian political elite in forming the government and in making nominations, the excluded and the defeated naturally rallied round the DLP: it was, as Selwyn Ryan says, 'a rally of the outs'. Soon the PDP faction - the Indian political elite -gained full command of the new party, and in January 1958 Maraj was elected party leader. The non-Indian elements had to take a back seat, and Trinidad entered a period of bitter party warfare: a racially polarized two-party system seemed to have been established.

For the DLP, the federal elections (March 1958) presented an opportunity for testing their strength and attacking the PNM on its record after eighteen months in office. The PNM, preoccupied with problems of government, and underestimating the DLP's vote-getting potential, staged a lack-lustre campaign with a relatively weak team of candidates, especially when contrasted with the DLP slate, which included such formidable political notables as Maraj, Gomes, Bryan and Roy Joseph. The result was a stunning victory for the DLP, which won six out of ten seats. It won all four seats where

Indians were in a majority and two seats where they were not: the eastern counties, won by Bryan, and St George East, taken by Gomes. These results were a personal triumph for Maraj, the DLP's chief vote-winner, and for the other old political hands in the party; but the PNM took some comfort from the fact that it had increased its share of the votes over 1956 (48 per cent as compared with 38.9 per cent) and had made inroads into 'enemy territory' like Tobago, where A. N. R. Robinson had defeated James.

Williams reacted to the PNM defeat with a speech in which he denounced the DLP for using race and religion to obtain votes and defeat his party. 'By hook or by crook they brought out the Indian vote', he declared, and he castigated appeals to race as the work of a 'recalcitrant and hostile minority of the West Indian nation masquerading as "the Indian nation" and prostituting the name of India for its selfish and reactionary political ends.' The speech was, in effect, a propaganda appeal to the black population: it was an appeal never again to let the DLP win by default, an appeal for racial counter-mobilization. It reflected the long-standing fear of the black middle class that the Indian political elite might 'seize' power, backed by the 'Indian block vote' and other disaffected elements. The speech acutely embarrassed Indian members of the PNM and three ministers threatened to resign; one of them, Winston Mahabir, felt moved to appeal publicly for tolerance and calm, for a recommitment by the PNM to multi-racialism and the 'spirit of Bandung' (Afro-Asian unity). But the damage had been done. In fact, the 1956 PNM victory had led immediately to heightened racial tensions as the black population began to think in terms of their 'right to govern', and the 1958 elections had further accentuated this development. Both parties had used race, the DLP, perhaps, more effectively. After 1958 open or disguised appeals to race became the major strategy of party politics.

Both of the two main ethnic groups responded to these appeals, but the Indians felt particularly alienated from the rise of Creole nationalism. By the middle of the twentieth century, Indo-Trinidadians had succeeded in rebuilding some of the key institutions of Indian culture. For many though not all, their values, life goals, beliefs and institutional structures differed from those of other ethnic groups; they had distinctive traditions in marriage, family, religious ceremonies, festivals, dance and music. Further, since the 1920s and 1930s Trinidad Indians had shown an increasing interest in India and its culture. Journals and papers owned by Indians, like the *East Indian Weekly* and the *Observer*, devoted considerable space to events in India. Mosques, temples and Hindu and Muslim schools were built, racially exclusive clubs and youth groups were founded. Well-to-do people began to travel to India, while visiting missionaries, musicians and dancers from the subcontinent helped to reinforce Indian culture; so did Indian films, records and literature.

In the 1950s the rural Hindus in particular were still largely untouched by the creolizing process, and for them the traditions and values of India took precedence over those of the West Indies or Trinidad.

For the rural Indian community, socialization took place mainly in the family, and to a lesser degree in the religious group. The basic unit of rural Indian society was the joint family, headed by the senior male member whose sons, with their wives and children, lived in his household. This family structure was characterized by the inferior status of the younger women, parental selection of mates, the rarity of divorce and the sharing of property. The individual's first allegiance was to his family, then to a wider circle of kinsmen; each person had a definite status in the kinship hierarchy, and the child was brought up to respect family and kinship authority patterns. Usually the family was close-knit - though the joint property system tended to cause conflict - and it closed ranks against all outsiders. According to Yogendra Malik, 'amoral familism' characterized the Indian community: the pursuit of family advancement was nearly always given priority over wider interests, and life was centred around family goals.+ Such a situation encouraged the perpetuation of ethnic identity; the rural Indian's loyalty was to his family, his village, his religion and his ethnic group.

Caste and religion were both important to the community. As a status symbol, membership in a high caste still carried social and political prestige, and the leadership of the Maha Sabha was invariably high-caste, but inter-caste marriages were increasingly common in the 1950s. Religion, however, played a critically important role in the Indian community. The great majority were Hindus, and the Maha Sabha, the organization of the largest Sanatanist Hindu group, became a very powerful force under Bhadase Maraj in the 1950s; he made it the strongest political base of the Hindu community. Nevertheless, despite the importance of religion and caste, there was a tendency towards greater ethnic solidarity in this period. Religious, caste or social differences were played down; when the ethnic group seemed to be threatened from the outside, ethnic loyalties would prevail. All the sub-groups within the Indian community felt some antipathy towards the Creoles, and this common fear or even hostility allowed the ethnic group to cohere; it promoted ingroup solidarity.

This hostility expressed itself in a strong opposition to Indian-black marriages, rationalized on grounds of cultural differences and a fear that the Indian identity would be lost. Since Indians tended to be less hostile to marriages with whites, it is clear that considerable prejudice against Creole blacks existed within the community (it is hardly necessary to state that this prejudice was generally mutual). On the whole, articulate Indians in the 1950s considered 'Creole culture' to be inferior to that of India, and they objected to the widespread idea (promoted by the PNM among many other groups and individuals) that Indians would inevitably be creolized; they distinguished between creolization and westernization, which in their view need not mean acceptance of Creole values. Many in the Indian leadership mistrusted the aims of the Creole nationalist party and tended to dismiss PNM nationalism as 'Negro nationalism'.

Furthermore, race tensions were heightened by the rise of an educated Indian middle class since the 1930s. Indian families showed great anxiety to educate their sons and train them for professions, and this development threatened the Creole middle class that dominated the civil service and the professions up to the 1950s and well beyond. Economically some Indians did well, dominating agriculture and transport (buses, taxis and trucks), and establishing many medium and a few large businesses. As the Creole middle class moved into power, resentments and jealousies between the two races were aggravated, and they were exploited by politicians of both groups for vote-getting purposes.

The other important development of the 1958-60 period was an apparent 'left turn' by the PNM, a development that centred on the Chaguaramas issue and the involvement of C.L.R. James in party affairs. James, a veteran Marxist of international stature, was invited back to Trinidad to edit the PNM paper in 1958, much to the alarm of senior party members close to Williams, who were disturbed by James's left-wing views and by Williams's apparent deference to the older man. Chaguaramas became an issue when Williams discovered that Governor Young had resisted the concession of the North West Peninsula to the USA in 1941 (see Chapter 10), but had been overruled. Williams changed his original position and demanded that the whole of Chaguaramas should be returned to Trinidad for the federal capital. A Joint Chaguaramas Commission (1958), with representatives of the USA, Britain and the Federation of the West Indies, simply stated that the USA should have a naval base in Trinidad and Chaguaramas was by far the best location, but the matter could be reopened in ten years; London indicated that Britain had no intention of asking the Americans to move the base. The PNM made Chaguaramas a public issue, spearheaded by James, and a new note of anti-imperialism crept into the rhetoric: in his famous 'From slavery to Chaguaramas' speech in July 1959, Williams declared 'we in the PNM did not form a political party in order to substitute American colonialism for the British colonialism we pledged to fight'. Trinidad's relations with the federal government were badly strained by the failure of the federal Prime Minister to push the issue, and by the beginning of 1960 Williams was publicly accusing the federal government of being 'a stooge for the Colonial Office'. In April 1960 the PNM staged the 'March for Chaguaramas', the militant high-point of PNM-sponsored nationalism.

No doubt this demonstration helped to convince the Colonial

Plate 14 The 'March in the Rain' to demand the return of Chaguaramas, Port of Spain, April 1960

Office that the issue would have to be negotiated, and London made an abrupt policy switch. In June 1960 British Prime Minister Harold Macmillan came to Trinidad, assured the government that he would open negotiations with the USA with Trinidad & Tobago as an independent participant, and told the West Indies to 'hurry up' to independence. For the PNM this was a victory on the crucial issue: Trinidad's right to negotiate with Britain and the USA as an equal partner on the Chaguaramas issue. Now the party could return, in 1960-1, to the moderate and accommodationist strategy it had adopted in 1956.

James, the major force behind the Chaguaramas agitation, was purged: the fourth Party Convention in March 1960 attacked him and his handling of the party paper, and shortly after he resigned his editorial post. Although he remained a party member until the following year, his effective influence was at an end. Free from James's promptings, and with negotiations over Chaguaramas about to begin, Williams publicly stated that he and his government were committed to the West: 'There can be no argument about that. That is the anchor of our foreign policy as we emerge into Independence.' Later in 1960 Williams put the matter even more forcibly when he declared that Trinidad was 'historically, geographically and economically' part of the West and warned that 'if the communists and fellow travellers were counting on him to pull their chestnuts out of the fire they would be disappointed'. The PNM's brief flirtation with radical anti-imperialism was over, and the Chaguaramas issue was amicably settled in negotiations during 1960. This was a reasonable settlement: the Americans agreed to abandon Wallerfield and Carlsen Field, but only part of the North West Peninsula; Teteron Bay would remain in their hands until 1977 at the latest. They also pledged to grant aid amounting to $30 million - not a very impressive figure - for infrastructural developments and for the construction of a college at St Augustine. In other words, partial withdrawal and foreign aid, exactly the kind of deal the DLP had advocated in 1957-8. The PNM radicals were disappointed, but their influence was waning, and James's rearguard efforts to push the PNM 'forward' - that is, leftward - ended with his break with the party in 1961.

On domestic issues, too, the PNM moved to accommodate with right-wing forces. The PNM's proposals for an integrated state school system had aroused bitter opposition from the Catholic Church. Many party leaders, especially the old teacher block, wanted to fight, but Williams and his senior Cabinet colleagues felt they should neutralize a contentious issue before the 1961 elections. At the end of 1960 the government reached a compromise that allowed the churches considerable freedom in rejecting changes in curricula and textbooks, and gave them the right to allocate 20 per cent of the places in the first forms of secondary schools 'as they saw fit'. While the so-called Concordat meant that the state could now transform the composition of the church schools through the 80 per cent quota (decided on the basis of a competitive examination) and that the appointment of teachers was now in the government's hands, the churches were left relatively free to carry on as before, and the 20 per cent concession gave them the right to assign scarce secondary school places at state expense to pupils less academically qualified than others who might go unplaced. Obviously the compromise was a significant concession to the Church and a blow to the PNM's egalitarian aims, but as a tactical move for neutralizing opposition it no doubt made good sense.

From Self-Government to Independence

The PNM could now concentrate on retaining power by winning the elections and then taking the country to independence, with the blessing of the imperial power, now showing signs of anxiety to rid itself of colonial embarrassments. Constitutional changes were the prelude. A 1959 Order in Council increased the number of Cabinet ministers to nine, including a Minister of Home Affairs with responsibility for police, security and immigration, and stated explicitly that the governor could only appoint and remove ministers on the advice of the Premier (formerly chief minister). The Premier would now preside over the Cabinet (the new name of the executive council) and the two official members would retain their seats but would not vote. In effect this was internal self-government, but without a fully representative legislature.

In 1961 a further constitutional change formally granted full internal self-government by requiring the governor to act on the advice of the Cabinet on all save a few matters. Since Trinidad was still a colony, the governor's reserve powers remained, but essentially the 1961 constitution gave him the very limited powers of a constitutional monarch. The other major change was the introduction of a bicameral legislature, consisting of a fully elected House of thirty members and a nominated senate consisting of spokesmen of the 'special interests' which might not be adequately represented in the elected chamber. It had been PNM policy since 1956 to press for a nominated senate, and it was a major concession to the traditional elite. The senate was to consist of twelve senators named by the Premier, two by the Leader of the Opposition, and seven by the governor to represent 'religious, social and economic interests'.

And the next step was to prepare the ground for the elections by changing the constituency boundaries and the electoral rules, to make sure that 1958 could not happen again. Legislation was enacted establishing a system of permanent voter registration by ID cards and introducing the use of voting machines. Both changes were attacked by DLP, which felt that the new system would confuse, intimidate or discourage the rural voter, who tended to be uneducated or even illiterate, and that the machines were easily rigged. In fact, while the changes in themselves were a step in the right direction - towards orderly, honest elections - they were introduced without any bipartisan consultation or negotiation, without any effort to defuse anxieties and fears, and so they widened political and racial divisions instead of leading to greater integration. Then a five-man Boundaries Commission, three of whom were PNM members, was given the task of redrawing constituency boundaries. There can be little doubt that the boundaries were systematically gerrymandered to favour the PNM, and to give the ruling party an excellent chance of winning all the seats except ten where Indians were in the majority and which the PNM in effect abandoned.

As an electoral machine the PNM was in good shape for the 1961 campaign; for five years there had been no open splits or public factional struggles, a revolutionary achievement in Trinidad politics. Its only important opponent, the DLP, had been torn by a bitter leadership struggle between Maraj and Rudranath Capildeo (see photo, p.232). Top party bosses had decided that Maraj was something of an embarrassment to the party because of his lack of formal education and sophistication, and because of his link with the Maha Sabha, which led people to identify the party with orthodox Hinduism. To win support from Muslims, Christian Indians and secular-minded, middle-class Hindus, and to match Williams's intellectual glamour, they turned to Capildeo, who was then the principal of the Trinidad Polytechnic. Capildeo was 'Trinidad's most educated man', a Ph.D. in mathematics and a fully qualified barrister, a member of a very prominent Hindu family but not himself identified with the Maha Sabha and not linked to discredited politicians. But the succession from Maraj to Capildeo involved bitter factional fights among the DLP leadership, and Capildeo later admitted how dismayed he was to find that he spent more time fighting his own party colleagues than the PNM. Moreover, Capildeo was physically and psychologically too frail to lead a party in a bitter election campaign; he was no politician, and throughout the 1961 campaign he was ill and on the verge of a breakdown. Still, the DLP tried hard to win the support of non-Indian elements, especially anti-PNM members of the old elite and people from the Syrian and Chinese minorities; it leant over backwards, in its choice of candidates, to prove that it was not exclusively an Indian faction. For the party needed the support of all the anti-PNM and uncommitted voters if it was to win.

This campaign was the roughest in Trinidad's history up to then, and by far the most racialist. Essentially it was a struggle between two ethnic groups for political power, and issues and policies took second place. The PNM asserted the right of the black nationalists to govern

Trinidad as the majority group; the DLP reacted with increasingly desperate rhetoric. Both parties appealed to race as their major strategy. DLP meetings in areas where Indians were not in the majority were ruthlessly disrupted by PNM supporters, especially in Port of Spain, and the DLP leadership accused the mainly black police of doing nothing. There was violence in the San Juan-St Augustine area, and a state of emergency was declared in several areas where Indians were the majority group; naturally the DLP thought that the objective was to terrorize its supporters. It seems fair to say that the campaign was marked by an aggressive determination by the PNM to defeat the DLP by any means.

The DLP leaders reacted in kind, and the tone of Capildeo's speeches became increasingly hysterical. In one speech, he said 'I have not come to bring peace, but to bring a sword. We have brought peace long enough and they cannot understand.' The climax was a DLP meeting in Port of Spain that was savagely disrupted by PNM hecklers; Capildeo told his supporters to break up PNM meetings, to march on Whitehall, to 'arm yourself with a weapon in order to take over this country' in self-defence, but 'if self-defence comes to violence, we are not going to stop at it'. These outbursts were clearly damaging to the DLP, however greatly Capildeo had been provoked, for they frightened away support which the party desperately needed.

For a time the country seemed poised on the brink of racial war. Then both sides pulled back: the government wisely did not detain Capildeo for his inflammatory rhetoric, while the DLP suspended open-air meetings in the last weeks and called on the people to pray for racial peace. But the damage had been done, and the DLP failed to win disaffected non-Indian groups; on the whole, the DLP leadership showed itself to be more sectarian, and less determined, than the PNM.

This election was fought primarily over the issues of race and power, or which racial group would govern the country on the eve of independence, and the voter turnout (88.11 per cent) revealed the high level of popular awareness of what was at stake. Research by political scientists like Ryan and Krishna Bahadoorsingh seems to show conclusively that race was the main determinant of voting. The results were a triumph for the PNM, which won twenty out of thirty seats with 58 per cent of the votes. Although the DLP did quite well in some of the urban seats, like San Fernando West, it only won the ten seats in which the Indian population exceeded 50 per cent. The PNM improved its position in the rural constituencies, taking two out of three seats in the eastern counties, both Tobago seats, and the two St Patrick seats in the oilbelt; Butler suffered a humiliating defeat in his La Brea stronghold. Perhaps these results owed something to gerrymandering, but on the whole the PNM was far better organized than the DLP and, under the charismatic direction of Williams, it had waged a brilliant campaign. Independence lay ahead, but after the bruising elections it seemed as if the PNM would take a deeply divided country into formal nationhood.

But first the PNM had to decide its policy with respect to the federation, now in its dying days.# In September 1961 Jamaicans opted to secede. Although the PNM refused to allow federation to be an issue in the elections, Williams was moving away from his earlier, strongly pro-federation stand; the Chaguaramas issue had severely strained his relations with the federal government, and he had been disillusioned by years of haggling with the other governments, especially Jamaica's, over the functions and powers of the central government. By the end of 1961 the party had decided that Trinidad should go into independence alone. Williams had no intention of allowing Britain to saddle Trinidad with responsibilities for the eight less developed territories in a truncated federation without Jamaica, and one can perhaps agree that this decision, harsh as it was, was the correct one. One from ten leaves nought, quipped Williams; and the PNM Convention early in 1962 announced the party's decision: Trinidad would go into independence alone, but any other island that wished to join Trinidad in a unitary state was free to do so, and the government would actively promote economic ties between the former federal territories. There was pro-federation support in the PNM, but the majority sentiment was clearly in favour of the decision; nationalism had won out over federal unionism, which had never gone very far or very deep in Trinidad. In fact the decision reflected, probably, a national consensus, but the DLP and many other groups and individuals felt that the public had not been properly consulted and that the party convention was hardly the correct forum for a final decision on such a matter. Williams ignored all political forces outside the PNM, he never attempted to establish a bipartisan approach to the federation issue, and he plunged the country into divisive political conflict on the very eve of independence.

As a result, the country's independence constitution had a stormy passage. It was drafted by the government (and notably by its constitutional adviser, Ellis Clarke), discussed in a public conference at Queen's Hall in Port of Spain, amended and sent to a joint Select Committee of Parliament, and finally submitted to the British government for approval and enactment. Although the Queen's Hall Conference (April 1962) was an innovative attempt to involve representatives of all important groups and sectors in the country in the constitutional debate, the draft had been framed unilaterally by the government without any consultation with the Opposition, and the chairman (Williams) kept a very tight rein on the proceedings. Partly to protest the chairman's actions, partly because the press was excluded, the DLP walked out of the first meeting and refused to come back, and this weakened the force of their criticisms. Essentially, the DLP (and other groups) sought to place checks on the Prime Minister's powers; to make the Elections and Boundaries Commission, the Public and Judicial Services Commissions, and the senate more independent of the government; and to entrench part of the constitution by requiring a three-quarters majority (instead of a two-thirds majority) in the House for amendment. These were constructive and legitimate amendments, but the PNM was in no mood to listen. In the Select Committee, the government and opposition disagreed on nearly every major issue. It was because of the bitter political conflicts of 1961-2 that government and opposition went to London for the Independence Conference (May 1962) with all the central issues still unsettled, and with the country in a state of racial polarization and acute tension.

At the Marlborough House Conference the DLP delegation reiterated its demands for a three-quarter majority in both Houses for amending the 'entrenched' clauses, and for guarantees that the civil service, the police and the proposed national guard would be more representative of the different races. It also called for elections before independence. Williams rejected all these demands, and deadlock ensued. In Trinidad tensions ran high; there is evidence that Indian extremists were arming themselves in secret. Probably recognizing that Trinidad was sitting on the very brink of racial war - and responding to pressure from an impatient Colonial Secretary, anxious to finish the whole business - Williams agreed to compromise, and made a statement in which he conceded major points to the DLP. A number of critically important clauses were 'specially entrenched' (requiring a three-quarters majority in the House and a two-thirds majority in the senate for amendment), Williams agreed to independent Elections and Boundaries Commissions, and he pledged to consult with the Leader of the Opposition on all important national issues and all appointments of a national character. Significantly, he promised to consult with the DLP on how best to reduce racial tensions. Capildeo accepted these assurances and concessions, and withdrew his opposition to immediate independence.

These were statesmanlike moves, even if they came at the eleventh hour. Williams had made major concessions, and in fact the DLP had achieved most of its aims with respect to limiting the powers of the executive and further entrenching important constitutional clauses. For his part, Capildeo had accepted the offered compromise and averted possible racial violence, even partition; he knew, of course, that Indians would have been the main sufferers in any physical conflict, since the armed forces were predominantly black, and presumably pro-PNM. As Capildeo put it, 'the decision confronting the leaders of the DLP was whether they should plunge the country into chaos with civil commotions and strife, or try to explore whatever reasonable avenue may be presented as the

Conference developed'.

Abruptly, tensions relaxed, and Trinidad and Tobago heaved a collective sigh of profound relief. Many people and many groups must have feared for the future in July-August 1962, but they kept their anxieties to themselves. An era of independence euphoria set in. It was the final culmination of a long historical process, by which political power was transferred from the imperial power, its expatriate civil servants and their allies in the planter-merchant community, to a Creole nationalist leadership. A heavy responsibility rested on the PNM, its leader, and the Creole middle class that dominated it. Apart from the urgent work of economic development and social justice, it was incumbent on the ruling party to attempt to build a truly national commitment from all the racial and economic groups which made up the society. These were the responsibilities and the opportunities that accompanied the possession of power, for Trinidad and Tobago had, at last, taken control of the destinies of their people.

---

1. See S. Ryan, *Race and Nationalism in Trinidad and Tobago* (Toronto, 1972).
2. See Y. Malik, *East Indians in Trinidad, a Study in Minority Politics* (Oxford, 1971).
3. The history of Trinidad's participation in the federation has not been discussed here, but it can be followed in Ryan, Gomes, Mordecai and Williams (see Select Bibliography).

Chronology of Major Events, 1498-1962

1498	Columbus sights Trinidad and Tobago
1592	Founding of St Joseph
1687-1708	Organization of Indian Missions by Capuchins
1699	Indians revolt at San Francisco de los Arenales
1725	Destruction of cocoa crop
1745	Cabildo of St Joseph rebels against governor
1757	Governor takes up residence in Port of Spain
1765	Direct trade between Spain and Trinidad authorized
1776	Decree authorizes settlement by foreign Catholics in Trinidad and other colonies
1777	Trinidad placed under jurisdiction of captain-general and intendant of Venezuela
1777	Arrival of French planters, including Roume de St Laurent
1783	Cedula of Population
1784	Arrival of Governor Chacon; cabildo moves to Port of Spain
1787	First sugar mill erected at Tragarete estate
1789	Beginning of French Revolution; Spain opens slave trade to her colonies
1791	Beginning of revolution in St Domingue (Haiti)
1794	Victor Hugues arrives in the Caribbean; French government abolishes slavery in the French empire
1796	Spain declares war on Britain
1797	Capture of Trinidad by Britain; Picton appointed military governor
1801	Picton appointed civil governor; Council of Advice established
1802	Trinidad ceded to Britain by Treaty of Amiens
1802-3	Commission of Government; resignation of Picton
1806	First arrival of Chinese immigrants to Trinidad
1807	Abolition of British slave trade
1810	Campaign for representative assembly rejected by Britain
1812	Registration of slaves begins
1813-28	Ralph Woodford Governor of Trinidad
1823	Free coloureds petition for civil rights
1824	Amelioration Order in Council
1825	Prohibition on importation of most slaves from the WI
1826	Repeal of some discriminatory laws against free coloureds
1827	Commission of Legal Enquiry reports
1829	Legal equality for free coloureds
1831	New Amelioration Order in Council
1832	Establishment of nominated legislative council
1834	Emancipation of slaves and beginning of Apprenticeship
1837	Daaga Mutiny at St Joseph
1838	End of Apprenticeship and complete emancipation; Mandingo Society petitions for repatriation to Africa

1839-40	Arrival of French and German immigrants
1840	Abolition of cabildo and establishment of Port of Spain town council
c.1840	Beginning of 'anglicization' policy
1841	Beginning of immigration of liberated Africans to Trinidad
1842-6	Trinidad's laws assimilated to those of England
1844	Ecclesiastical Ordinance establishes the Church of England in Trinidad
1845	Arrival of first Indian immigrants
1846	Sugar Duties Act; fall in sugar prices; arrival of first Portuguese immigrants from Madeira
1846-54	Lord Harris Governor of Trinidad
1847-8	Economic and financial crisis; Indian immigration stopped
1851	Resumption of Indian immigration; establishment of government primary schools (Ward schools)
1853	Beginning of immigration of indentured Chinese labourers
1854	Immigration Ordinance No.24 of 1854
1857	Establishment of Queen's Collegiate School; first successful oil-well drilled in Trinidad
1862	Five-year contracts for indentured Indians allowed; Unofficial majority in legislative council granted
1863	Establishment of St Mary's College
1866	Incorporation of Colonial Company
1866-7	Walter Darwent drills oilwells at Aripero
1866-70	Arthur Gordon Governor of Trinidad
1868	Canadian Presbyterian Mission to Indians begins its work
1869	Crown lands opened up to small purchasers; land commutation scheme for Indians begins
1870	Establishment of Queen's Royal College; dual system in primary education set up; Church of England disestablished in Trinidad
c.1870	Expansion of cocoa industry begins
1872	Erection of Usine St Madeleine
1876	Opening of Trinidad's first public railway (to Arima)
1881	Carnival riots in Port of Spain
1882	Beginning of cane-farming
1884	Hosein massacre in San Fernando; Carnival riots in Princes Town and San Fernando
1884-5	Depression in sugar industry
1885-91	William Robinson Governor of Trinidad; attempts to diversify the economy and establish minor crops
1885-9	First reform movement; failed by 1889
1887	Royal Franchise Commission
1889	Tobago linked to Trinidad in a federal union
1892-5	Second reform movement; rejected by Chamberlain in 1895
1895-7	Second depression in sugar industry
1897	West India Royal Commission; establishment of Trinidad Workingmen's Association (TWA) and the East Indian National Association (EINA)
1898	Tobago becomes a Ward of the united Colony of Trinidad and Tobago; abolition of Port of Spain borough council; end of Unofficial majority in legislative council
1901	Formation of branches of Pan-African Association in Trinidad

1902	Brussels Convention ends bounties on beet sugar exports; Randolph Rust begins drilling for oil at Guayaguare; formation of Rate-Payers Association
1902-3	Agitation against government's water policy
1903	Water Riots: Red House burnt, sixteen killed
1904	First black appointed to legislature (C.P.David)
1907-9	Guapo-Point Fortin area opened up for oil
1910	TWA establishes links with British Labour Party
1911-13	Refineries built at Point Fortin and Brighton
1912	First Indian appointed to legislature (G.Fitzpatrick)
1913	Establishment of United British Oilfields of Trinidad (UBOT) and Trinidad Leaseholds Ltd (TLL)
1914	Refinery at Pointe-à-Pierre opened; first exports
1914-17	Re-establishment of elected Port of Spain borough council
1914-18	First World War; war service by BWI Regiment
1914-20	Rapid expansion of cocoa production and cultivation
1914-24	Great expansion in oil industry
1917	End of Indian immigration to Trinidad
1918	Habitual Idlers Ordinance; revival of TWA
1919-20	Labour unrest, strikes and disturbances
1920	Fyzabad area opened up by Apex for oil; collapse of cocoa prices on the world market
1920-34	Depressed prices for cocoa and sugar, some estates abandoned
1921	Final end of indenture in Trinidad (January 1)
1921-22	Wood Commission
1923	A.A.Cipriani elected president of TWA
1925	Trinidad's first elections to the legislative council; Cipriani elected; Agricultural Bank established
1925-31	Growth of TWA throughout Trinidad and Tobago
1928	First appearance of cocoa witchbroom disease
1929-30	Olivier Commission on sugar industry
1929-39	Worldwide Great Depression affects Trinidad
1931	Divorce Bill controversy
1931-3	Appearance of *The Beacon*
1932	Trade Union Ordinance
1933	Record low prices for cocoa
1934	Strikes and riots by sugar workers; formation of Negro Welfare Association; Cipriani's leadership begins to be challenged; TWA becomes Trinidad Labour Party (TLP)
1935	Apex Oilfields strike and hunger march; emergence of Butler; formation of Trinidad Citizens League by Rienzi and Butler
1935-6	Protests against the invasion of Ethiopia
1936-7	Butler agitates among the oil workers
1937	Oil workers strike; island-wide strikes and riots follow; Forster Commission; formation of unions; dismissal of Governor Fletcher; Butler tried and imprisoned; establishment of Caroni Ltd
1938	Appointment of Industrial Adviser; Trade Disputes Ordinance;more unions formed
1938-39	West India Royal Commission (Moyne Commission)
1938-41	Extension and modernization of Pointe-à-Pierre refinery
1938-46	Wartime boom for oil industry

1939	Trade Union Council established in Trinidad
1939-45	Second World War; Butler and others detained
1941	Cession of North West Peninsula and Wallerfield to USA
1941-5	Construction and operation of US bases in Trinidad; rapid decline in production of sugar
1942	Trade unions given right of peaceful picketing and immunity from actions in tort
1943	Marine drilling for oil begins
1944	Report of Franchise Committee; retirement of Rienzi from politics
1945	Butler released, launches his union; adult suffrage granted; death of Cipriani
1946	First elections with adult suffrage; first woman appointed to legislature (Audrey Jeffers)
1946-7	Strikes and labour unrest in oil and sugar; riots in city
1947	F. W. Dalley's first report on labour
1947-8	Constitutional Reform Committee
1948	Eric Williams returns with the Caribbean Commission
1950	Constitutional change gives elected members a majority in both legislative and executive councils and sets up 'quasi-ministerial' system; general elections; Butler party excluded from executive council; beginning of tax incentives to pioneer industries
1950-6	Albert Gomes heads 'quasi-ministerial' regime
1951	Commonwealth Sugar Agreement
1952	Formation of West Indian Independence Party (WIIP); first electricity in Tobago
1953	Formation of People's Democratic Party (PDP)
1954	Dalley's second report; Williams debates with Dom B. Matthews; exploitation of Soldado marine oilfield begins
1955	Elections postponed to September 1956; Williams leaves Caribbean Commission; he opens University of Woodford Square
1956	Constitutional change establishes a Cabinet with a chief minister responsible to the legislature; formation of People's National Movement (PNM); PNM wins thirteen seats in general elections; formation of first PNM government (1956-61)
1956-7	Texaco acquires TLL and Shell buys out UBOT
1957	Formation of Democratic Labour Party (DLP)
1958	Inauguration of federation; first federal election; DLP wins six out of ten Trinidad seats; C. L. R. James returns to Trinidad to edit PNM paper; Joint Chaguaramas Commission
1959	Establishment of Industrial Development Corporation
1959-60	Campaign for return of Chaguaramas
1960	Chaguaramas withdrawal negotiated; 'Concordat' signed
1960-1	James breaks with Williams and PNM
1961	Constitutional change grants full internal self-government; general elections: PNM wins twenty seats out of thirty, forms second PNM government (1961-6); first woman elected to Parliament (Isabel Teshea)
1962	Dissolution of federation; national Independence (August 31); Trinmar established to take over marine oil operations

Select Bibliography

Items marked * were found to be particularly valuable.

Books

Anthony, M. and Carr, A. (eds), *David Frost Introduces Trinidad* (London, 1975).

Armstrong, E., *Import Substitution in Jamaica and Trinidad and Tobago* (Jamaica, 1967).

Bahadoorsingh, K., *Trinidad Electoral Politics, the Persistence of the Race Factor* (London, 1968).

Beachey, R., *The British West Indian Sugar Industry in the Late 19th Century* (Oxford, 1957).

Bodu, I., *Trinidadiana* (Port of Spain, 1890).

Borde, P.G.L., *Histoire de l'île de la Trinidad sous le gouvernement espagnol* (Paris, 1876 and 1882).

Bowman, H. and J., *Crusoe's Island in the Caribbean* (New York, 1939).

Braithwaite, L., *Social Stratification in Trinidad* (Jamaica, 1975).

*Brereton, B., *Race Relations in Colonial Trinidad, 1870-1900* (Cambridge, 1979).

Bridges, Y., *Child of the Tropics, Victorian Memoirs*, edited by N.Guppy (London, 1980).

Burnley, W., *Observations on the Present Condition of the Island of Trinidad* (Port of Spain, 1842).

Calder-Marshall, A., *Glory Dead* (London, 1939).

Carmichael, A.C., *Domestic Manners and Social Condition of the White, Coloured and Negro Population of the West Indies* (London, 1834).

Carmichael, G., *The History of the West Indian Islands of Trinidad and Tobago* (London, 1961).

Chapman, J. K., *The Career of A. H. Gordon, first Lord Stanmore 1829-1912* (Toronto, 1964).

Clifford, B., *Proconsul* (London, 1964).

Cohen, D.W. and Greene, J.P. (eds), *Neither Slave nor Free* (Baltimore, 1972).

Collens, J.H., *A Guide to Trinidad* (London, 1888).

Craig, H., *The Legislative Council of Trinidad and Tobago* (London, 1952).

de Verteuil, A., *Sir Louis de Verteuil, His Life and Times* (Port of Spain, 1973).

de Verteuil, L., *Trinidad* (London, 1858 and 1884).

*Fraser, L.M., *History of Trinidad* (Port of Spain, 1891 and 1892).

Gamble, W.H., *Trinidad, Historical and Descriptive* (London, 1866).

*Gomes, A., *Through a Maze of Colour* (Port of Spain, 1974).

Gordon, S., *A Century of West Indian Education* (London, 1963).

Gordon, S., *Reports and Repercussions in West Indian Education, 1835-1933* (London, 1968).

Green, W., *British Slave Emancipation* (Oxford, 1976).
Henry, Z., *Labour Relations and Industrial Conflict in Commonwbalth Caribbean Countries* (Port of Spain, 1972).
Hill, E., *The Trinidad Carnival* (Austin, Texas, 1972).
Hollis, C., *A Brief History of Trinidad under the Spanish Crown* (Port of Spain, 1941).
Jacobs, W.R., *Butler versus the King* (Port of Spain, 1975).
James, C.L.R., *Party Politics in the West Indies* (San Juan, 1962).
James, C.L.R., *Life of A.A. Cipriani* (Nelson, Lancs, 1962).
James, C.L.R., *Beyond a Boundary* (London, 1963).
Joseph, E.L., *History of Trinidad* (London, 1970).
Kingsley, C., *At Last, a Christmas in the West Indies* (London, 1871).
Kirpalani, M. et al. (eds), *Indian Centenary Review* (Port of Spain, 1945).
Klass, M., *East Indians in Trinidad* (New York, 1961).
Knowles, W., *Trade Union Development and Industrial Relations in the British West Indies* (Berkeley, 1959).
La Guerre, J. (ed.), *Calcutta to Caroni* (London, 1974).
*Laurence, K.O., *Immigration into the West Indies in the 19th Century* (Barbados, 1972).
Lewis, W.A., *Labour in the West Indies* (London, 1977)
McCallum, P., *Travels in Trinidad during the Months of February, March and April 1803* (Liverpool, 1805).
Mahabir, W., *In and Out of Politics* (Port of Spain, 1978).
*Malik, Y., *East Indians in Trinidad, a Study in Minority Politics* (Oxford, 1971).
Manning, H.T., *British Colonial Government after the American Revolution* (Yale, 1933).
Mathieson, W.L., *British Slavery and its Abolition* (London, 1926).
Mathieson, W.L., *British Slave Emancipation* (London, 1932).
Mathieson, W.L., *The Sugar Colonies and Governor Eyre* (London, 1936).
Mavrogordato, O., *Voices in the Street* (Port of Spain, 1977).
*Millette, J., *The Genesis of Crown Colony Government* (Curepe, 1970).
Mordecai, J., *The West Indies: the Federal Negotiations* (London, 1968).
Morton, S.E., *John Morton of Trinidad* (Toronto, 1916).
Murray, D.J., *The West Indies and the Development of Colonial Government* (Oxford, 1965).
*Naipaul, V., *The Loss of Eldorado* (London, 1969).
*Newson, L., *Aboriginal and Spanish Colonial Trinidad* (London, 1976).
Niehoff, A. and J., *East Indians in the West Indies* (Milwaukee, 1960).
*Noel, J., *Trinidad, Provincia de Venezuela* (Caracas, 1972).
O'Connor, P.E.T., *Some Trinidad Yesterdays* (Port of Spain, 1978).
*Ottley, C.R., *The Story of Tobago* (Port of Spain and Kingston, 1973).
*Oxaal, I., *Black Intellectuals Come to Power* (Cambridge, Mass., 1968).
Philip, J-B., *An Address to the Rt Hon Earl Bathurst ...* (London, 1824).
Rampersad, F., *Growth and Structural Change in the Economy of Trinidad and Tobago, 1951-61* (Mona, Jamaica, n.d.).
Reis, C., *A History of the Constitution or Government of Trinidad* (Port of Spain, 1929).
Rennie, B., *The History of the Working Class in the 20th Century (19191956): the Trinidad and Tobago Experience* (Port of Spain, 1973).

Robinson, H.B., *Memoirs of Lieut.-Gen. Sir Thomas Picton*(London,1836).
*Ryan, S., *Race and Nationalism in Trinidad and Tobago* (Toronto, 1972).
Sander, R. (ed.), *From Trinidad: an Anthology of Early West Indian Writing* (London, 1978).
Sewell, W., *Ordeal of Free Labour in the British West Indies* (New York, 1860).
*Shephard, C.Y., *The Cacao Industry in Trinidad* (Port of Spain, 1932).
Stephen, J., *The Crisis of the Sugar Colonies* (London, 1802; New York, 1969).
Thomas, J.J., *Froudacity* (London, 1889 and 1969).
Weller, J., *East Indian Indenture in Trinidad* (Puerto Rico, 1967).
Will, H.A., *Constitutional Change in the British West Indies 1880-1903* (Oxford, 1970).
*Williams, E.E., *History of the People of Trinidad and Tobago* (London, 1964).
Williams, E.E., *Inward Hunger* (London, 1969).
*Wood, D., *Trinidad in Transition* (Oxford, 1968).

Articles

Brereton, B., `The Negro middle class of Trinidad in the later 19th century', in *Social Groups and Institutions in the History of the Caribbean,* Association of Caribbean Historians (Puerto Rico, 1975).
Brereton, B., `The foundations of prejudice: Indians and Africans in the 19th century', in *Caribbean Issues*,1 (1), 1974.
Campbell, C. , `The death of the cabildo of Port of Spain, Trinidad', in *Social Groups and Institutions in the History of the Caribbean* (op. cit.).
*Campbell, C., 'Jonas Mohammed Bath and the free Mandingos in Trinidad', in *Pan-African Journal,* 7 (2), 1974.
Campbell, C., 'Mahammedu Sisei of Gambia and Trinidad, c.1788-1838', in *African Studies Assoc. of the WI Bulletin,* 7, 1974.
Caribbean Quarterly: Trinidad Carnival Issue, vo1.4, 1956 (several items).
Carrington, E., 'Industrialisation in Trinidad and Tobago since 1950', in *New World Quarterly,* 4 (2), 1968.
Carrington, E., ''The post-war political economy of Trinidad and Tobago', in *New World Quarterly,* 4 (1), 1967.
Elkins, W., 'Black power in the British West Indies: the Trinidad longshoremen's strike of 1919', in *Science and Society,* 33 (1), 1969.
Elkins, W., 'Hercules and the Society of Peoples of African Origin', in *Caribbean Studies,* 2 (4), 1972.
Haraksingh, K., 'Indian leadership in the indenture period', in *Caribbean Issues,* 2 (3), 1976.
Henry, R., 'A note on income distribution and poverty in Trinidad and Tobago', in *C.S.O. Research Paper,* 8, October 1975.
*Higman, B., 'African and Creole slave family patterns in Trinidad', in *Journal of Family History,* 3, 1978.
Johnson, H., 'Immigration and the sugar industry in Trinidad during the last quarter of the 19th century', in *Journal of Caribbean History,* 3, November 1971.
Johnson, H., 'The origins and early development of cane-farming in Trinidad 1882-1906', in *Journal of Caribbean History,* 5, November 1972.

Johnson, H., 'Oil, imperial policy and the Trinidad disturbances, 1937', in *Journal of Imperial and Commonwealth History*, 4 (1), 1975.
Joseph, C. L., 'The British West Indies Regiment 1914-18', in *Journal of Caribbean History*, 2, May 1971.
La Guerre, J., 'The general elections of 1946 in Trinidad and Tobago', in *Social and Economic Studies*, 21 (2), 1972.
Laurence, K.O., 'The settlement of free Negroes in Trinidad before Emancipation', in *Caribbean Quarterly*, 9 (1 and 2), 1963.
Laurence, K.O., 'The Trinidad Water Riots of 1903: reflections of an eye-witness', in *Caribbean Quarterly*, 15 (4), 1969.
Lewis, G., 'The Trinidad and Tobago general elections of 1961', in *Caribbean Studies*, 2 (2), 1962.
Martin, T., 'Revolutionary upheaval in Trinidad, 1919', in *Journal of* Negro *History*, LVIII (3), 1973.
Ramesar, M., 'The position of the East Indians in Trinidad', in *Social Groups and Institutions in the History of the Caribbean* (op. cit.).
Ramesar, M., 'Patterns of regional settlement and economic activity by immigrant groups in Trinidad 1851-1900', in *Social and Economic Studies*, 25 (3), 1976.
Riviere, W., 'Labour shortage in the BWI after emancipation', in *Journal of Caribbean History*, 4, 1972.
Ryan, S., 'The struggle for Afro-Indian solidarity in Trinidad', in *Trinidad and Tobago Index,* 4, 1966.
*Samaroo, B., 'The Trinidad Workingmen's Association and ... popular protest in a Crown Colony', in *Social and Economic Studies*, 21(2),1972.
Samaroo, B., 'C.P.David, a case study in the emergence of the black man in Trinidad politics', in *Journal of Caribbean History*, 3, November 1971.
Samaroo, B., 'Introduction' to *The Beacon* (reprinted New York, 1977).
Spackman, A., 'Constitutional development in Trinidad and Tobago', in *Social and Economic Studies*, 14 (4), 1965.
Warner, M., 'Africans in 19th century Trinidad', in *African Studies Assoc. of the WI Bulletin*, 5 and 6, 1972 and 1973.
Williams, E.E.,'My relations with the Caribbean Commission, 1943-1955', (Port of Spain, 1955).

Unpublished Theses and Papers

*Basdeo, S., 'Labour organisation and labour reform in Trinidad, 1919-1939', Ph.D., Dalhousie, 1975.
Brereton, B., 'The Trinidad reform movement in the later 19th century', paper presented to 5th Conference of Caribbean Historians, Trinidad, 1973.
Campbell, C., 'The development of education in Trinidad 1834-70', Ph.D., University of the West Indies (UWI), 1973.
*Campbell, C., 'The transition from Spanish law to English law in Trinidad before and after emancipation', paper presented to 7th Conference of Caribbean Historians, Jamaica, 1975.
*Campbell, C., 'The wealth of mulatto men: Trinidad 1813-28', seminar paper, Dept of History, UWI, Jamaica, 1976.
Campbell, C., 'The attack on paper equality: the politics of the coloureds in Trinidad 1832-46', seminar paper, Dept of History, UWI, Jamaica, 1977.

Craig, S., 'Smiles and blood', UWI, Trinidad, 1974.
*Goodridge, C., 'Land labour and immigration in Trinidad 1783-1833', Ph.D., Cambridge, 1969.
Harewood, T.A., 'The Caribbean mineral economy: the case of Trinidad and Tobago 1951-65', M.A., McGill, 1969.
Ince, B.A., 'Politics before the PNM: a study of parties in British Trinidad', Ph.D., New York University, 1965.
Jacobs, W.R., 'The role of some labour movements in the political process in Trinidad 1937-50'. M.Sc., UWI, 1969.
Jacobs, W,R., 'The politics of protest in Trinidad: the strikes and disturbances of 1937', paper presented to 5th Conference of Caribbean Historians, Trinidad, 1973.
*Johnson, H., `Crown Colony government in Trinidad 1870-1897', D.Phil., Oxford, 1969.
Maingot, A.P., '19th century Trinidad, a discussion of the relative position of the French Creole group in the society', M.A., University of Puerto Rico, 1962.
*Mulchansingh, V., 'The origins, growth and development of the oil industry in Trinidad and its impact on the economy, 1857-1965', Ph.D., Queen's University Dublin, 1967.
Ramesar, M., `Indian immigration into Trinidad 1897-1917', M.A., UWI, 1973.
*Samaroo, B., 'Constitutional and political development of Trinidad 1898-1925', Ph.D., London, 1969.
Samaroo, B., 'The making of the 1946 constitution in Trinidad', paper presented to 5th Conference of Caribbean Historians, Trinidad, 1973.
*Singh, K.. 'Economy and polity in Trinidad, 1917-38', Ph.D., UWI, 1975.
Singh, K., 'A.C.Rienzi and the labour movement in Trinidad, 1925-1944', paper presented to 11th Conference of Caribbean Historians, Curaçao, 1979.
*Tikasingh, G., 'The establishment of the Indians in Trinidad, 1870--1900', Ph.D., UWI, 1976.
*Titus, N., 'Amelioration and emancipation in Trinidad, 1812-34', M. A., UWI, 1974.

Official Reports

1827: Report of Commissioners of Legal Enquiry on the Colony of Trinidad
1888: Report and Evidence of Royal Franchise Commission (Trinidad)
1897: Report and Evidence of West India Royal Commission
1930: Report of the West Indies Sugar Commission (Olivier Report)
1937: Report of Commission on the Trinidad and Tobago Disturbances (Forster Report)
1939: Report of Maj. G. Orde Brown on Labour Conditions in the W.I.
1945: Report of West India Royal Commission (Moyne Report)
1948: Report of Comission to Enquire into the Working of the Sugar Industry in Trinidad (Soulbery Report)
1947: Report by F. W. Dalley on Trade Union Organization and Industrial Relations in Trinidad
1954: Report by F. W. Dalley on General Industrial Conditions and Labour Relations in Trinidad

Index